Disco
West Central Adirondacks

A Guide to the Western Wildernesses
and the Moose River Plains

Discover the
West Central Adirondacks

A Guide to the Western Wildernesses and the Moose River Plains

Barbara McMartin
Lee M. Brenning

Prepared with the assistance of Dennis Conroy and
John and Sandy Edwards

Backcountry Publications
Woodstock, Vermont

An Invitation to the Reader

Over time trails can be rerouted and signs and landmarks altered. If you find that changes have occurred on the routes described in this book, please let us know so that corrections may be made in future editions. The author and publisher also welcome other comments and suggestions. Address all correspondence to:

Editor
Discover the Adirondack Series
Backcountry Publications
P.O. Box 175
Woodstock, VT 05091

Library of Congress Cataloging-in-Publication Data

McMartin, Barbara.
  Discover the west central Adirondacks.

  (Discover the Adirondacks series)
  Bibliography: p.
  Includes index.
  1. Outdoor recreation—New York (State)—Adirondack Park—Guide-books. 2. Adirondack Park (N.Y.)—Guide-books. I. Brenning, Lee M., 1955-   . II. Title. III. Series.
GV191.42.M373 1988   917.47′53   88-16674
ISBN 0-942440-45-5 (pbk.)

Published by Backcountry Publications, Inc.
Woodstock, Vermont 05091

Printed in the United States of America by McNaughton & Gunn
Typesetting by Sant Bani Press
Series design by Leslie Fry
Layout by Barbara McMartin
Maps by Richard Widhu

Photograph Credits
Barbara McMartin, cover, 2, 12, 23, 42, 69, 72, 74, 83, 87, 88, 94, 109, 114, 134, 137, 142, 149, 154, 159, 165, 171, 174, 176, 291
Lee M. Brenning, 6, 187, 193, 198, 201, 204, 208, 222, 226, 229, 234, 237, 241, 248, 256, 261, 270, 275, 277, 285, 287
John Edwards, 36, 63, 92, 131, 146, 163
Dennis Conroy, 50, 54, 57, 166
Edythe Robbins, 107

Photographs
Cover: *Cedar Lakes from the dam at the outlet*
Page 2: *Oxbow on the Indian River*
Page 6: *Windfall Pond*

Acknowledgements

As we began to discover the extent of the trail system and the places to be explored in this large west central region, we had to call on an ever-increasing number of friends and experts for help. Barbara's husband, W. Alec Reid, not only hiked a lot of trails, he continued to make excellent prints of the pictures we took. Lee's wife, Georgie, hiked with him on almost all the trails he covered, not only providing field support, but augmenting his perceptions with her own woods' intuition.

DEC staff and rangers have been most helpful. Margaret Baldwin, cartographer, and John Keating of the Real Property Office, helped us discover much historical information from valuable DEC records. Rangers John Seifts, Piseco; Thomas Eakin, Lake Pleasant; Doug Riedman, Old Forge; Terry Perkins, Stillwater; and Gary McChesney, Raquette Lake, answered questions and offered advice, corrections, and new information. Ranger Gary Lee did all of that and more, for he read most of the manuscript, added information only he would know about, and corrected trail maps and the underlying USGS base maps so that the maps in this guide are probably the only correct printed version for much of the area.

We wish also to thank Gerold Pepper, the librarian at the Adirondack Museum; Jim Dawson, another author in this series who contributed geological background to this guide; and Francis B. Rosevear, who serves as the historian for the series and makes us aware of Colvin's exploits in the area we have researched.

Jay O'Hern is writing a book on the history of the Moose River Plains. He and Paul Sirtoli, with whom he shares adventures, not only provided us with background material, they wrote two sections describing remote bushwhacks. Their stories of several other exploits challenged us to ever greater explorations.

Joe Conway, author and historian from Woodgate, answered our queries for Moose River Plains history by conducting interviews with several people who worked in the Plains in the critical post-war years. He conveyed the remembrances of Norbert and Ed Kornmeier and Gerald Van Alstyne and sent along several valuable maps.

Daisy Kelley of Sagamore Institute not only gave us information on Sagamore, she led us on exploratory hikes of some nearby trails. Howard Kirschenbaum and John Friauf added to our knowledge of Sagamore.

Pat Flood and Bob McCormack of International Paper Company supplied information and maps of the Perkins Clearing Tract.

Many people hiked with us. Edythe Robbins and Chuck Bennett made it possible for us to do several extended trips. Brian McDonnell, a natural guide, was great support for the longest of these trips.

Dennis Conroy researched and wrote up trails near Indian Lake and some in the Moose River Plains. John and Sandy Edwards accompanied us on several trips, extending our range. They also struck off on their own on several really long adventures, among them Yale Brook, West Mountain, and Lost Pond and made excellent written and photographic records of their trips.

More than any previous guide in this series, this one is the result of collaborative efforts of a number of individuals. It would not have been possible to cover such a large area as effectively without their help, so we are deeply indebted to all of them. Besides, learning from them and sharing the trails and historical discoveries with them was for us a large part of the thrill of preparing the guide.

Contents

The Northern Tier   165

Ha-de-ron-dah Wilderness Area   185

From Old Forge to Eagle Bay   209

Along the Uncas-Browns Tract Road   279

References and Other Resources   290

Index   292

Crossing the South Branch of the West Canada Creek

Introduction

THE LANDS DESCRIBED in *Discover the West Central Adirondacks* represent a variety of wilderness areas. The Adirondack Park includes very little land that has been continuously preserved, and only tiny pockets of old-growth forest exist in this region of the park. Here, most of the land that is now called wilderness was cut over. Some of it was logged so lightly and so long ago that today the forests resemble old-growth forests. Some of it was logged very heavily and very recently, belying its wilderness designation. Yet, out of this variety, New Yorkers are creating the wilderness of the future, for once the state acquires land within the park boundaries, the state consititution demands that it can never be logged again.

Scattered through these wilderness forests are an abundance of lakes and ponds, more than a hundred of them, many among the handsomest in the park, all entirely owned by the state. These gems will only improve as the forests surrounding them mature.

Adventures in this guide will take you to many lakes and all sorts of forests. All the stages in the re-creation of wilderness are found in the west central region. Nowhere in the park is the disparity of the age of forests as evident as it is here, and each step in forest succession offers the outdoors person a different experience.

The guide includes four areas, which because of their size and inaccessibility are considered Wilderness by the State Land Master Plan. Bordering them are Wild Forest Areas with easily accessible recreation. In this upside down world of creating wilderness, some of the most majestic forests are in these Wild Forest areas while there are Wilderness Areas with some of the scrubbiest stands the state has ever acquired.

Stands of tremendous maples and yellow birch with a scattering of large hemlock mark parts of the Wild Forest near Piseco and Sacandaga lakes. To the north, tracts around the West Canada Lakes Wilderness were logged within the last seventy years, but those lakes (West, South, Mud, and Brooktrout) are today surrounded with maturing stands that are becoming real complements to their wilderness setting. The eastern part of this region was logged within the last few decades. Part of Pillsbury and Whitney lakes and all of Otter and Little Moose were recently added to the Forest Preserve.

The northern part of the West Canada Lakes Wilderness where it touches the Moose River Plains Wild Forest was logged so heavily about twenty-five years ago that it is still covered only with dense stands of small trees. The Plains includes more than twenty lakes and ponds, some over a mile in length, most reached by very short trails. A small part of the Moose River Plains was never logged, and because of the sterile, wet, sandy soil, some of it has no forest cover at all. Other parts are covered with fully mature black spruce, taller here than almost anywhere else, but these only grow to sixty feet tall at most. Tall pines and tamarack dot other parts of the Plains. Further north, blowdown leveled forest that had been part of the Forest Preserve for nearly a century.

The woodsman's axe barely touched the forest stands in the Blue Ridge Wilderness south of Blue Mountain and Raquette lakes. In contrast, parts of the forest near Sagamore and Mohegan lakes and Bear Pond were heavily cut in the last two decades.

North of the Fulton Chain Lakes, the story is equally variable. Magnificent stands of maple, yellow birch, pine, and hemlock lie near parts of the Uncas Road and west of Queer Lake in the Pigeon Lake Wilderness Area. Other parts as well as much of the Ha-de-ron-dah Wilderness are just recovering from fires, most started by the railroads, that destroyed all the forest cover.

Throughout this region are lakes where only the cry of loons or the splash of jumping fish break the quiet. But, for some lakes, the stillness has become an oppressive silence, for no fish survive in them. The shadow of acid rain is greater here than in any other part of the park.

In spite of the disturbed lakes and the forests not yet recovered, the west central region beckons you to discover a world of wilderness recreation — the true get-away places of the Adirondacks. There are many miles of level trails as well as a network of well-maintained dirt roads in the Moose River Plains. Lakes in the Plains like Beaver, Squaw, and Indian can be as serene as Sampson, Spruce, and the West Canadas; and the forests surrounding them are equally spectacular. Here, access to wilderness lakes is not limited to those who hike long distances or enjoy bushwhacks. The vast majority of lakes in this guide are reached by a trail, and a relatively easy one at that.

How to Use the Discover Guides

The regional guides in the *Discover the Adirondacks* series will tell you enough about each area so that you can enjoy it in many different ways at any time of year. Each guide will acquaint you with that region's access roads and trailheads, its trails and unmarked paths, some bushwhack routes and canoe trips, and its best picnic spots, campsites, and ski-touring routes. At the same time, the guides will introduce you to valleys, mountains, cliffs, scenic views, lakes, streams, and a myriad of other natural features.

Some of the destinations are within walking distance of the major highways that ring the areas, while others are miles deep into the wilderness. Each description will enable you to determine the best excursion for you and to enjoy the natural features you will pass, whether you are on a summer day hike or a winter ski-touring trek. The sections are grouped in chapters according to their access points. Each chapter contains a brief introduction to that area's history and the old settlements and industries that have all but disappeared into the wilderness. Throughout the guide you will find accounts of the geological forces that shaped features of the land, mention of unusual wildflowers, and descriptions of forest stands.

It is our hope that you will find this guide not only an invitation to know and enjoy the woods but a companion for all your adventures there.

MAPS AND NOMENCLATURE

The DeLorme Atlas is the best reference for town roads, but it does not show state land. The Adirondack North Country Regional Map shows all state land including acquisitions through 1986. It is currently being updated. Write Adirondack North Country Association, 183 Broadway, Saranac Lake, NY 12983.

This guide contains maps showing all the routes mentioned and is adequate for the marked trails, even though the maps are based on the 1954 series. You may want to carry the new metric USGS (United States Geological Service) topographic maps, on which most of the land forms and drainages are more accurately shown. The region is covered by the following new, double 7.5 by 15 minute maps: Honnedaga Lake, West Canada Lake, Page Mtn., Piseco Lake, Old Forge, Wakeley Mtn., Indian Lake, Eagle Bay, Raquette Lake, Blue Mountain Lake, and Beaver River.

The guide maps were taken from parts of Piseco, Lake Pleasant, Ohio, Old Forge, West Canada Lakes, Indian Lake, Raquette Lake, McKeever, and Big Moose quadrangles. In this guide, they are reproduced at a scale of 1 inch = 1 mile.

Maps are available locally in many sporting goods stores. You can order maps from USGS Map Distribution Branch, Box 25286, Denver Federal Center, Denver, CO 80225. They are currently more easily obtained from a private source, Timely Discount Topos. (1-800-821-7609).

The guide uses the spelling given in the USGS but local variations are noted.

Maps are available locally in many sporting goods stores. You can order maps from USGS Map Distribution Branch, Box 25286, Denver Federal Center, Denver, CO 80225. They are currently more easily obtained from a private source, Timely Discount Topos. You can call them at 1-800-821-7609; with your credit card number they will ship maps within a week.

The guide uses the spelling given in the USGS but local variations are noted.

DISTANCE AND TIME

Distance along the routes is measured from the USGS survey maps and is accurate to within ten percent. It is given in miles, feet, or yards except where local signs use metric measure. Distance is a variable factor in comparing routes along paths or bushwhacks. Few hikers gauge distance accurately even on well-defined trails.

Time is given as an additional gauge for the length of routes. This provides a better understanding of the difficulty of the terrain, the change of elevation, and the problems of finding a suitable course. Average time for walking trails is 2 miles an hour, 3 miles if the way is level and well defined; for paths, 1½ to 2 miles an hour; and for bushwhacks, 1 mile an hour.

Vertical rise usually refers to the change in elevation along a route up a single hill or mountain; *elevation change* generally refers to the cumulative change in elevation where a route crosses several hills or mountains.

A line stating distance, time, and vertical rise or elevation change is given with the title of each section describing trails and most paths, but not for less distinct paths and bushwhacks for which such information is too variable to summarize. Distance and times are for *one way only*, unless otherwise stated. The text tells you how to put together several routes into a longer trek that will occupy a day or more.

TYPES OF ROUTES

Each section of this guide generally describes a route or a place. Included in the descriptions are such basic information as the suitability for different levels of woods experience, walking (or skiing, paddling, and climbing) times, distances, directions to the access, and, of course, directions along the route itself. The following definitions clarify the terms used in this book.

A route is considered a *trail* if it is so designated by the New York State permitted on them in winter when there is sufficient snow cover. The guide indicates trails not heavily used where skiing and snowmobiling may be compatible, but a skier must always be cautious on a snowmobile trail. Hikers can enjoy both ski and snowmobile trails.

A *path* is an informal and unmarked route with a clearly defined foot tread. These traditional routes, worn by fishermen and hunters to favorite spots, are great for hiking. A path, however, is not necessarily kept open, and fallen trees and new growth sometimes obliterate its course. The paths that cross wet meadows or open fields often become concealed by lush growth. You should always carry a map and compass when you are following an unmarked path and you should keep track of your location.

There is a safe prescription for walking paths. In a group of three or more hikers, stringing out along a narrow path will permit the leader to scout until the path disappears, at which point at least one member of the party should still be standing on an obvious part of the path. If that hiker remains standing while those in front range out to find the path, the whole group can continue safely after a matter of moments.

Hikers in the north country often use the term *bushwhack* to describe an uncharted and unmarked trip. Sometimes bushwhacking literally means pushing brush aside, but it usually connotes a variety of cross-country walks.

Bushwhacks are an important part of this regional guide series because of the shortage of marked trails throughout much of the Adirondack Park and the abundance of little-known and highly desirable destinations for which no visible routes exist. Although experienced bushwhackers may reach these destinations with not much more help than the knowledge of their location, I think most hikers will appreciate these simple descriptions that point out the easiest and most interesting routes and the possible pitfalls. In general, descriptions for bushwhacks are less detailed than those for paths or trails; it is assumed that those who bushwhack have a greater knowledge of the woods than those who walk marked routes.

Bushwhack is defined as any trip on which you make your way through the woods without a trail, path, or the visible foot tread of other hikers and without markings, signs, or blazes. It also means you will make your way by following a route chosen on a contour map, aided by a compass, using streambeds, valleys, abandoned roads, and obvious ridges as guides. Most bushwhacks require navigating by both contour map and compass, and an understanding of the terrain.

Bushwhack distances are not given in precise tenths of a mile. They are estimates representing the shortest distance one could travel between

Bushwhack is defined as any trip on which you make your way through the woods without a trail, path, or the visible foot tread of other hikers and without markings, signs, or blazes. It also means you will make your way by following a route chosen on a contour map, aided by a compass, using streambeds, valleys, abandoned roads, and obvious ridges as guides. Most bushwhacks require navigating by both contour map and compass, and an understanding of the terrain.

Bushwhack distances are not given in precise tenths of a mile. They are estimates representing the shortest distance one could travel between points. This reinforces the fact that each hiker's cross-country route will be different, yielding different mileages.

A bushwhack is said to be *easy* if the route is along a stream, a lakeshore, a reasonably obvious abandoned roadway, or some similarly well-defined feature. A short route to the summit of a hill or a small mountain can often be easy. A bushwhack is termed *moderate* if a simple route can be defined on a contour map and followed with the aid of a compass. Previous experience is necessary. A bushwhack is rated *difficult* if it entails a complex route, necessitating advanced knowledge of navigation by compass and reading contour maps and land features.

Compass directions are given in degrees from magnetic north and in degrees from true north. The text will usually specify which reference is used, but if no reference is given the degrees refer to magnetic north.

The guide occasionally refers to old *blazed* lines or trails. The word "blaze" comes from the French *blesser* and means to cut or wound. Early loggers and settlers made deep slashes in good-sized trees with an axe to mark property lines and trails. Hunters and fishermen have also often made slashes with knives and, though they are not as deep as axe cuts, they can still be seen. *It is now, and has been for many years, illegal to deface trees in the Forest Preserve in this manner.* Following an old blazed path for miles in dense woods is often a challenging but good way to reach a trailless destination.

You may see *yellow paint daubs on a line of trees.* These lines usually indicate the boundary between private and public lands. Individuals have also used different colors of paint to mark informal routes from time to time. Although it is not legal to mark trails on state land, this guide does refer to such informally marked paths.

All *vehicular traffic*, except snowmobiles on their designated trails, *is prohibited* in the Forest Preserve. Vehicles are allowed on town roads and some roads that pass through state land to reach private inholdings. These roads are described in the guide, and soon the DEC will start marking those old roads that are open to vehicles. Most old roads referred to here distance, time, and elevation change for the trail. For unmarked routes, such information is given only within the text of each section—partly to allow for the great variations in the way hikers approach an unmarked route, and partly to emphasize the difficulty of those routes.

Protecting the Land

Most of the land described in these guides is in the *Forest Preserve,* land set aside a century ago. No trees may be cut on this state land. All of it is open to the public. The *Adirondack Park Agency* has responsibility for the Wilderness, Primitive, and Wild Forest guidelines that govern use of the Forest Preserve. Care and custody of these state lands is left to the Department of Environmental Conservation, which is in the process of producing Unit Management Plans for the roughly 130 separate Forest Preserve areas.

Camping is permitted throughout the public lands except at elevations above 4000 feet and within 150 feet of water or 150 feet of trails. In certain fragile areas, camping is restricted to specific locations, and the state is using a new No Camping disk to mark fragile spots. *Permits* for camping on state lands are needed only for stays that exceed three days or for groups of more than ten campers. Permits can be obtained from the local rangers, who are listed in the area phone books under New York State Department of Environmental Conservation.

Only dead and downed wood can be used for *campfires.* Build fires only when absolutely necessary; carry a small stove for cooking. Build fires at designated fire rings or on rocks or gravel. Fire is dangerous and can travel rapidly through the duff or organic soil, burning roots and spreading through the forest. Douse fires with water, and be sure they are completely out and cold before you leave.

Private lands are generally not open to the public, though some individuals have granted public access across their land to state land. It is always wise to ask before crossing private lands. Be very respectful of private landowners so that public access will continue to be granted. Never enter private lands that have been posted unless you have the owner's permission. Unless the text expressly identifies an area as state-owned Forest Preserve or private land whose owner permits unrestricted public passage, the inclusion of a walk description in this guide does not imply public right-of-way.

Burn combustible trash and carry out everything else.

Most *wildflowers and ferns* mentioned in the text are protected by law. Do not pick them or try to transplant them.

Safety in the Woods

It is best *not to walk alone*. Make sure someone knows where you are heading and when you are expected back.

Carry water or other liquids with you. Not only are the mountains dry, but the recent spread of *Giardia* makes many streams suspect. I have an aluminum fuel bottle especially for carrying water; it is virtually indestructible and has a deep screw that prevents leaking.

Carry a small *day pack* with insect repellent, flashlight, first aid kit, emergency food rations, waterproof matches, jackknife, whistle, rain gear, and a wool sweater, even for summer hiking. Wear layers of wool and waterproof clothing in winter and carry an extra sweater and socks. If you plan to camp, consult a good outfitter or a camping organization for the essentials. Better yet, make your first few trips with an experienced leader or with a group.

Always carry a *map and compass*. You may also want to carry an altimeter to judge your progress on bushwhack climbs.

Wear *glasses* when bushwhacking. The risk to your eyes of a small protruding branch makes this a necessity.

Carry *binoculars* for birding as well as for viewing distant peaks.

Use great care near the *edges of cliffs* and when *crossing streams* by hopping rocks in the streambed. Never bushwhack unless you have gained a measure of woods experience. If you are a novice in the out-of-doors, join a hiking group or hire the services of one of the many outfitters in the north country. As you get to know the land, you can progress from the standard trails to the more difficult and more satisfyingly remote routes. Then you will really begin to discover the Adirondacks.

Southern West Canada Lakes Wilderness

THE WEST CANADA Lakes Wilderness is an hour-glass shaped high plateau that is higher than any other Adirondack land mass. With over 160,000 acres it is the second largest Wilderness Area (after the High Peaks) in the park. Although many trails penetrate its narrow core, parts of it are trackless, making it the most remote and secret area in the park. Contributing to this sense of remoteness in the south are its boundaries: the West Canada Creek on the west, which is bridged only on private land, and the South Branch of the West Canada Creek, which has but one bridge where it defines the Wilderness Area's southern border. The interior of the southern corner has no marked trails. Traveling here is so difficult that only two bushwhacks are suggested. Fortunately, one road and one snowmobile complex on the periphery of the area offer easy routes that give you a taste of the vast southern prong.

The Adirondack League Club's posted lands block access to the northwest of the prong. The Wilmurt Tract blocks easy access to the Metcalfs, a series of distant ponds. Wilmurt at 2458 feet elevation is the highest settled lake in the Adirondacks. Its camps were built by vacationers from the western part of the state, and its owners permit *no one* on their lands.

The history of log driving on the West Canada Creek is mentioned in the Southwestern guide in this Discover Series, and it is described in vivid detail in Harvey Dunham's *Adirondack French Louie* and David Beetle's *The West Canadas*. Even though this was one of the first regions to be logged in the Adirondacks (Henry Noble floated logs down the creek before 1800), most of the land bordered by the creek and its South Branch was purchased by the state or acquired by tax sale nearly a hundred years ago. The creeks conceal spectacular forests as well as a dozen inviting lakes.

1 South Branch of the West Canada Creek, near Fort Noble Mountain

Picnic spot, map 1

A charming short trail leads 0.6 mile north from NY 8 to the banks of the South Branch of the West Canada Creek. The road begins 1.9 miles east of the bridge at Nobleboro, less than 0.5 mile east of the Herkimer-Hamilton County Line. The path is through deep forest and leads to a short climb over a bank beside the river, where there is a delightful place to picnic and even to camp, though until recently, this led to a much more exciting destination.

The path was the beginning of the trail to Fort Noble Mountain, which served as one of Verplanck Colvin's triangulation points in his Adirondack survey. A fire observation platform was placed on the mountain in 1910. A steel fire tower stood there from 1910 until 1985. There is currently no view from the mountain top. In its last few years, when the tower stood abandoned, you could still climb its rickety stairs for the view. However, even to do this you had to ford the South Branch, no mean feat even in low water, because the great hikers' suspension bridge was removed about 1980. It was considered nonconforming use according to the State Land Master Plan. The bridge's huge nonconforming concrete piers remain, however.

You can find remnants of the trail north of the river, but the last outlook on the summit has filled in, so shortly, only the tower's piers will remain as a reminder of this favorite trail with its fine view into the heart of the West Canadas.

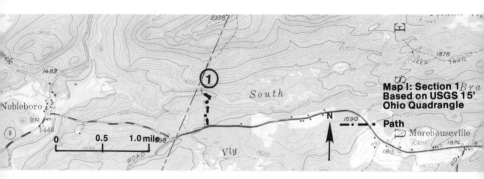

Map 1: Section 1
Based on USGS 15'
Ohio Quadrangle

Path

G Lake

Map II: Sections 2-4, 6-9 Based on USGS 15' Piseco Lake Quadrangle

Trail
Path
Bushwhack
Road

0   0.5   1.0 mile

N

2   South Branch of the West Canada Creek, Mountain Home Road

Bushwhack, map II

Mountain Home Road heads northeast from NY 8, 1.5 miles west of Hoffmeister or 1.5 miles east of Morehouseville. At 0.7 mile the road crosses the South Branch of the West Canada Creek and curves east to follow the north shore of the creek. At 1.5 miles, Wilmurt Road forks left, north, leading to private and posted lands around Wilmurt Lake.

Pavement ends about a half mile past Wilmurt Road, and just beyond, at 2 miles from NY 8, there is a large turnaround, which, lacking anything better, is the best place to park. There are places farther along, but most would block private accesses; and by the time you reach state land, the road may be too rugged for ordinary vehicles. The road continues past private camps for another half mile. Extensive lawns in front of these camps overlook The Floe, the widening of the South Branch. At the last camp, where the road turns into a narrow track, there are No Parking signs. This is the beginning of state land.

The road, now passable only by four-wheel drive vehicles, curves around the lower slopes of Signal Mountain, reaching a fork at 3.1 miles. The way right leads downhill. In slightly more than a hundred yards it reaches a ford on the South Branch, a crossing that four-wheel drive vehicles can make in low water. This road continues east-northeast for 1.2 miles to the private and posted lands surrounding Pine Lake.

The way straight is barricaded in 100 yards. The walk description starts here at 0.0 mile. The roadway descends to cross Mad Tom Brook at the boundary of the West Canada Lakes Wilderness Area. The old bridge here is washed out, but you can make a dry crossing on rocks in low water. The old dug roadway has been cleared and is easy to follow. The grade is gently uphill, but since the track was cut into the steep hillside of Signal Mountain it collects water, making wet walking, in fact in normal times this whole route is wet walking.

The climb northwest is followed by rolling terrain and a curve to the north. You traverse a hardwood hill that drops steeply to your right. There are through-the-trees glimpses of the bluff above Pine Lake and northeast to G Lake Mountain. A curve to the east and a descent brings you at 1.1 miles to the crossing of Roaring Brook, where remnants of a logging bridge are visible. A lovely camping site occupies a hemlock knoll on the northwest quadrant of the crossing. Several deadfalls fill the trail, which then becomes more open. You are walking in a lovely open maple glade with tall, mature trees. Decaying old wooden culverts fail to keep the roadway dry. Ferns line the route; look especially for the rare dissected grape fern, *Botrychium dissectum*. At 1.8 miles you cross Wagoner Brook where there is a nice campsite on the north side of the roadway.

The roadway climbs slightly and begins a long level traverse. It is filling with maple and beech starts. A faint blaze on a tree marks the old track that branched left here, leading ultimately to Jones Brook. This track is hard to follow—a real map and compass challenge.

Near the end of the level, the roadway approaches meadows surrounding the South Branch and two streams that meet it here: Twin Lakes and G Lake outlets. You cross two small brooks, one on a very old bridge. The roadway, visible because it is quite straight, is now filling with spruce and balsam. There is a spruce bog on your left, then the roadway angles down to your right to approach the creek at the site of an old bridge.

This point is frustrating; it is three miles short of T Lake and the valley ahead offers very difficult walking. A local ranger calls it a "real ankle-twister." A flagged route here to the base of T Lake falls might provide a safer route than the one described in section 8. You could follow the west shore of the creek as far as Beaudry Brook, about 0.5 mile, and use that brook as a guide to the high country of the Metcalfs, but this is a very long bushwhack that would lead to the top of the Metcalf Range and down to the lakes that lie northwest of the range. The only other routes to the Metcalfs are from private land at Wilmurt Lake, which is not open to the public, or the bushwhack described in section 5. The West Canada Lakes are the accessible heart of this wilderness, the Metcalfs are its most hidden recesses.

3 G Lake

Hiking, camping, snowshoeing, cross-country skiing, fishing
0.4 mile, ten minutes, relatively level, map II

G Lake is vaguely shaped like a G, hence the name. It sits on a high plateau surrounded by small mountains 2.5 miles north of NY 8. Its access road is at the Arietta-Morehouse Town Line, 2.45 miles west of the West Shore Road of Piseco. The road to this state acquisition, which was made within the past ten years, is considered a town road, hence it is open in summer and passable much of the time to ordinary vehicles. However, the road is not plowed in winter, which makes the distance to the lake the full

2.5 miles with a 100-foot descent to the valley of Big Marsh and a climb of 200 feet to the lake.

From the barrier at 2.1 miles, it is such a short walk to the lake that it is very easy to bring in a canoe. There are lovely campsites beneath the pine stands that surround the site of a house that stood on the eastern lobe of the lake. Your view from that spot is of the eastern lobe, with only a glimpse beyond of the larger part of the lake. The shoreline here is sandy, but there are leeches in the lake.

As you head toward the lake, watch at 0.2 mile from the barrier where the road bends to the northeast. A less-traveled road heads northwest down a small draw toward the peninsula that almost cuts G Lake in two. The road turns west along the south shore of the western lobe, then snakes around the western shores of G Lake toward the dam on the outlet. At the closest approach to the peninsula, 0.2 mile from the main access road, a roadway/path heads north along the peninsula and gradually peters out. It is fun to walk along it for a better look at the lake. The peninsula has some lovely deep woods plants, and its shores are bordered with yellow bladderwort.

In winter, the 2.5-mile approach makes an excellent ski trail, which you can vary by skiing either east or west along the snowmobile trail in the valley of Big Marsh. You begin to see the marsh 0.9 mile north on the G Lake Road from NY 8 and cross the snowmobile trail at 1.1 miles. To the east there is a long stretch of open vlies, so you can ski through them or ski the trail that continues east, section 4. The trail is currently flooded and cannot be walked more than 0.15 mile east of G Lake Road. You can ski or walk to the west where the snowmobile trail follows a high valley that marks the divide between Big Marsh and Alder Brook.

4 | Piseco to The Floe on the South Branch

Snowmobile trail, cross-country skiing
9.5 miles of trail, several possible loops, 200-foot elevation change, map II

A 7-mile snowmobile trail connects Hoffmeister on the west with Irondequoit Bay on Piseco on the east. It follows a valley route, with NY 8 high on the slopes to the south. There are two side snowmobile trails and the town road to G Lake, section 3, which lead north to the valley trail, making it possible to ski several different loops from one point along NY 8.

The eastern end begins at Piseco Lake Lodge, which is a store and restaurant (a good place for a hot lunch), on the West Shore Road, 0.2 mile north of NY 8. The trail leads west for 0.7 mile to a trailer park on the shore of Evergreen Lake that is a dammed portion of Big Marsh. The trail heads west along Evergreen Lake to marshes at its western end and intersects the G Lake Road at 2.4 miles. Because of the trailer park, only the western end of this route is attractive for skiers.

The route continues west along an old road through a high valley; drainage changes here from east to west toward Alder Brook. At 3.2 miles there is a marked intersection with the 1.3-mile-long connector trail from NY 8 that heads north from that highway 3 miles west of West Shore Road and 0.1 mile east of the eastern loop of Alder Brook Road. This connector is fairly steep at first, then levels in spruce swamps. Together with G Lake Road, it makes a good, short, 3.2-mile loop with possible extensions to G Lake or Big Marsh.

Now heading west through Alder Brook valley, the trail meets a trail from Bear Path Inn at 4.4 miles. This inn is 4 miles west of the West Shore Road of Piseco Lake. From a bluff behind the Bear Path Inn there is a good view to the northwest of the Metcalf Mountains across the valley of the South Branch of the West Canada Creek. A short connector trail through private land just west of the bluff leads steeply down the hillside to the state-marked snowmobile trail. Another route, also unmarked, just to the west is less steep, but traverses private land. Both routes join halfway down the slope.

The main snowmobile trail continues west through the valley which is becoming wider. At 5.2 miles you cross a small brook not far from its confluence with Alder Brook, which you will see shortly. Just short of 6 miles the trail approaches the marshes that border The Floe, a partially man-made widening of the South Branch of the West Canada Creek. Here, conditions permitting, you can ski out on The Floe to several small evergreen-covered islands. Mountain Home, the site of an old hotel, sits north across The Floe.

From the east edge of The Floe, the trail curves south and climbs to Hoffmeister, joining NY 8 at 1857-foot elevation, 7.2 miles from Piseco. There is a dense grove of young hemlock halfway up the hill that becomes progressively steeper but not as steep as the approach to Bear Path Inn. You can ski a shorter, 3.8-mile loop from NY 8 using just this western end of the trail near The Floe with a connector from Bear Path Inn. This route is through lovely forests in the valley, and the high point is an approach to the south side of The Floe.

5 Southwestern Corner of the West Canada Lakes Wilderness Area

Extended bushwhacks and snowshoe trips, Piseco Lake and Ohio 15' USGS quadrangles

Lack of good public access makes this area extremely difficult to explore. The poor driving conditions on Haskell Road and the physical problems of crossing the West Canada Creek hinder access from the west. Private lands along the South Branch of the West Canada Creek prevent entry from the south from NY 8. Even if you ford the South Branch on Forest Preserve land near the abandoned trail to Fort Noble Mountain, you will have miles of bushwhacking ahead of you before you reach features of the interior. If you solve the above problems however, you will find this to be one of the wildest areas in the state where solitude is almost guaranteed. Paths do exist along the edges of some of the major ponds, lakes, and waterways, but these are used infrequently, mostly by sportsmen from nearby camps or private clubs.

Several ridges and mountains have rocky outcrops inviting the explorer to discover the views to be had from their tops. Polack, Baldface, and Spruce mountains are among the summits worthy of attention. Many streams, vlies, ponds, and lakes found between the hills support a variety of wildlife, although, because of their high elevation, these waters are severely impacted by acid precipitation. The remote and beautiful Metcalf Lakes were once abundant with native trout, and you may wish to follow a path up Metcalf Brook from the West Canada Creek, testing the waters as you go to see how they fare in modern times.

Alternatively, you can bushwhack up the escarpment from the path along the South Branch of the West Canada Creek, section 2. Either this or a trek from the west along Metcalf Creek suggests a winter backpack trip when you could explore the frozen surface of the Metcalf Lakes. All the routes to those lakes are sufficiently difficult that only those experienced in deep-woods navigation should attempt them, and those individuals are capable of devising their own routes. The experienced deep-woods navigator can find weeks of enjoyment here and because such places as this exist, others will want to hone their backwoods skills to visit them.

Piseco Lake Area

SETTLERS REACHED PISECO in the 1820s via a road from Lake Pleasant. Land between Spy Lake and Piseco Lake was bought on speculation by the Van Rennselaer family in 1835. The town remained small until Andrew K. Morehouse bought land at the north end of Piseco as well as several lots to the north in the Oxbow Tract. With exaggeration and unrealistic promises about the fertility of the land, he induced many settlers to come to the town he laid out on the north shore of Piseco Lake. As many as three hundred people came to the town where he built a store, mills, and a hotel. But whether from the climate, the harshness of the land, or the rigidity of his contracts with those who bought his land, the community failed, and within a decade only a few families were left.

In a second spurt, Piseco grew during the 1870s and 1880s, with the building of several mills and tanneries. However, the hemlock was soon exhausted, and the land north of Piseco was sold to the state, some of it as early as 1877. Before 1900 all the land north of Piseco and around Oxbow Lake except the settlements near the roads was returned to the state. With one hundred years to recover, the forests around Piseco are now some of the most beautiful in the Park. Several good trails, including the Northville-Placid Trail, a new ski trail, and some beautiful snowmobile trails lead to destinations in these forests.

The state owns most of the northwest shore of the lake, and three lovely state campgrounds are on waterfronts along that shore. From NY 8 and the West Shore Piseco Road, Point Comfort Campground is 1.2 miles north; Little Sand Point, 3.2 miles; Poplar Point, 4.2 miles; Piseco Village, 6.3 miles.

6 Echo Cliffs

Hiking, views
0.75 mile, 1 1/3 hours round trip, 700-foot vertical rise, map II

A short and very worn trail leads from West Shore Road Piseco to a magnificent cliff top on a knob on the side of Panther Mountain. The trailhead is 2.6 miles north of NY 8, and there is roadside parking opposite the trailhead. The guide board at the trailhead is confusing. It states

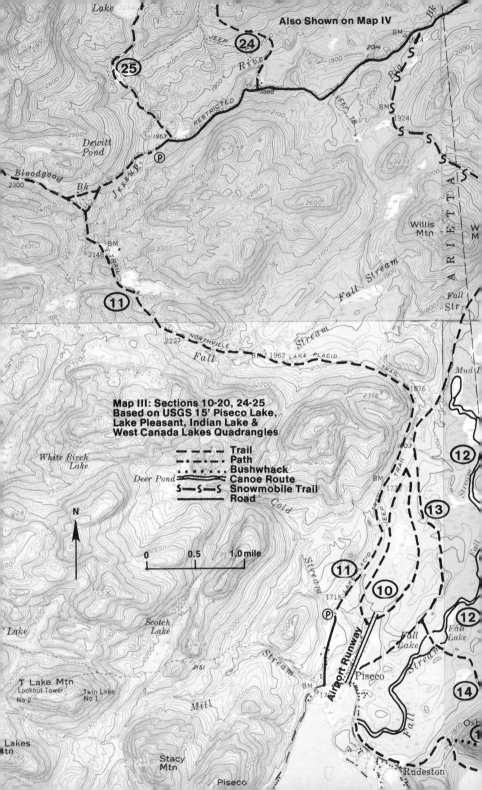

Also Shown on Map IV

Map III: Sections 10-20, 24-25
Based on USGS 15' Piseco Lake,
Lake Pleasant, Indian Lake &
West Canada Lakes Quadrangles

Trail
Path
Bushwhack
Canoe Route
Snowmobile Trail
Road

N

0   0.5   1.0 mile

Panther Mountain, 1048 feet. Well, that is how high the summit of Panther Mountain rises above Piseco Lake, but the cliffs—the destination of the trail—are not on the summit.

It is unfortunate that such a lovely and easy trail is so eroded and has received so little maintenance. Water drains into the trail and has eroded it; there are no water bars.

Aside from the condition of the trail, however, this is a perfect little hike. The trail begins to the north, swings west to begin climbing, then winds generally northwest and fairly steeply. Watch as the grade begins to ease; there are several views in the 0.1 mile through the trees to the cliffs above on your right. At 0.5 mile, the trail has reached the 2100-foot level in a draw. Land now slopes sharply away on your right. The trail turns into the draw between the knob and the mountain proper, which is lined with cliffs. It follows the east side of that draw, climbing steeply to emerge on an open grassy spot from which there are spectacular views east across Spy Lake to the Silver Lake Wilderness.

7 T Lake

Hiking, snowshoeing, camping
3.65 miles, 2 hours, 1000-foot elevation change, map II

The state-marked trail to T Lake begins from the Poplar Point Campground, 4.2 miles north of NY 8 on the West Shore Road of Piseco. The trail begins just south of the campground entrance and a day-use parking fee is charged. T Lake is remote and offers a lean-to for camping, though the lean-to needs to be rebuilt. This trail was marked about 1975 to avoid the private lands followed by the traditional and prettier trail along Mill Stream.

The trail heads west along the southern flanks of Piseco Mountain, climbing fairly steeply through a lovely hardwood forest. At 0.7 mile you traverse a boulder strewn col, with a knob to the south and cliffs that face the mountain to the north. The narrow path leads toward the draw between Piseco and Stacy mountains, then follows the south slopes of Stacy, reaching a height-of-land on that mountain at 1.2 miles. A long, gentle descent follows. As you approach the valley you follow and cross a small stream, then at 1.9 miles in a clearing, you cross Mill Stream, having descended 250 feet. The confluence of the streams, which flow over pink feldspar, is quite lovely.

The trail, now heading north, climbs the flanks of T Lake Mountain and at 2.5 miles, near a rock outcrop, makes a sharp turn to the west. The trail continues climbing and passes the turnoff that once led to the fire tower on T Lake Mountain. That tower has been removed, and there is no view without it. In fact, the tower was removed so long ago that it is almost impossible to spot the trail junction. At 3.2 miles, the grade eases. You are high above the fault valley that forms T Lake and can look across a small arm of that lake to mountains to the north. The trail is wide and level and at just short of 3.7 miles descends to the lean-to on the eastern part of upside-down T.

8 T Lake Falls

Hiking, snowshoeing, camping
5.45 miles, 3 hours, 1000-foot elevation change, map II

This trail begins as for T Lake and continues for 1.8 miles past the lean-to along the outlet valley to the most spectacular falls in the Adirondacks. T Lake Falls plunges 350 feet over a rounded rock escarpment into a tiny pool that is part of the headwaters of the South Branch of the West Canada Creek.

The rounded top of the falls makes it a very dangerous place, and unfortunately many hikers over the years have failed to appreciate that danger. There have been many injuries and several fatalities. As a result, the state has officially closed and is not maintaining the 1.8 miles of trail west of T Lake at present. You can still walk the route, but it is becoming difficult. And, if you do walk it, be sure to follow these cautions: Do not approach the top of the falls, there is no place from which you can see the bottom because of the curved rock base. If you want to descend to the base of the falls, walk either north or south and descend through the trees. To cross the stream to the north, do so only well upstream from the top of the falls. This side has lots of bare rock to negotiate. It is safer to descend on the south side, which has better footings and hand-holds. This is not an easy place to enjoy and certainly no place for children or pets.

The trail west from the T Lake Lean-to is gorgeous as it passes through a deep evergreen forest beside the western portion of the T then descends beside the natural rock dam that holds back the lake. You walk beside a small rock gorge then emerge beside a beaver meadow 0.6 mile from the lean-to. Here the trail may be flooded. A second rock ledge holds back the

outlet here. At 1 mile, the trail drops to the level of a second beaver flow that continues west for 0.5 mile. This is a favorite place, full of birds, with handsome ground cover beneath the spruce that border the trail.

Beyond the end of the meadow, the valley narrows and the trail begins to descend into a small gorge. At 1.8 miles you emerge at the top of the waterfall, but the only view you should expect is to the Metcalf Mountains across the South Branch valley.

There is a camping spot on the north side of the outlet stream. Dense spruce cover the top of the escarpment. Several paths lead through the spruce and down to open rock, but remember to stay in the woods as you descend, even if it is difficult going.

9 Twin Lakes

Bushwhack, map II

The local ranger has proposed a safer route to the base of T Lake Falls. It involves heading to Twin Lakes from the present trail and circling around to the base of Eagle Cliff before approaching the base of T Lake Falls from the south. Without commenting on the merits of the route, it is obvious that Twin Lakes (a misnomer since the lakes are of vastly unequal size) are no rival for T Lake.

From the clearing and the Mill Stream crossing on the T Lake Trail, head west of north, about 240° magnetic, generally following the stream, but leaving and continuing on the course where the going is easier. In places, the open hardwood forest has a thick understory of hobblebush. You pass beneath the ledges on the south face of T Lake Mountain, then descend to the lakeshore. The 1.4-mile bushwhack takes over an hour.

The remains of an old bridge lies underwater between the two lakes, which nevertheless seem to be lower than normal with wide mucky shores. The lakes appear to be quite shallow, with many lily pads. Remains of a campsite with a stove can be found on the shoreline.

A compass heading northeast from the ponds through the draw takes you over 0.5 mile in less than half an hour to the T at T Lake, just to the west of the lean-to.

10 Piseco Airport Ski Trail

Cross-country skiing
5 miles (8 kilometers), 2 hours, relatively level, map III

A very handsome 8 kilometer, 5 mile, ski track has been cut through the wonderfully mature mixed hardwood and hemlock forest that fills the flat Fall Stream valley. This forest owes its beauty to the fact that the state has owned it for nearly a century. The forest is so good that this would make a delightful deep woods walk if it were not for the fact that only the minimal clearing and marking that is needed for winter has been done, so the trail is rather brushy and walking is not easy.

The trail, a counterclockwise loop, starts on the east side of Piseco Airport. North of the airport building, 0.6 mile from NY 8, arrows direct you into the woods to the east of the runway. The track heads generally north for 4 kilometers (the trail is described in metric measure because that is the way it is marked), then turns south to complete the loop along 0.25 mile of a dirt road that approaches the airport from the west, across the runway and south of the beginning point. The ski trail intersects an old trail, an alternate beginning to the Northville-Placid Trail, section 11, 0.3 mile north of this road that continues to private lands. This alternate is currently blocked by much windfall.

The route is occasionally along an old roadway, and there are some swampy areas, which are of no concern in winter. Huge maples and yellow birch are interspersed with tall stands of hemlock that exceed two feet in diameter. Dark patches of conifers, balsam and red spruce, fill the wetter pockets. The tall canopy shades out the understory so you can see great distances through the forest, summer or winter. You meet a slightly younger forest between the 4 and 6 kilometer marks. In fact, the best forest seems to be closest to the airport.

The trail twists and turns in its north-south course with no important changes in contour. One confusing marking near the north end will undoubtedly be corrected before this guide is printed—the route was extended to make it exactly 8 kilometers long and a cross-over bore the same yellow markings at the trail.

11 Northville-Placid Trail to Spruce Lake

Hiking, camping, fishing, skiing
9.8 miles, 4½ hours, 765-foot elevation change, maps III and IV

The blue-marked Northville-Placid Trail to Spruce Lake has long been the only way to reach the lake, and it is the southern entrance to the West Canada Lakes Wilderness. The last 2.45 miles of the trail and notes on Spruce Lake and its three lean-tos are given in section 24, which describes a much shorter route to the lake. The handsome southern section of trail will remain of interest for end-to-enders, those for whom the feat of walking the entire length of the Northville-Placid Trail is the main attraction. The time given does not take into account carrying a pack, and those who merely want to camp at Spruce Lake will undoubtedly use the nearer trailhead from International Paper Company land.

Haskell Road is 2.2 miles west of NY 8 on Old Piseco Road. Use the parking turnout 0.7 mile north and walk across the bridge over Cold Stream. The beginning of the trail crosses private land, and there is the possibility the trailhead will be relocated near the Piseco Airport, which is just east of Haskell Road.

The trail begins in a deep, rich, mature forest of evergreens, on a level route at the edge of the broad, flat valley that stretches east to Fall Stream and north for 4 miles. The registration box is across the bridge, past the last house, and just beyond it is a red-marked trail stating 0.75 mile to Piseco Airport. The way is really flat. Short of 0.9 mile, the trail crosses a stream. The forest of big trees contains some evergreens mixed among the large yellow birch and maples, and the walking is fairly smooth.

Gradually, the trail climbs the hillside to the west, and wet areas begin to appear in the trail. At 2 miles you pass a bigger stream, then a couple smaller intermittent streams. You feel as if you are on the edge of an escarpment—the trail is seventy feet or more above the valley floor, and there are ledges on the mountain to the right, west.

You have been heading just east of north and now the trail makes a big right angle bend so that you end up heading just north of west and climbing significantly for the first time. You pass a wind-throw area where quite a number of large trees lie prone, all facing in the same direction, northwest. Perhaps these are skeletons from the 1950 hurricane. There is a huge erratic on the lip of the escarpment. You are climbing steadily now in a much more disturbed forest with lots of beech starts interspersed among a few giant trees. The trail crosses several more intermittent streams, all still flowing to your right. The trail is muddy as well as strewn with rocks and stones.

At 3.1 miles the grade eases. You are still on a hillside with rock ledges on your left and the Fall Stream valley on your right. The trail traverses a stretch of grassy quagmire. In fact, muddy spots mark the next mile of trail where small washes drop north from the hillside. The trail is along such level terrain that it is easily flooded. At 4.5 miles you approach Fall Stream. There is a campsite on both sides of the stream here. Rock steps take the trail across the stream at an acute angle.

Following Fall Stream, the trail begins to climb through a narrowing valley. You climb for 1.3 miles through the valley, most of the time well away from the stream, on the north side of its valley. With a couple of short exceptions, the 250-foot ascent is gentle. There is an old Forest Preserve marker at the height-of-land at the former International Paper Company boundary line. This point now marks a change of drainage. At 5.8 miles, the trail begins to descend and marshes become visible to the northeast. At 6.1 miles you pass the site of an old camp with an old trash heep. Modern campers have stopped here, too, since the spot is a bit over halfway to Spruce Lake.

Skirting the vly, the headwaters of the Jessup River, the trail traverses a spruce swamp, then climbs over a knoll. Just beyond the brow of the knoll, a side path leads to an old flooded area on the vly—perhaps a flood dam for logging. Another descent leads past a huge glacial erratic to a hop-a-rock crossing of another branch of the Jessup at 7 miles. A spot used by campers is too close to the stream to be appropriate. Just beyond there is a small field with a No Camping sign. Campers appear to have used a site to the north of it on the side of a small gorge. The trail makes a moderate climb through a draw for 0.35 mile to come close to the woods road from Perkins Clearing, section 24. It is 0.8 mile beyond to the crossing of Bloodgood Brook where at 8.15 miles you are 1.65 miles from Spruce Lake.

12 Fall and Vly Lakes

Canoeing
12 miles round trip, 5 hours, map III

Fall Stream is a wonderful flat-water canoe trip into the long, marsh-filled valley that stretches north from Piseco between a range of unnamed small hills to the west and a series of conical knob hills to the east. Easy canoeing through this scenic area where a variety of plants border the stream makes this a great trip. You do have to carry over a few small beaver dams—an average of half a dozen has been counted over the years. But, if the current higher dam—nearly two feet tall—holds just downstream from the outlet of Vly Lake, an additional 3 miles of canoeing will remain available. With the higher water you can canoe northwest nearly 0.5 mile from Vly Lake into Mud Lake and over a mile upstream on the inlet of Vly Lake.

The beginning of this canoe trip is from Old Piseco Road, 1.6 miles west of NY 8. On the west side of the bridge over Fall Stream, a short roadway leads across a snowmobile trail to a canoe launching spot. Permission may be required from the Irondequoit Club to the west that owns the property. No camping, picnicking, or fires are permitted in this area, and be careful not to leave any litter. The shoulders of the main road are wide enough for cars to pull off; this avoids blocking the launch road. There is an alternate beginning, 0.25 mile to the east along a concealed and muddy roadway that would require a 0.2-mile carry to the stream.

There are rapids downstream from the snowmobile bridge but the way north and east is all flat water. In early August great clumps of cardinal flowers greet you as you start upstream. The first beaver dam may be quite close to the beginning. The stream heads east toward Oxbow Mountain and passes a place where boats are tied up. This site is at the end of a dirt track that begins from Old Piseco Road 0.4 mile to the east of the bridge and could be an alternate beginning for the canoe trip, though it, too, crosses private lands.

The stream turns north beside clumps of buttonbush with its flowers like white pins in a pincushion. The purple of pickerel weed reflects in the stream.

After a mile you pass a dock that leads to a house and at 1.5 miles you enter Fall Lake. North of Fall Lake the stream is narrower as it winds about the lowlands. Watch for turtlehead on the shore. At times the twisted route is through alder swamps; at times tall hemlock, spruce, and maple crowd the shores that are accented by a very few tall pines.

At about 3.3 miles you see a cable stretched across the stream. Here is the only place you really have to watch for rocks in the stream. As the valley opens up to the north, you can begin to see the hill that lies west of Vly Lake. Waterwillows and monkey flowers dot the shore. Yellow warblers, kingbirds, cedar waxwings, and black ducks are among the many birds you will see. There are more beaver dams to cross, then at 5.3 miles

you see another cable over the stream. There is a camping spot to the east and, just beyond, another good spot high on the west bank. Within five minutes you enter Vly Lake.

There is a camping site high on the west shore—one of the few flat places on the slopes of Vly Lake Mountain, but watch out for poison ivy! Farther north are rocks that provide a favorite picnic spot. The view from here is south toward Piseco Mountain. The long, unnamed ridge traversed by the Northville-Placid trail is to the right, north, followed by the cut through which that trail passes. Next, going north, another unnamed ridge is in the background, with Willis Mountain in the foreground. Potash is the most northerly mountain visible.

The inlet comes through a long marshy prong that extends south into the lake. The small stream that leads to Mud Lake is just to the west of this prong. Fall Stream is deeply tannin colored; in contrast, Mud Lake is a tiny crystal-clear, shallow pond.

13 From Piseco to Fawn Lake

Snowmobile trail, cross-country skiing, hiking
9.6 miles, 4½ hours, relatively level, map III

Rarely does a snowmobile trail offer such a wonderful day in the woods, whether in summer or winter, as this varied forest route. The reasons for its beauty are simple: most of the trail is through mature forests, uncut for over a century. It is certainly one of the half dozen best forest walks in this guide in both summer and winter, and it is so good that it is described twice, once in each direction.

For the trip from west to east, leave a car at your destination, the parking turnout on the shore of Sacandaga Lake. To find it, drive west on NY 8 from Old Piseco Road for just short of 4 miles to the western end of Fish Mountain Road. Head north, going straight at the first intersection and turning left, west, when you reach the lakeshore, 1.2 miles from NY 8. The easiest way to navigate these roads is to follow the signs for Roads End, a lodge that is just west of this intersection. Continue past Roads End to the end of the road, 0.7 mile from the intersection, to a marked parking area.

The western end of the trail begins at Piseco Airport, 2 miles northwest of NY 8 along Old Piseco Road. (Maps may refer to this as Piseco Lake Road, but the sign at NY 8 says Old Piseco Road.) A sign at the entrance

Fall Stream

to the airport gives mileages to Oxbow Inn, 3.1 miles; Big Brook, 9.2 miles; Sacandaga Lake, 9.4 miles; and Speculator, 14.6 miles.

Park in the airport parking area and head east into the woods right behind the lot. In 0.2 mile there is a marked left turn; right leads to a private inholding on Fall Stream. Another path from the airport joins the trail farther north. You are on a wide woods road headed east of north through a mature hardwood forest. At 0.8 mile you reach a fork: the way right leads 2.3 miles to Oxbow Lake via Fall Lake, section 14.

Stay left, straight, on gently rolling terrain. Wetlands lie to the west of the trail, and at 1.3 miles you cross a small bridge. Your route is now west of north, and the forest is beautifully mixed with large hemlock. Just short of 2 miles you jog right and can see a swamp ahead. The stream through this circular swamp has been flooded by beaver in the past. You can just about stay dry hopping on grass hummocks across the swamp to a bridge on the north side. The trail curves about on level contour, both east and west of north. You cross a ridge of spruce, then drop into a swale with a sort of cirque around the northwest. The trail turns easterly, and at 3 miles you reach a stream with another fairly good bridge, not far from the 1803 benchmark.

The trail, east of north now, is following a definite old road along the edge of marshes that drop down to Mud Lake, which is out of sight behind to the east. You cross a ridge of notable maples, then dip to cross a huge bridge over Fall Stream at 4.5 miles. The trail heads east and in 200 yards forks sharply north again, away from the roadbed it has been following. This cut route continues just east of north with the steep slopes of Willis Mountain to the left, west.

At 5.2 miles you reach a junction. The unmarked trail north leads to Mossy Vly and Big Brook along a snowmobile trail that circles Potash Mountain, mostly on International Paper Company roads. As a result of the 1985 land swap, IP now owns much of Potash Mountain and has begun to log its slopes. The eastern portion of that circuit through Mossy Vly is currently flooded and impossible to walk. The western part is along the road south from Perkins Clearing.

The sharp right fork leads uphill; signs point to Sacandaga and Fawn lakes. The route is now southeast for 0.5 mile to a right angle that turns to the east, left. A side road, which confusingly still has snowmobile markers, heads west of south from this bend downhill into a swamp. Take the left turn and shortly (at 5.9 miles) you reach the high bridge over Willis Vly. Fawn Lake Vly lies northeast. Both vlies are bordered with huge black and red spruce, tamarack, and thick stands of alders.

The trail, now southeast, climbs slightly to a balsam-covered knoll, then winds about constantly changing elevation and direction. The forest is impressive with huge maples and occasional black cherries. You are walking in a forest that looks as it must have when the first Europeans arrived. Here the knolls are covered with a large proportion of huge red spruce, many over two feet in diameter and eighty feet tall. One giant beside the trail is over eight feet in circumference!

At 7.8 miles you reach a lovely flooded vly; beaver have managed to float the bridge across it. Shortly beyond you see Fawn Lake through the trees, and at 8.2 miles you cross its outlet on another high bridge. For 0.4 mile you walk along the north shore of Fawn Lake, then turn south for another mile to reach the western parking area at 9.6 miles. See sections 16 and 17 for more details of Fawn Lake.

14 Oxbow Ski Loop

Snowmobile trail, cross-country skiing
4.4 miles, 2½ hours, relatively level, map III

This snowmobile trail makes a superb loop from Piseco Airport. A portion of the trail along Old Piseco Road is adjacent to private land, in fact almost in many backyards. You may wish to make a loop that avoids this part by finishing at Rudeston, 1.1 miles northwest of NY 8. If you ski the entire circuit, the length is 5.5 miles. Remember, this is a snowmobile trail, so watch out for them. You cannot hike this trail as it is routed across two lakes, so be sure their surfaces are frozen.

From Piseco Airport follow the snowmobile trail north for 0.8 mile and turn east at the junction, section 13. The trail descends gently to the northwest corner of Fall Lake, cuts across the lake, and at 1.2 miles heads southeast. If Fall Stream is securely frozen, and it has such a slight flow that it often is, you can extend the trip by skiing north or south along it.

To the southeast of Fall Lake, the trail heads through the woods with little change in grade, then crosses a large vly from which Oxbow Mountain is visible. At 1.9 miles, the trail reenters the woods and circles north around the mountain, to approach Oxbow Lake at 2.4 miles in a deep, hemlock-bordered bay.

Ski south from the bay (the lake may be windy and full of snowmobiles). You can end your trip as the snowmobilers do at Oxbow Lodge on the southeast corner of the lake. Or, you can ski down the lake for about 1 mile to a bay on its southern flanks where you pick up the trail heading west. It climbs slightly and hugs the base of the mountain for 0.5 mile before turning southwest and winding over several small rises as it takes a circuitous route toward Old Piseco Road. Several downhill runs end at a gravel pit, at 4.2 miles, and just beyond it the trail heads northwest immediately behind a row of houses.

Again you can end the trip where the trail approaches the road, or continue paralleling the road to return to the airport.

15   Oxbow Mountain
Bushwhack after a canoe trip, map III

Oxbow Mountain is a steep, conical mountain. Its shape is repeated in numerous little hills that lie in the glacial valley north of Piseco. This one has sharp cliffs on its southern face and a lovely perch atop them that overlooks Piseco Lake and Rudeston Hill.

To reach the foot of the mountain, rent a boat at Oxbow Lodge, or put a canoe in where Oxbow Outlet crosses Old Piseco Road, 0.2 mile west of NY 8. The local fire company fills its truck here, so you cannot park right at the outlet. Instead, pull off on the shoulder further west.

Oxbow Outlet is a handsome tamarack swamp with many bog plants along the northern shore. Paddle northeast for 0.8 mile to the beginning of the snowmobile trail of section 14. You are below the steepest part of the mountain, so walk a bit east before heading up the mountain, approaching it from the east. Pick your way up the steep slopes, watching out for loose rock. This scree can be dangerous. As you approach the tiny summit, head south, looking for the opening that indicates the cliff tops. They are about 30 feet below the summit of this 570-foot mountain.

You can retrace your steps or continue across the summit and head down in a westerly direction. While the eastern slopes are dry, probably burned, with oak, ironwood, and basswood among the beech and maples, the western slopes are deeply shaded with hemlock. The walking is easier, and it is not difficult to avoid the ledges that become so steep close to the south face. From the bottom of the mountain head south, and you quickly pick up the snowmobile trail about 0.5 mile from your canoe.

Jessup River Wild Forest

LANDS ALONG NY 8 and NY 30 bordering the West Canada Lakes Wilderness Area make up the Jessup River Wild Forest. There has been a track called the Albany Road through this region since the early 1800s. Authorized as a state road on June 19, 1812, it was to be the first road to traverse the southern Adirondacks and was projected to run from "Albany to some place near the foot of sloop navigation on the river St. Lawrence." Since a primitive road already existed from Albany to Sir William Johnson's "Fish House" near the Sacandaga River, the proposed extension was often referred to as the Fish House-Russell Road.

Eddy's map of 1818 shows an essentially straight route from Lake Pleasant to the St. Lawrence county line, following the east boundary of Totten and Crossfield townships 1-5 and the west boundary of townships 40 (Raquette Lake), 39, and 38. The state *Map of the Adirondack Forest* (1896) shows a similar route; but, between Raquette Lake and Albany Lake (now Nehasane Lake) on the Beaver River, later editions cease to show any "north-south" trail.

From Lake Pleasant, the Albany Road took the route of the old road to Perkins Clearing and on to Sled Harbor. From Sled Harbor, the route was through the pass north of Pillsbury Mountain, the same as the modern trail, section 31, then north past Cedar Lakes to Little Moose Lake. The trail past Pillsbury Mountain is still known as the "Old Military Road," although Donaldson has plausibly shown that none of the three early state roads through the Adirondacks was built as a military road.

Curiously, none of the modern routes through the Moose River Plains reflects a part of the Albany Road.

Today the route north from Lake Pleasant passes through International Paper Company land and the Jessup River Wild Forest. A number of snowmobile trails wind through both areas. Some, through beautiful forests owned by the state for a century or more, make excellent ski trails and are described. Others are so heavily used by snowmobiles that skiing is not advised, except possibly during the week.

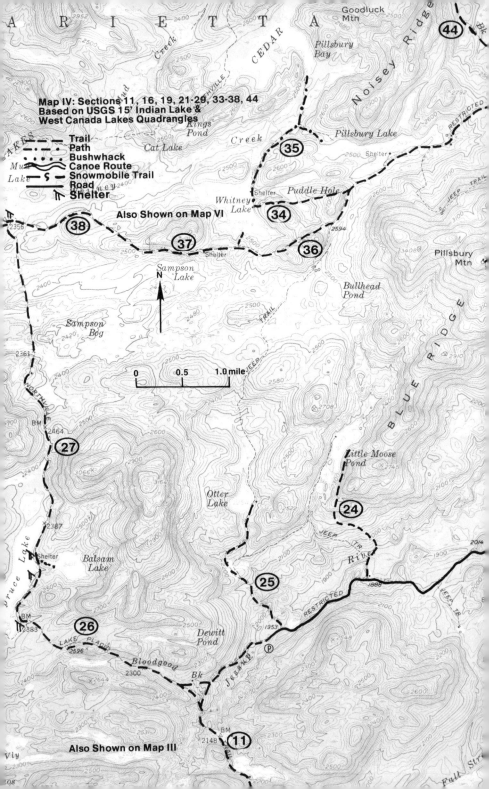

Map IV: Sections 11, 16, 19, 21-29, 33-38, 44
Based on USGS 15' Indian Lake &
West Canada Lakes Quadrangles

Trail
Path
Bushwhack
Canoe Route
Snowmobile Trail
Road
Shelter

Also Shown on Map VI

Also Shown on Map III

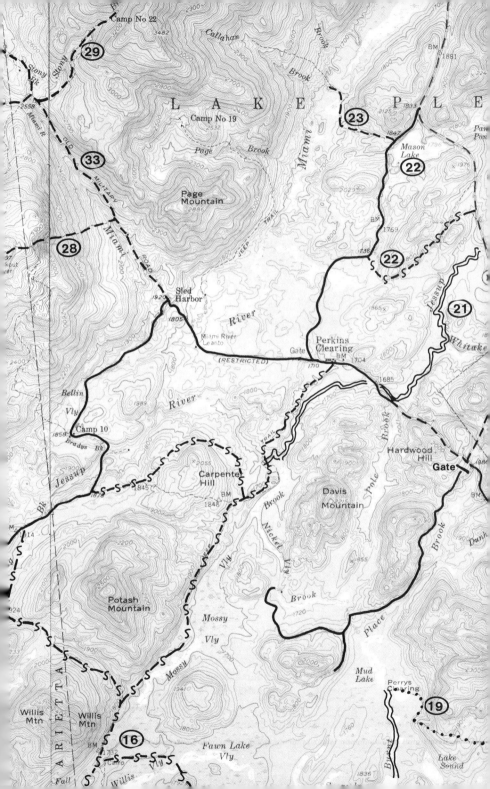

Erratic on Fawn Lake Snowmobile Trail

16 Snowmobile Trail from Fawn Lake to Piseco

Hiking, picnicking, snowshoeing, cross-country skiing
9.6 miles, 4 hours, relatively level, maps III and IV

The marked snowmobile trail from the northwest side of Sacandaga Lake to Piseco Airport is described as a hiking trail in section 13. This section describes the trail in the opposite direction, emphasizing it as a winter route when skiers will not encounter many snowmobiles, except on weekends.

The trail signs give different mileages for the two directions, 9.8 and 9.4 miles, depending on which end of the trail you start on. Reverse the directions of section 13, leaving a car at Piseco Airport. Return to the eastern trailhead near Sacandaga Lake where a DEC sign indicates "Fawn Lake Outlet 1.0 mile, Valley Lake 4.2 miles, Piseco Airport 9.8 miles." Do not believe all of it. There is no Valley Lake, and in case it is just a printing error, the trail does not reach Vly Lake at all.

Start northwest along the roadway and within 50 feet reach a barrier to all motorized vehicles except snowmobiles. The beginning of the trail has some very large white pines, mixed with deciduous trees and balsam fir, not surprising since the state has owned the land since 1877.

At 0.2 mile, the trail forks; straight ahead the route goes to the shore of Fawn Lake for fishing (section 17); the snowmobile/hiking trail goes right to pass northeast of the lake. In twenty minutes you go down into a hemlock grove, and you can see the lake on your left. In less than a half hour, you reach the two camping sites at the end of the lake. They are used by fishermen who have taken some nice lake trout out of this large, deep lake. After a five minute walk beyond, at 1.4 miles, you cross a plank bridge over the outlet and skirt the northern end of the lake. At 1.8 miles you cross another stream flowing northwest out of a beaver meadow. In one hour you reach a height-of-land and from there the trail drops to Willis Vly and crosses this tributary of Fall Stream. The bridge here at 3.7 miles is a nice place for lunch.

Two hundred yards beyond the bridge, there is a bend in the trail, which turns westerly. At 4.4 miles you reach a junction; right leads to Perkins Clearing and Big Brook Trail, straight ahead leads to Piseco Airport. From the junction, the Piseco Airport trail angles south. An hour and a half from your car, at 5 miles, you cross fast-flowing Fall Stream. Shortly beyond, in winter, if you leave the trail, you can see Mud Lake on your left and the marshes that surround it. From here the trail runs about 200° from magnetic north and follows along the edge of a hill in beautiful hardwoods, paralleling Fall Stream. It is a nice open trail for hiking and skiing, and small brooks have bridges or can be jumped.

At 7.4 miles, beaver have dammed a stream, and it is not skiable in late spring. However, the entire route is easily skied in under four hours. Allow longer for hiking.

Since the trail is packed by snowmobiles, there is usually snow on it until late March making delightful spring skiing. From the eastern trailhead, you can shorten the route to a comfortable round trip to Willis Vly and Fall Stream that takes less than four hours, including lunch. From the airport, western, end you can ski into the beaver overflow and back in less than two hours.

17   Fawn Lake Paths

Hiking, fishing, camping, skiing, map III

There are two lovely paths connected with the eastern end of the snowmobile trail described in section 16. From that trailhead walk along the snowmobile trail for five minutes, 0.2 mile, and take a left, unmarked fork. You may spot a local snowmobile trail sign. The cover is scrubby with a few really big pines. You head generally northwest and in five minutes more, at 0.5 mile, you can see the water of Fawn Lake.

This beautiful shoreline is laden with pinxter bushes, a spectacular border of pink blooms about Memorial Day weekend, when the blackflies are nearing their peak. The path, which follows an old roadway, is so flat and easy that wheeling a canoe along it to the lake is very easy. The lake is shallow with sandy shores and lovely swimming beaches.

Paths lead both north and south along the shoreline to several campsites. The tall hemlock groves that border the lake have an open understory, an almost park-like appearance. Woodferns are mingled on the forest floor among wintergreen and dewdrop. The northern path disappears before the last camping spot, which is most easily reached by boat. This path crosses several small streams and can be wet, but it is a gorgeous shoreline with tall pines, polypody capped erratics, and places to camp. The northern sites have lovely views to Fish Mountain in the south and one has Oxbow visible through the draw at the southern end of the lake.

Another unmarked path leads from the head of the lake along the snowmobile trail through a draw for 0.5 mile to Sacandaga Lake. To walk it, begin on the snowmobile trail and stay right along it until you reach the planking that bridges the marshy area at the foot of the lake. The walk is quite level, through tall stands of maples and yellow birch with huge pines. You reach the planking after a twenty-five-minute walk, about 1 mile. You can see the lake through the trees on your left, and on your right, there is a faint path.

Follow this path a little north of east, using faded yellow blazes to guide you. You walk through a stand of huge hemlock, climbing slightly to traverse a hillside with a hemlock stand below. Lush ferns fill the wet lowlands. After about a ten-minute walk you reach a fork. The way left leads less than 100 yards to a spring. The way right leads to a big, deep bay on Sacandaga Lake. To the left of it there is a lovely rock promontory, to the right a hemlock and pine covered peninsula. It is a delightful place for a picnic, about a forty-minute walk from your car.

18 Moffit Beach Campground Nature Trail
Short trail, map III

The Moffit Beach Nature Trail offers a ten-minute walk through a mature hemlock stand that covers a knoll in the campground. The trail is too short to walk, unless you are staying at the campground, for it hardly justifies the day-use fee charged. However, it is a pleasant loop through a beautiful, open, park-like woods along the trail that begins from a field near campsite #259.

19 Mud Lake
Bushwhack or canoe trip, map III

A 3-mile track once led from Page Road west of Moffit Beach Campground north and west over low hills to Mud Lake, a widening of Burnt Place Brook. The track was marked as a snowmobile trail in the 1970s. A short portion of the track at the beginning of the trail at Page Road crosses private land, and the owner objected to the trail crossing. Hence, the trail is now closed and not maintained.

However, it is possible to reach the trail by bushwhacking northeast from the Moffit Beach Campground along the east side of Hatchery Brook. In fact, the local ranger has intended flagging just such a route. It is hoped that it will be done as soon as the Unit Management Plan is adopted. At present, the trail is growing in and will become too difficult to follow if it is not maintained. The forests throughout this area are really lovely, and this trail could offer a good walk in the future.

If you just want to reach Mud Lake, there is a better way to do it than walking. Canoe from the Moffit Beach Campground (there is a marked boat launch site) west then north to the very northernmost bay of Sacandaga Lake. It is about a 2-mile trip. Burnt Place Brook is a deep, slack channel that flows into the bay. After 0.8 mile it narrows, but remains deep as it winds through marshes, vlies, and spruce swamps. The only obstacles are a couple of low beaver dams. Another 0.5 mile of meandering brook opens into Mud Lake, a badly named, beautiful pond. There is a campsite on the south shore on the only bit of firm ground near the lake. Burnt Place Brook continues broad and deep for at least 0.3 mile above Mud Lake.

Looking south across Fawn Lake

20   Near Fish Mountain

Cross-country skiing, bushwhacking, map III

The main snowmobile trail from Sacandaga Lake to Oxbow Lake makes a loop beneath the slopes of Fish Mountain. The trail is too heavily used for weekend skiing, but if you go midweek, it offers a good 3.5-mile circuit. There are several access points: A southern one is at the north shore of Oxbow Lake at the end of Oxbow Road. Parking here is limited. The northern access is at the shore of Sacandaga Lake, again with limited parking. To find access near Fish Mountain, turn north from the western end of Fish Mountain Road for 0.7 mile and turn left. The snowmobile trail crosses the end of this road just beyond the Fish Mountain Cemetery.

The road that passes the cemetery also gives access to Fish Mountain. The summit is mostly state land. If you head toward magnetic north you can climb this steep little cone, which has a large triangular summit 540 feet from the road. There are cliffs and openings below the summit to the north and west, one with views of the Oxbow Lake and a western one with views across Fall Stream.

21 Jessup River

Canoeing, camping, fishing, map IV

It is surprising and exciting to find a memorable experience where you least expect it. You cross the Jessup River 6.5 miles north of the Village of Speculator and the intersection of NY 8 and 30. The river does not look like much, but will delight you with a secluded, easy trip, a place for overnight camping, and some deep holes for fishing or swimming.

Turn west on a dirt road immediately south of the bridge. Head down a short, sharp hill to a parking place beside the river. Slide your canoe into the gently flowing stream and paddle upstream. (You can also go downstream to where Cannon Brook comes in on the right, but below that there are rapids where the river flows down into Indian Lake.)

It is easy to paddle against the gentle current in summer and fall, although early spring with high water could be strenuous. The river winds around, going west, then almost south, as it meanders among red spruce and balsam. The shoreline is alder and brush choked. Stark dead trees make interesting reflections in the still water. The bottom, seen through tea-colored water, is a series of sandy ripples. The sand builds up on the inside of the bends, and rushing spring floods have carved out deep pools in the sandy glacial till.

Sticks gnawed by beavers float along the banks. Twenty minutes upstream you will see a pile of cuttings. These are stored in a row—not formed in a beaver house—for these are bank beavers who dig tunnels in the sand banks and cache their winter food just outside. After thirty minutes, there is a low tree blocking most of the stream, but near the left bank there is enough water to paddle past it. After forty minutes, high ground to the south enables large white pines to crown the ridge. Just as the stream winds right away from the rocky, high bank, there is a level place to camp under tall trees. This is all state land, so you can camp here or anywhere along the river, as long as you stay 150 feet back from the stream. A sandy beach and a deep pool invite a swim or a place to fish.

Shortly beyond, at the head of the next loop, a large tree blocks the river. You can climb out on it and slide your canoe over, but it is easier to take out on the sand spit to the south of the log and slide your boat across the weeds 20 feet to the upstream loop.

After paddling for an hour and twenty minutes, you reach Whitaker Lake Outlet, which comes in on the left, east. It is a small, blocked stream that you may not even notice unless you hear running water. You are only

1.4 miles as the crow flies from the highway, but easily twice that distance along the river's twisting course.

Continuing on, there are several large loops and then another ridge develops on the left. In fall, you may see ducks or a resting goose in this remote section. In summer there are warblers in the shurbs beside the stream. The river gets smaller, and after paddling for an hour and fifty minutes, your way is blocked by several trees. This point is about a half mile downstream from the snowmobile bridge, which crosses the Jessup southeast of Perkins Clearing. You can portage around the logs, but the stream is smaller, and you are likely to find more log jams.

This spot is less than 2 direct miles from the highway, four miles by the winding river. If you turn here, it is thirty-five minutes back to the log, which must be portaged, forty minutes to the camp spot. With the help of the current, it is only an hour before you again hear civilization, all too short a time to enjoy this pretty, meandering stream.

22 Mason Lake and Snowmobile Trail

Canoeing, camping, fishing, hiking, cross-country skiing
1.6-mile trail, 1.7-mile dirt road, 1½ hours, relatively level,
map IV

Mason Lake lies to the west of NY 30, 8 miles north of Speculator; its eastern shore is within 50 feet of the parking area beside the highway. It stretches south and west for almost a mile. The far end has a contorted shoreline of spruce-covered promontories projecting into marshes that surround the narrowing outlet.

A dirt road, 0.4 mile north along NY 30, heads southwest along the northwestern shore of Mason Lake. There are a dozen or so good campsites along the road, many between the road and the water. It is easy to launch a canoe from any of those sites. This is not a formal campground area, so camping is allowed for up to three days without a permit. The one drawback is that almost every site is fully occupied on every warm weather weekend. It is too close to the road to give a sense of solitude, but it is handsome, and a visit midweek with canoe offers a couple hours of delightful exploring.

There is one snowmobile trail near Mason Lake that is all on state land, making it attractive for skiers, who, nevertheless, may wish to avoid winter weekends when there is much snowmobile traffic. The 1.6-mile segment of trail is pleasant enough for hiking as well. It follows the route of one of the

Bridge over Willis Vly

old roads headed toward Perkins Clearing, and connects NY 30 north of the Jessup River with the Perkins Clearing Road southwest of Mason Lake. You can combine it with a walk along the two roads for a 4.7-mile loop from Mason Lake.

Turn south off NY 30 on the dirt road past Mason Lake for 1.7 miles where the trail heads south as the road turns west. There is a barrier two hundred yards down the trail, just before it reaches the outlet of Mason Lake. A wide, solid bridge crosses the stream. Telephone wires are strung on creosoted poles the entire length of this route, and you will note that many are very splintered, particularly about eight feet off the ground. There is something about creosote that attracts black bears and they wreak havoc on these poles!

A wet area shortly beyond the bridge is no problem even in summer. The route takes a generally level contour around a small hill, going from south to east to northeast. To the right of the trail is a dense spruce and balsam thicket. Low moss-decorated ledges line the hillside to your left. You cross a number of little streams flowing from left to right into the swamp, but they are easily jumped or skied over. At 1 mile the trail climbs a gentle slope between two hills and beyond is a swampy area that the road loops around. Then, at 1.3 miles the road forks and the main route turns right and downhill. You reach the trailhead on NY 30 at 1.6 miles. It is 1.4 miles south of the Perkins Clearing Road, and would be a better beginning spot for a winter ski trip as there is adequate parking on the road here.

23 Miami River

Hiking, camping, fishing
1 mile, 30 minutes, 160-foot elevation change, map IV

A short, pleasant, but not-well-marked trail heads west from the campsite that is on the knoll to the left, north, side of the road beside Mason Lake and 0.45 mile from NY 30. There is no guideboard and so few red markers that it might be called an unmarked footpath.

The very narrow footpath leads through scrubby forest, cuts across a very small open marsh, and continues relatively straight and slightly downhill. The forest quickly improves and even large hemlock line the ravine that the path follows, then crosses, to continue following almost down to the level of the Miami, where at 0.7 mile, the path turns north along the river valley. The path seems to disappear in wet marshes near the river, but you can find a cable crossing. The path does continue west, to the north of Callahan Brook, but it is only infrequently used by hunters and is very faint.

On the return, blowdowns might confuse a couple places in the path, but in this direction there are lots of informal red and orange blazes to keep you on the correct route.

Perkins Clearing

A CONSTITUTIONALLY APPROVED land swap, completed in 1984 between the state and International Paper Company (IP), has given the hiking, fishing, and hunting public a series of new trailheads that lead to destinations on state land, sometimes making much shorter trails than existed in the past. In addition to the trails from Sled Harbor, described in the chapter, "The Heart of the West Canadas," trails from IP land lead to Pillsbury Mountain, Otter Lake and Little Moose Pond, and a real shortcut to Spruce Lake.

IP's principal route through the area does not follow exactly the traditional route, but it does pass Perkins Clearing, which is remembered mostly as a place on the way to some place else. The road continues on to Sled Harbor, where horse-drawn, wheeled-carts were exchanged for sleds that were loaded with supplies for the lumber and hunting camps in the West Canadas and Cedar Lakes. Dunham recounts in *Adirondack French Louie* that sometimes twenty or thirty or more sleds could be seen lying around at Sled Harbor.

IP will keep the road south of Sled Harbor open to the public. Much of it is used by IP's logging trucks and some bridges have recently been improved. There are a few rough places on hills, but with care, you can drive an ordinary vehicle to the very end. Mileages given below are to places important for hikers. Mileages in the eastern area where IP is currently logging are not given.

Mileages to and along International Paper Company's Access Roads
Mileages north from Speculator

0.0   Speculator
2.9   IP Road South

4.25   Snowmobile trail opposite Whittaker Lake Road
6.6   Jessup River
8.0   Mason Lake
8.4   Road to Perkins Clearing
12.1   Lewey Lake Campground

Perkins Clearing Road

0.0   at NY 30
0.4+   Trail to Miami River from Campsite
     Several campsites, canoe launching sites
2.4   Marshes both sides of road, view west to Page Mountain
3.4   Intersection, straight to IP Headquarters building, snowmobile
     trails and Perkins Clearing

Turn right, west, at 3.4 miles

4.4   Intersection, logging road, stay straight
4.45   Miami River
5.05   Sled Harbor, parking in gravel pit, trailhead for West Canada
     Wilderness
5.1   Intersection, road right, northwest, leads to Pillsbury
     Mountain, Cedar Lakes, and the West Canadas; stay straight
5.8   Bridge over Miami River
7.2   Intersection, gravel pit, site of Camp No. 10. Road right, west
     leads to beginning of old jeep trail to Pillsbury.

Turn left, east, at 7.2 miles

7.6   Bridge over the Jessup River
8.2   Stay right, the way left leads to new IP logging roads
8.5   Stream Crossing
9.3   Stay straight; a left turn, east, is the Big Brook Snowmobile
     Trail
11.1   Road right, west, leads to Little Moose Pond
12.2   Bridge over the Jessup River
12.3   Road right, west, leads to Otter Lake
12.7   Barrier at end of road, trail registration, beginning of
     connector trail to Northville-Placid Trail and Spruce Lake

24 Little Moose Pond

Path on old logging roads; hiking, camping, fishing
1.9 miles, 50 minutes, 400-foot elevation change, maps III and
IV

Logging roads will continue for some time to provide access paths to both Little Moose Pond and Otter Lake, which were acquired by the state from International Paper Company in the land swap. These roads are filling in with brambles and small trees in places, but the roadways were so well constructed that they will remain obvious for some time to come, hopefully until the Unit Management Plans are completed and the decision is made to mark state trails to both bodies of water.

Turn off from the main IP road on the side road to Little Moose Pond 11.1 miles from NY 30. Mileages are given from this turn. The side road is drivable for only a short distance, so park and walk along it. In the space of just a hundred yards on a warm summer day, Milberts Tortoise, Green Commas, White Admirals, and Fritillaries were spotted along the roadway—a feast of butterflies.

The roadway descends to a bridge over the Jessup River in 0.25 mile. You are still on IP land, so no camping is permitted near the river. The road heads east along the north shore of the Jessup River and 250 yards from the bridge, there is a left fork, uphill. (The logging road continues east along the river.)

At 0.5 mile, you reach state land, and there is a barrier against vehicular traffic. Follow the roadway straight through an open field and up. At a second field, stay to the left to find the continuing roadway/path. You walk along a level for a time, then at 1.2 miles turn north along a draw—a deep valley is developing on your left, to the west. You are headed northwest and begin to climb again, this time to a height of land at 1.5 miles. Where the roadway descends to the north it is very washed out, so it is rough walking and steep as you descend to the level of Little Moose Pond, reaching it at 1.9 miles.

Beavers have recently flooded the pond, killing the spruce and balsam that line its shores and leaving a border of rusty-brown stumps. There is a beautiful erratic on the eastern shore and huge yellow birch among the spruce. At the outlet an old bridge has washed out and lies just below the beaver dam. Large rocks fill the outlet and below it there is another small pond and a meadow, also created by the beaver. A path along the west side leads to a camping spot where once there was a cabin. Looking northeast along the length of the pond, you see Pillsbury Mountain.

25 Otter Lake

Path along old logging roads, hiking, camping, fishing
2 miles, 1 hour, 250-foot elevation change, maps III and IV

Otter Lake is easy to reach, if you can negotiate the one really confusing place on the logging roads that lead to it.

The IP road crosses the Jessup River at 12.2 miles and 0.1 mile beyond a roadway turns north. In 150 yards you reach a barrier with a No-Motorized-Vehicles sign. The roadway climbs a small hill to a field of berries—and a good place to sight bear. You cross this field, which was once a log staging area, continue uphill beside a pretty little stream to a second staging area, then at 0.6 mile, no more than a fifteen-minute walk, you descend to a hop-a-rock crossing of that stream.

North of the stream crossing the roadway heads more steeply up. Skid roads fork off to the left, but the main road is obvious. At 0.9 mile you see a small stream on your right where the roadway enters a large grass-filled field. This was the site of a cabin and the road/path to Otter Lake forked right to cut across this field. It is almost impossible to find the route in the tall grass and field flowers, so stay briefly on the obvious roadway you have been following, which continues along the left side of the field. Just as the road enters the woods again, turn right, cross a stream that is not shown on the USGS, and pick up the proper roadway that becomes obvious again as soon as it enters the road from the field. (Note that the left fork begins to climb steeply as it reenters the woods, so you should not be tempted to follow it.)

The path to Otter Lake now heads northwest and slightly uphill; two fainter tracks fork from it, one to the right, the other to the left, all within 200 yards of the field. As the proper route levels off, it approaches the outlet of Otter Lake, a handsome stream that you follow to the pond. There are several very wet places in the roadway. A path forks left to the outlet as you approach the pond, but it is terribly wet. A second fork leads to a cabin site quite close to the pond, which is quite a handsome place with pond lilies, and an evergreen border.

If you continue along the roadway that follows the east shore, you reach the site of the old cabin, where there is considerable trash. The roadway continues behind the cabin—it led north for 3.5 miles to intersect with the Whitney Lake Trail. You can follow it for a ways, but the north end of the track where it traversed marshes is totally overgrown.

Waterfall on the outlet of Sampsons Bog

26   Perkins Clearing to Spruce and Balsam Lakes

Hiking, camping, fishing
4.4 miles to northern lean-to, 2 hours, 550-foot elevation change, map IV

Spruce Lake is a mile-and-a-quarter-long, spruce-bordered lake with three lean-tos and good trout fishing. It used to be that the only way to reach it was along the Northville-Placid Trail, a 9.8-mile walk from Piseco. The land swap with International Paper Company provides a trailhead at the southwest corner of IP land where the south end of Spruce Lake is but 3.5 miles away.

From the trailhead (see the mileage and direction chart), continue southwest along the road beyond the barrier. The road climbs and contours around the hillside. Within ten minutes, about 0.5 mile, you cross the outlet of Dewitt Pond. The second culvert, 0.2 mile beyond, carries Bloodgood Brook under the road. Immediately beyond it an unused logging road heads right, steeply uphill. There is a lone blue disk beside the fork.

You can turn uphill and follow the roadway beside Bloodgood Brook steeply uphill to a field where Tin Can Camp once stood. A pathway leads through the field to the west, across the brook, and on to intersect the Northville-Placid Trail at 1.3 miles. Alternately, you can continue along the main road beyond its crossing of Bloodgood Brook; the roadway climbs for 0.2 mile then begins to descend. A guide board directs you right 0.4 mile from the brook, into deeper woods to the Northville-Placid Trail. Head uphill for 0.4 mile to reach the intersection with the shortcut trail. (The way left leads to Piseco.)

The path and the Northville-Placid Trail intersect near Bloodgood Brook where the trail appears to be at the edge of an old settlement area; there are fields to the north, and the trail is level and muddy. At 1.7 miles, the trail crosses Bloodgood Brook. Here a roadway used to lead straight ahead, but you make a right turn. The trail is still muddy as you walk along the side of a valley, which is low on your left now. A small stream joins the trail to make it even muddier. Finally the trail crosses the stream, and you continue uphill, a little north of west. At 2.3 miles you reach a height-of-land; the walk from the barrier has been less than an hour, and you have less than a half hour to go to reach the southern end of the lake.

From the height-of-land, the trail descends to a forest of huge trees that occupies the level terrain southeast of the lake. An arrow directs you right, downhill, at 2.6 miles. It is wet walking through the spruce swamps and there is a wet crossing of a small stream that flows to the left, southwest. A marsh opens on your right at 3.3 miles, and you continue through spruce and balsam to a sharp right turn at 3.4 miles. If you go straight at the turn, you pass a lean-to, then reach a campsite at shoreline.

There is a faint path around the south shore of the lake, but it is all wet walking. Spruce Lake is surrounded by dense spruce and balsam stands, and you can reach the lake easily at only a few points, most of them near the three lean-tos. The trail north along the lakeshore is through the spruce stands, where roots and muddy spots again make walking difficult. A campsite sits on a ledge about 0.2 mile north of the southern lean-to. Planking and wet spots continue north where the trail stays out of sight of the lake. A faint path forks left, 0.7 mile north along the lakeshore. The spot is unmarked, but the path leads to a second lean-to on a promontory above the lake. Beyond the fork, the trail descends, crosses a mucky area within sight of Spruce Lake, and at 0.9 mile you cross the outlet of Balsam Lake. Poor trail conditions slow the 0.9-mile walk along Spruce Lake, so this section takes at least a half hour.

There is a faint path on the north side of the outlet of Balsam, and in a ten-minute walk, partly bushwhack, you can reach that lake, but again, thick spruce prevent you from walking around it or enjoying much of the shoreline.

On the Northville-Placid Trail, about 60 yards beyond the outlet stream of Balsam Lake, a sign indicates a lean-to to the left, and there is a faint path leading to this one that sits near the lakeshore.

27 Spruce Lake to the Headwaters of West Canada Creek

Hiking, camping, fishing
4.1 miles, 2¼ hours, 80-foot elevation change, maps III and IV

This segment begins at Spruce Lake's northern lean-to near Balsam Lake Outlet, 4.4 miles from the Perkins Clearing Trailhead. From here, 0.0 mile, the Northville-Placid Trail continues north and fairly dry in a good hardwood forest through which you can still catch glimpses of the lake. At 0.4 mile, the trail is again wet and out of sight of the lake. Shortly there is a wet area with no bridges to make crossing easier. A second intermittent stream crossing is also wet, but there are stones to step on.

Just short of 1 mile from the lean-to, the trail emerges at the side of the large vly that is north of Spruce Lake. The trail is close to a vly, and crosses a stream flowing into it at 1.2 miles. A gradual uphill follows, and at 1.5 miles you reach a benchmark (2464 feet) in the middle of the trail. The trail descends from the height-of-land through a draw with a small brook that the trail crosses several times. Lots of turtlehead and trillium grow in this wet forest. At 2 miles the trail begins a gradual climb beyond an old corduroy crossing. Then a steep downgrade with more slippery corduroy leads to a fork at 2.65 miles. The trail right goes to the bridge over Sampson's Bog Outlet.

Take time for a detour left to a stretch of nice pools in the outlet and a lovely waterfall. It is possible to cross the creek on stones below the waterfall and continue on the path back up until it intersects the blue trail again.

From the bridge the trail north climbs a small hill, passes a campsite, and swings abruptly right to head northeast through a beautiful hardwood forest. In the next few minutes you cross two creeks, and the second is followed by a steep uphill with old corduroy. The trail levels off, descends, then at 3.55 miles it crosses another stream with a little bit of a pond to the east.

After a series of ups and downs, there is another long (more than 50 yards) mucky area, a short hill, then a sign at 3.7 miles indicating the West Canada Creek Lean-to is 0.5 mile away. Within five minutes you have your first view of the West Canada Creek. The trail beside the creek is in a very wet area, in fact you have to make your own path here. Just beyond there is a trail intersection; the way right leads to Sampson Lake, section 38, and Perkins Clearing. The blue trail straight ahead leads 100 yards to the bridge over the creek at the outlet of Mud Lake. The lean-to sits on a knoll just beyond. Sections 33 through 43 describe the heart of the West Canadas, which lies just beyond the bridge.

28   Pillsbury Mountain

Fire tower, hiking, views
2.8 miles, 2 hours, 1677-foot vertical rise, maps IV and VI

Climb to the fire tower on Pillsbury on a clear day to study the mountains and lakes of the West Canada Lake Wilderness. Be sure and make the trip if you plan to bushwhack to any of that region's cliff-faced mountains. The understanding this view gives is very important.

You can begin the trail from Sled Harbor, and walk the gentle 1.2 miles to the new trailhead along the Old Military Road, which also leads toward Pillsbury Lake or the Cedar Lakes. It takes no more than half an hour to walk to this point, gaining 260 feet in the process. Alternatively, you can drive that 1.2 miles to a new, primitive 15-car parking area. Ordinary cars have used this section of road in summer, and four-wheel-drive vehicles have no problem at all. The road follows the Miami River to the new parking area, with the Pillsbury Trailhead to the left.

The trail, marked with red, descends nearly 100 feet to cross the Miami River, which is here small enough so the rock-hop-crossing is dry. Then in less than 1.1 miles, the trail will climb over 1200 feet. It is a steep and steady climb to the south of west. You are in a mixed hardwood forest dominated by yellow birch and maples; few erratics line the way. At 1.9 miles, about 3000 feet in elevation, you pass a large yellow birch that has wrapped its roots around one huge erratic. Shortly beyond, the grade seems to ease, but it is an illusion, for immediately there is a steep, wet area where the trail has worn to bedrock. Sphagnum clings to the mountainside here. Spruce, with sorrel beneath, line the trail. Watch for a side trail to the right that hikers have worn to avoid the worst stretch.

At 3250 feet, 2.2 miles, the trail traverses the mountainside in an open field of hay scented ferns. Then it climbs again in zigzags on the narrow ridge line. At 3400 feet, where the trail levels briefly, there is a concealed side route to the left—it is the old roadway down the south flanks of the mountain. You can still find the route at this end, but it is filled with balsam fir and blowdowns. The southern end is clear for the first 0.8 mile, then disappears behind one of IP's leasehold camps. The route is too overgrown to offer an alternate to this marked trail.

The trail dips, then climbs sharply in the final steep pitch, and at 2.5 miles begins a relatively level traverse to the south side of the summit knob. From rocks below the tower there is a view south to Speculator. From the tower you can see a panorama that begins with the IP lands to the southeast, and going clockwise, the newly acquired Little Moose Lake lies west of south, Sampson Bog is more distant, Whitney Lake is directly west, with South Lake just in front of it and to the left and Mud Lake to the right. You can spot the slide on South Lake Mountain and the range of cliffs on West Lake Mountain. North of West Lake Mountain is Kitty Cobble; together they are the two highest peaks on the western horizon. Only a couple pieces of the Cedar Lakes are visible, but the massif of Little Moose and Manbury mountains behind clearly shows three sets of cliffs.

To the north lies the Cedar River Flow with Sugarloaf Mountain clearly defined in the valley beyond and Wakely to the west of it. To the northeast Snowy's cliffs often glisten in the sun.

In the scrubby forest along the summit ridge you can spot grey-cheeked thrush and boreal chickadees.

You need less than one and a half hours to return to the car, but watch your footing if the ground is wet!

29 Blue Ridge Mountain
Difficult bushwhack, maps IV and VI

In 1872, only two weeks into the first year of the Adirondack Survey, Colvin noted this peak from (Little) Moose Lake at the head of the South Branch of the Moose; his guides named it Mount Colvin. Just ten years later, having found it ideal as a key peak for extending his triangulation project to the west, Colvin renamed the peak Cloud Cap.

Cloud Cap lies south of Snowy Mountain and is almost as high. It is the highest of the various Adirondack peaks named Blue Ridge. Today, Blue Ridge is a trailless summit, wooded on top, but with views north to west from a little below the top. In the forties it was bushwhacked from the Sucker Brook Trail. A shorter approach was explored for this guide from the Perkins Clearing side via the former woods road to abandoned Camp 22; a hasty search of the wooded summit did not uncover Colvin's bolt #67, the triangulation mark that he placed on this peak. Spruce grow right down to the edge of the round-topped cliffs, making it dangerous as well as difficult to try and reach the views from them.

It is still quite easy to reach the site of Camp 22. The cliffs are shown on the accompanying map, but no bushwhack route is shown because no easy route has been found. This is a trip only for those experienced with map and compass.

A DEC map shows Lewey Mountain with the name Cloud Cap, but the latitude and longitude date in Colvin's *1897 Report* prove that Cloud Cap is the modern Blue Ridge.

The best and easiest place to study the cliffs before trying such a bushwhack is from a canoe on Cedar River Flow.

Lewey Lake

30 Lewey Lake and the Miami River
Canoeing, map V

Lewey Lake has a really lovely state campground with a convenient boat launch site. You can spend a delightful half-day canoeing the 1.3-mile length of the lake and for several miles up its inlet, the Miami River, which twists and bends in a broad valley. To launch from the campground, a day-use fee is charged in season.

Out on the lake, Snowy Mountain dominates the view north. As you canoe south, the view is of the long chain of mountains with Lewey in the north, then Cellar and Page to the southwest.

The Miami River empties into Lewey Lake about midway across the grass fields at the southwest end of the lake. Your canoe lets you sneak up on groups of mergansers and other ducks. The valley is as wide as the lake and the river winds across it from side to side in a series of oxbows. You pass the wide channel where Cellar Brook comes in, then gradually work to the eastern shore. You canoe from spruce knolls on the eastern shore to alder patches and back toward the forested eastern bank. One spruce knoll has a lovely picnic site.

You can canoe upstream for about 2 miles as the crow flies, nearly twice that distance of meandering stream. Well upstream, there is a cable crossing then some short rapids, but you can still go upstream. Finally, there in an area of tall and beautiful forest, the stream narrows between alder-choked banks, and the rapids make further progress just too difficult. You must turn about just as the valley narrows to dense forests close to both banks of the stream.

Lewey Lake

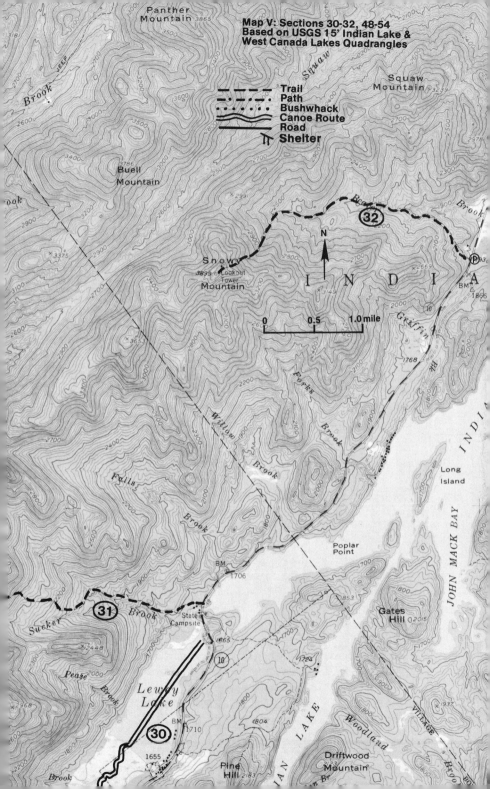

Map V: Sections 30-32, 48-54
Based on USGS 15' Indian Lake &
West Canada Lakes Quadrangles

Trail
Path
Bushwhack
Canoe Route
Road
Shelter

N

0   0.5   1.0 mile

Panther Mountain

Squaw Mountain

Buell Mountain

Snowy Mountain
Lookout Tower

I N D I A

Bear Brook

Griffin Bk.

Forks Brook

Willow Brook

Falls Brook

Long Island

JOHN MACK BAY

Poplar Point

Gates Hill

Sucker Brook

State Campsite

Lewey Lake

Pease Brook

Pine Hill

Driftwood Mountain

Woodland

VILLAGE Brook

I N D I A N   L A K E

31

32

30

10

P

Snowy Mountain from Lewey Lake

31 Sucker Brook—Colvin Brook Trail

Hiking, camping
8 miles, 4½ hours, 1230-foot vertical rise to height-of-land,
530-foot descent to Cedar River at Colvin Brook Lean-to, maps
V and VI

This is the longest, most strenuous, and most beautiful approach to the heart of the West Canadas. You can also use this trail for a good through-trip from Lewey Lake to the Cedar River Flow.

Just north of the bridge over the outlet of Lewey Lake into Indian Lake, a road heads west into the portion of the Lewey Lake campground that gives access to sites along the channel. Within 150 feet of NY 8 there is a small brown building beside the road. The trail begins to the west of the building, where a trailhead sign warns you that the nearest shelter is the Colvin Brook Lean-to, 6.95 miles away.

The trail begins as a narrow path, leading gently uphill, then down to intersect a woods road coming from the campground. The trail follows the woods road briefly and then heads west again. There are plenty of red markers to make this crossover obvious. Shortly you hear Sucker Brook down in the deep hemlock gorge on your left. The trail is beside this lovely gorge for all too short a time.

At 0.8 mile the trail begins to pull away from the Sucker Brook Valley, then crosses one small tributary and a second, which it follows briefly. The trail approaches a tributary of Sucker Brook, and at 2020-feet elevation and 1.6 miles, the trail makes a sharp bend to the south to cross a large tributary of Sucker Brook. The trail loops back close to the main brook at 1.8 miles, and turns west again.

The next stretch is far from the brook, with gentler grade and even a level stretch. There is another tributary of Sucker Brook to cross at 3.3 miles, beyond which the trail becomes steeper. Someone has camped right in the trail here! You are climbing fairly steeply now through a tall beech-birch-maple forest, making a traverse to the southwest to cross the head of a ravine at 3.1 miles. There is a confusing rerouting of the trail here; it is very steep and both branches rejoin to the west of the crossing. The next 0.5 mile is a steep traverse of a hillside and through open patches in the trees you can see Lewey Lake. Just beyond a huge boulder the grade eases, and at 3.6 miles you reach a height-of-land at 2880 feet.

The saddle is a pleasant place with flocks of warblers in spring and fall and lush *dryopteris* stands including the mountain woodfern. *dryopteris campyloptera*. Actually, birding for deep woods species is good all along the upper level of this trail. You will hear the call of the hermit thrush as you walk.

The path descending to the west is much narrower as it winds its way through fern covered slopes beneath a tall hardwood forest. You can see great distances through the forest as you wind down on the north slopes of a developing draw. You cross a seep at 4.1 miles, perhaps the beginning of Colvin Brook. This draw develops into a big gorge below and to your right. The forest is open enough so that you have a view across to Cellar and Blue Ridge mountains. At 4.6 miles you cross yet another small stream that flows from the flanks of Lewey Mountain. It drops steeply to your left to join Colvin Brook, which has become a substantial stream. Here you begin a long level traverse through a deep ferny woods. At 5.0 miles you approach Colvin Brook just upstream from an oxbow loop, which has been dammed downstream by a huge (ten-foot-tall) beaver dam. This narrow gorge is a strange place for a beaver!

The trail continues beside the stream through the deep gorge and the way has become almost level. The trail follows what was once an old roadway, though you are sure you are on it only briefly. Then, at 5.6 miles your walk slows as the trail is directed across to the left bank of the stream, then back. It repeats this pair of crossings three more times, as the meandering stream is pushed alternately against the steep-walled left bank, then to the steep right one. There are big boulders to step on at most of the

View of Indian Lake from Snowy Mountain

crossings. It is slow walking, though. After the third pair of crossings, the stream turns abruptly to the right, but you immediately recross it to avoid the steep gravelly bank on the right. Gradually, the banks surrounding the brook diminish, and you end with a cross to the left bank and head away from the brook at 6.6 miles, just as the brook turns sharply north. The trail seems to be lost in a meadow of tall goldenrod and asters; stay to the left of the meadow. Markings direct you right into an alder swamp, where you twice cross a small stream. For 100 yards or so, the trail is bound to confuse you. Then it climbs to a spruce stand, just a few feet in elevation above the alders, and circles around the edge of the marshes to approach the lean-to that sits beside the Cedar River.

There is no bridge across the Cedar near the lean-to. A row of rocks angling downstream just below the lean-to may serve to support a dry crossing—at least in dry weather. The river is wide here, and from the overgrown banks on the west side, you have a view across the marshes downstream on the river to Cellar and Blue Ridge mountains. The continuing trail to connect with the Northville-Placid Trail is described in section 53.

32 Snowy Mountain

Hiking
3.8 miles one way, 6 hours round trip, 2100-foot vertical rise,
map V

In 1920, T. Morris Longstreth wrote about a trip to Snowy in his book
called *The Adirondacks.*

> In every view that is to refresh the memory, there must remain one chief
> delight. And from Snowy it is not the tumble of green rollers, not even the
> timber blanket that I would climb to see most of all. There is a little ledge on
> the western side from which the slope swoops down into a perfect
> amphitheater. The soaring sides sing evenly to rest. From the ledge the arms
> of mountains appear to enclose it. . . . Long did we lie on the moss of the
> ledge, steeping in the sunshine, and the calm of the marvelous bowl below. It
> was a vision of serenity worth far greater struggle to attain. We forgot for a
> moment that we were on a planet that was mad.

The view to the northeast across Indian Lake to the High Peaks may be
more spectacular and popular, but the view from this ledge remains as
Longstreth described it, the perfect spot for contemplating the vast and
quiet Adirondacks. For nearly six decades, hikers were rewarded with a
360 degree panorama from the fire tower. Its closing forces hikers to
scramble about the summit looking for other openings like the one found
by Longstreth. With a bit of exploration, you can find vistas in every
direction, recreating the panorama in pieces.

Snowy has enormous appeal; it is the southern Adirondacks' highest
peak, the most majestic in the range west of Indian Lake. Its cliffs are a
beacon for hikers sighting from many other mountains. Snowy's steep
upper slopes means the mountain has been cursed with some of the worst
of trail conditions. Recent work by the Adirondack Mountain Club trail
crews has improved conditions on wet portions of the lower trail with long
string of boardwalks; new stairs and waterbars built durably of rock correct
seepages on the lower slopes. The upper, steep slopes are still in bad shape,
but two proposals should be in place in the next few years. One calls for
some kind of ladder up the small cliffs at the very top, another calls for
rerouting the trail away from the direct course of the old telephone line
and back to the old trail, which zigzagged as much as possible up the steep
summit slopes.

The parking area on NY 30 is full on every clear summer day. The red-
marked trail begins across the road. After a short rise, it crosses several
intermittent streams and winds up and down, passing from taller forest

near the road to shorter stands on the more wind-swept slopes. At 1 mile, you approach the valley of Beaver Brook, which is north of the trail. Shortly the stream is visible and herd paths lead to it and to camping sites along its north bank. At 1.2 miles, you cross the stream and traverse a knoll on the north shore of the valley. You descend from the knoll to cross a stream that often sports a string of beaver dams.

The muddy sections of trail that follow, as well as the previous ones, all have boardwalks. As the trail beings to rise, you again approach Beaver Brook, which is here composed of several braided streams as it picks up other small drainages. The trail crosses the stream for the last time at just short of 2 miles. The hour-long walk thus far has been remarkably level. You begin to climb as the trail follows a small gorge on the brook. The trail continues close to the brook. At 2400-foot elevation, the trail becomes steeper and angles south. As you gain altitude, the trail zigzags through fern fields. There is a campsite 100 yards to the left of the trail above the 2800-foot level. You reach a relatively level stretch at 3100 feet with a through-the-trees view. You continue traversing south, until at the 3200-foot level, almost two hours and nearly 3 miles into the climb, you reach the beginning of the steep bedrock steps, covered with exposed roots and loose rocks, and made slippery with water coursing down the trail. The first real lookout just beyond reveals MacIntyre, Colden, Marcy, Gothics, Saddleback, Slide, Avalanche Pass, Colvin, Blake, and Dix, with Giant behind.

For 0.6 mile, the trail continues in large steps over boulders, slippery when wet, which is most of the time. Several spots are badly eroded, unstable, and even dangerous. At just short of 3800 feet and 3.8 miles, you cross below a ledge, where you have to scramble up to a small field where all signs of the fire observer's cabin have been removed. From here, head west toward the summit, turning right within 150 feet to the western lookout on top the cliff. The tower is another 200 yards to the west, and paths lead in all directions for the different smaller views now available.

The Heart of the West Canadas

THE HEART OF the West Canada Lakes Wilderness is a circle that encompasses the highest region of lakes in the Adirondacks. On that circle lie the three lakes known as the West Canadas: West Lake at 2368 feet and South and Mud lakes at 2345 feet. Also on the circle are the Cedar Lakes at 2442 feet, Whitney Lake at 2456 feet, and Pillsbury Lake at 2493 feet.

This chapter describes that circle with excursions from it, dividing each segment into separate sections so you can decide how best to plan a camping trip into the region. You have to backpack, for no day trip will let you enjoy the circuit. Camping, fishing, swimming, and hiking are a part of every segment.

Almost every approach to the West Canadas has a drawback. Every route but one traverses logged and disturbed lands, so that the forest that ought to accompany this heart of the wilderness does not appear until you have walked toward it for several miles. None of the routes are short, but they should not be, for this is a wilderness to be protected. No day trip can even sample the beauties of the clusters of lakes. The West Canada Wilderness requires backpacking, and a week-long stay offers only a sample of this wilderness.

What is the mystique of wilderness, if not its remoteness? But remoteness has not always been the prime appeal of the West Canadas. For fifty years it was possible to fly into the lakes to fish. Before that logging roads led to camps that catered to sportsmen. The lakes were, in a sense, far away, but easy for many to reach. Until recently, logging has been carried on close to the eastern boundary and within the past thirty years very near the northwestern boundary of this wilderness.

Fishing has always been great in these lakes and for years almost every visitor was a fisherman. The Northville-Placid Trail cuts across the heart of the West Canadas, but increasingly hikers have come to plumb its secrets, using routes other than the through trail. It is no longer just a sportsman's paradise, but everyone who visits comes away with the thought, "don't tell about this place, it is so beautiful, no one else should know about it."

Four approaches to the heart of the West Canadas, from Spruce Lake to the south, section 27, from Brooktrout Lake to the northwest, section 78, from the Cedar River Flow, sections 48 and 49, and from Sled Harbor on the west, described in this chapter, are roughly equal in length and difficulty. Each route gives access to the central circle of trails, and this chapter describes a route through the heart of the West Canadas starting from one point on that circle. Obviously, trips can begin from the other points.

Note: The mileages given here are not those given on DEC signs or in DEC's brochure on the Northville-Placid Trail, West Canada Lakes Section. Both sources contain errors that we hope this guide corrects. The times represent carrying a full backpack and are therefore slightly slower than those in other places in the guide.

Adirondack French Louie, by Harvey Dunham, describes that famous woodsman and places him at various haunts in the West Canadas in the 1870s and 1880s. His exploits—hunting, fishing, trapping, and living off this vast area—are entertainingly recorded in that volume. Dunham also tells of the logging that occurred there as early as 1880. Although logging proceeded up West Canada Creek before the turn of the century, old Conservation Department maps place the first logging around the Cedar Lakes after 1905 and with logging only touching Mud Lake in 1912.

The eastern shores of the Cedar Lakes, Good Luck Mountain, and the land south to Cat Lake and Kings Pond were purchased by the state in 1899. Logging ceased there shortly after. The Buell Brook region was acquired by the state in 1894.

Three-fourths of Township 8, Totten and Crossfield Patent in the heart of the West Canadas, the part that did not include the lakes, was purchased by the state in 1900 for $3.33 an acre. The rest, five thousand acres that included the lakes, was purchased in 1921, and logging continued near them until about 1918. Oddly enough, in this century, logs were not floated down the West Canada Creek, but were trucked north to Cedar Lakes and from there out to mills. In spite of its accessibility by roads, most of it was only logged for soft woods, and this practice, combined with the deep rich soils, has allowed this region to return to the forests that complement its beautiful lakes.

Logging continued near the eastern lakes, Pillsbury and Whitney, until the 1970s. Logging continues along much of the northeastern approach not far from the Cedar Lakes.

33 Sled Harbor to Pillsbury Lake

Hiking, camping, fishing
4.8 miles, 2½ hours, 640-foot elevation change, maps IV and VI

Pillsbury Lake is the most accessible of the West Canada Wilderness lakes. It is a mile and a quarter long, making it nice to have a canoe or inflatable boat.

From the parking area at Sled Harbor, walk or drive the 1.2 miles to the Pillsbury Mountain Trailhead, see section 28. Walking, you will discover the roadway is sporadically marked with red trail disks. It traverses the northeast side of the valley of the Miami River where it cuts between Pillsbury and Page mountains. Part of the time you hear the river, but barely see it. Almost all of the route is gently uphill.

In thirty minutes, you reach a junction. Here, at 1.2 miles, the foot trail to Pillsbury Mountain, section 28, turns left. Your road-trail continues gently uphill, overlooking the deep valley to the southwest with occasional glimpses of Pillsbury Mountain through the trees. Several huge erratics lie near the trail. At 1.8 miles you cross an intermittent stream, and shortly beyond there is a site where campers have stopped. The way is still up, and there is a steep and eroded section of road at 2.4 miles. Then the way levels off, and you reach a clearing at 2.8 miles. An unmarked log road, the way to Camp 22, section 29, forks right at the beginning of the clearing. A guide board in the clearing gives mileages straight ahead to Cedar Lakes, section 44. For Pillsbury, take the left fork, headed west.

The trail continues uphill and in 400 yards passes an old roadway forking left and uphill. You are in land that until the 1983 land swap belonged to International Paper Company. The forest is small and scrubby and log landings punctuate the road-trail. The roadway begins a long, gentle downhill and reaches the site of a cabin in a huge field at 3.9 miles. Clumps of monkshood and roses mark the settlement that existed for a hundred years.

A roadway leads right from the field, past an enormous garbage dump to a new beaver flow on an inlet of Pillsbury Lake. You want to continue straight ahead, southwest, through the field, where you again see trail markers. There is a bridge 200 yards from the clearing. The trail is flat and muddy and narrowly cut between the thick stands of spruce and balsam that line Pillsbury Lake. At 4.4 miles you pass a drying beaver flow—all of this part of the trail is routed through low spruce flats. You cross a ridge and at 4.7 miles turn left toward the lean-to at the lake.

There are other tent sites near the lean-to but few paths through the dense growth at shoreline and very few places where it is easy to reach the shore, making it really desirable to have a canoe or boat.

34 Pillsbury to Whitney Lake, the Whitney Lake Path

Trail, path
1.8 miles, 1 hour, 200-foot elevation change, maps IV and VI

Two good campsites crown knolls on the east side of Whitney Lake. At present, and perhaps until 1994, float planes are allowed to land on Whitney Lake. They bring fishermen to these campsites and a third on the west shore of the lake. This route is not now officially marked, but will become the shortest and best route to Whitney when flights cease.

From the Pillsbury Lean-to, head south, over a low ridge, then west on the red trail. Beaver have flooded the trail below the ridge, and there is a stream crossing on a decrepit bridge. You are close enough to the lake for occasional glimpses of it, then the trail turns south and begins to climb. Watch as the trail begins to climb and you see a field to the right, west, of the trail. On the far side of the field, there is a faint path heading uphill. This is the beginning of the path to Whitney Lake. The route becomes much more obvious as it enters deep woods and heads generally west or a little south of west toward Whitney Lake. The path climbs fairly steeply up the slopes of a small hill, rising nearly 200 feet above the level of Pillsbury Lake. (It is curious that this path climbs so much, especially when the old route was a much leveler one to the north near Puddle Hole.) The path descends through a narrow draw and circles around the north side of a small hill. Occasional blazes and flags mark the way, but this is an unmarked route, so watch your compass headings.

The path approaches the southern campsite on Whitney's east shore through blowdown, in a field that has burned. A rock slab leads cleanly to water. A faint path heads north along the shore. It circles inland around the bay formed by the outlet of Puddle Hole and leads to the second and

South bay of Whitney Lake

larger campsite. Here, because of tree cutting and over use, there is room for several tents.

Whitney has a lovely, jagged shoreline with tall, stately spruce bordering most of it. The fishing is good, a canoe is almost a necessity, and loons nest here.

35 Whitney to Pillsbury Bay on Cedar Lakes and the Western Arm of Pillsbury Lake

Paths, maps IV and VI

The traditional sportsman's path between these three lakes has been kept open by the interior ranger. He has even rerouted a part of it from its former course to circle a huge new beaver-flooded marsh that is now a good-sized pond. Fishermen who fly into Whitney use the route as the shortest way to the other two lakes.

The path heads north from the northern campsite on Whitney, past a small tent site, and through a handsome grove of big white birch and spruce. Parts of the pathway are filling in with witch hopple and small maples, but it is really a clear route. Blazes and red paint daubs mark most of the route. The path heads along a ridge with Whitney's long, thin outlet barely visible through the trees.

The path is in a beautiful forest of large balsam and spruce and winds generally north along a series of ridges. After 0.6 mile, nearly a twenty-minute walk, the path is at the edge of a steep ridge, an esker perhaps, with a twenty-foot drop to the right and Pillsbury Lake Outlet to the left, west. Deadfalls obscure the path a bit here. It turns right, and crosses the outlet of Pillsbury Lake. Shortly you see a large marsh on your left, west. The path follows the marsh, headed northeast.

After nearly forty minutes of walking, the path takes a sharp turn to the left and crosses a small stream that flows from right to left. If you look to the west about fifty feet short (south) of the crossing, you spot a pyramid-shaped erratic, a blaze on a tree, and a faint footpath. A blazed route heads right, east, uphill here over a low shoulder of Noisey Ridge headed east. The route, descends from the ridge, turns left, and reaches the rocky outlet of Pillsbury Lake, a ten-minute walk of 0.4 mile from the Cedar Lakes path.

The Cedar Lakes path makes the sharp left then continues north from the stream crossing to the new beaver dam on the long chain of marshes that lie southeast of Pillsbury Lake. Fishermen walk across the dam and continue north on the west side of the flow. Within five minutes you reach the old path; the way right is flooded, but the way left leads north for a less than ten-minute walk to Pillsbury Bay on Cedar Lakes. The 1.6-mile walk from Whitney Lake takes the better part of an hour, partly because the path is occasionally obscured, partly because there is rough walking.

36 Pillsbury Lake to the South Shore of Whitney Lake

Hiking, camping
2.4 miles, 1 1/2 hours, 200-foot elevation change, maps IV and VI

The main trail from Pillsbury Lake to Whitney is marked with red disks. It heads south from the lean-to, over a rise, and through a flooded area. At

0.6 mile, the trail begins to climb—the old roadway is eroded and rocky. (The field to the right of the trail here marks the beginning of the Whitney Lake path, section 34.)

You are still in a forest that has been logged, not long ago, so it is not a pretty place. There are several log landings. The road curves southwest around a hillside. At about 1 mile from the Pillsbury Lean-to, the trail makes a couple right turns away from the roadbed to avoid marshy areas. Here the logging road, where it is to the south of the trail, out of sight of the marked trail, splits. The way straight ahead once led to a camp not far from Bullhead Pond. That road used to continue over the hill to Otter Lake, section 25, but only the southern part of that road exists. Beyond the site of the camp, the road disappears in marshes.

The red trail rejoins the roadway, taking a more westerly course along the north side of a hill. Gradually the forest improves and there are lovely hillsides of ferns beneath taller trees. The trail is a series of ups and downs, crossing an intermittent stream, and circling around two more small hills. At 1.8 miles, look down the slopes to your right—the water of Whitney Lake is visible through the trees. The trail is on the slopes above the lake. Watch at 2 miles where the trail is briefly level. A flagged and faint path heads north, down the slope, intersecting in 100 yards another flagged route that leads west back up to the red trail, then past the site of a camp that was burned after the land swap, past a garbage dump, and steeply down the remains of a float plane landing. There are no good campsites nearby and no paths along the lakeshore. However, there is a lovely bay sheltered by a rock peninsula capped with spruce. Several small rock islands, all spruce covered, fill the bays at this end of the lake.

37 Whitney Lake to Sampson Lake

0.9 mile, 30 minutes, 140-foot elevation change, maps IV and VI

The red trail south of Whitney Lake continues west on the ridge above the lake. The ridge narrows, and 0.4 mile from the fork to Whitney the trail crosses to the left side of the ridge and begins to drop off it. There is already a view of Sampson to the left through the trees. The trail is very wet and at 0.5 mile there is a spring on the south side of the trail. The old shelter is 100 yards beyond; the site, with fireplace, makes a good, dry place to camp. Red flags alert you to the place to turn off the trail. At 0.7

mile there is a marked fork left, downhill, for 0.2 mile to a new lean-to on Sampson Lake. The way down to the lake is very steep, muddy, and difficult, and Sampson Lake's shores are marshy.

38 Sampson Lake to the Bridge over the West Canada Creek near Mud Lake

2.5 miles, 1 1/4 hours, relatively level, maps IV and VI

From the turnoff to Sampson Lake Lean-to, the red trail west offers some of the most beautiful walking in the West Canadas. For a few minutes you can still see the lake through the trees—you are walking on the edge of a hill. There are lovely ferns underfoot, among them rattlesnake and silvery glade fern. The level walk ends with a slight rise and a turn slightly to the north at 0.6 mile. Then the trail descends to the level of a spruce bog at 1.2 miles and continues northwest. The trail descends some more, then curves southwest as it rounds a small hill. The forest changes to hardwoods, then back to spruce as the trail approaches a marked intersection.

The way south, left, leads to Spruce Lake Lean-to and Piseco along the blue marked Northville-Placid Trail, section 27. The way right, marked for Cedar River Headquarters and the site of the West Canada Ranger Headquarters, is also the blue Northville-Placid Trail. Turn right for a few feet to cross the West Canada Creek at the outlet of Mud Lake. Just upslope from the bridge is the West Canada Creek Lean-to. A path from it leads north 100 yards to another campsite on the shore of Mud Lake. From here there are beautiful views north over the vlies surrounding Mud Lake with their great blue herons and deer splashing in the lily pads. This is the province of Johnny Leaf, a trapper and hunter and contemporary of French Louie, who had a rough bark shack on the Mud Lake dam.

There is also a path along the west bank of the creek heading south. The view from the bridge is lovely, and significant, as the birthplace of that mighty creek. Standing on the bridge you can imagine the scene nearly a hundred years ago. In 1891, a flood dam was built at the bridge site to provide water to float logs down the West Canada Creek. According to Dunham, "one of the biggest, if not the biggest, log-drives in the history of the whole North Woods went down the old West Creek in the spring of 1895. To be exact, it was 20,194,156 feet board measure."

Mud Lake near bridge over the West Canada Creek

39 Past South Lake to West Lake
1.2 miles, 40 minutes, relatively level, map VI

The short portion of Northville-Placid Trail from the West Canada Creek crossing to South Lake and on to the site where the West Lake Ranger Headquarters stood until 1986 is one of the prettiest stretches in the whole circuit.

From the lean-to above the crossing, the trail heads southwest to cross an esker ridge and descend to a deep hemlock woods. Just as the trail reaches the sand plain that separates the three lakes, at 0.5 mile there is a path (sometimes wet) left of the lean-to on the shore of South Lake. There are many campsites in the flat area nearby. South Lake has a great sand beach. From the lean-to you can look across the long bridge over the marshes at South Lake's outlet to the cliffs behind West Lake. When a west wind blows over the lake to the lean-to, it helps to keep the bugs away, but sometimes drives rain into it.

Crossing West Lake Outlet

Beyond the path to the lean-to, blueberries and Labrador tea border the spit of land, a causeway, that approaches the outlet. Across the long bridge, the trail at 0.7 miles again enters the deep woods of a spruce swamp with a lovely ferny understory. The trail crosses a ridge and turns left below it, then climbs a second ridge. Very quickly you see the water of West Lake. A path leads left at just over 1 mile to a lean-to. From here you can look across West Lake to the mountain with cliffs behind it.

The trail turns northeast along lakeshore and reaches an intersection in a grass field. Headquarters used to be on the lakeshore here, but all that remains are the rock foundations and French Louie's fireplace. Legend has it that the fabled garter snakes you will see in the foundations—and there are an incredible number—used to live under the ranger's porch, but were supposed to be descendants of the snakes French Louie kept in his flour barrel to keep the flour free of insects. French Louie's house (hotel) served visiting hunters and fishermen until his death in 1915. Then George Wilson took over the establishment and ran it until the state bought it in

1921. The Ranger Headquarters cabin was built on the site, which commands a view of the lake.

The shores of Mud, South, and West lakes were logged twice, once shortly after 1900 and again just before the land was sold to the state by Union Bag and Paper Company, which retained a timber reservation. The logging took most of the spruce, but no hardwoods. And, sixty-five years of inactivity have been great enough to return the spruce to their former nobility.

West Lake's shoreline is filled with pinxter bushes, a lovely sight in spring. As with all the interior lakes, exploring is best from a canoe or inflatable raft.

40 The Slide on Mountain West of South Lake

Bushwhack, map VI

From the Northville-Placid Trail just north of the outlet of South Lake, bushwhack toward magnetic west through a spruce swamp. It is spongy and treacherous underfoot. Gradually the woods begin to open up. As the terrain becomes steeper, you have to seek out the easiest walking route between small ledges and small and large boulders. They are moss covered and the holes between them are traps for your feet. It would be easier if you took a more direct route, slightly to the north, toward the summit, but stay on this course if you want to reach the slide.

At 2700-feet elevation, 1.5 miles from the start, you reach abrupt ledges that force you to scramble up and over a tangle of growth clinging to the steep rock. Shortly you are at the base of a rock slide, one hundred feet long, that leads almost to the summit, but falls short of reaching it by a few minutes scramble. The rock face is steep and offers few hand and foot holds. Climbing along the edge is advisable. There is a wonderful panorama from the top part of the slide.

The same adventurous bushwhackers who described this route tell of continuing on to make a circuit to Northrup (where there was a logging camp) and Mica lakes and back to the Northville-Placid Trail; but anyone who is capable of making such a trek is capable of figuring out the details with map and compass. The ledges southeast of Northrup Lake are an obstacle to be avoided, as is the ring of wet spruce swamp that circles the larger of the Mica lakes.

41   Along West Lake to Brooktrout Lake
2.55 miles, 2 hours, relatively level, map VI

A yellow-marked trail heads west from site of West Lake Rangers Headquarters, through a spruce swamp to a bridge over the outlet of West Lake. From there it continues for 0.3 mile through a spruce-walled corridor to a lean-to that sits back from the sandy shore of a deep blue-green bay of West Lake. Boulders border the bay's protecting arm. There is a spring by the lean-to.

The trail goes west beside the lean-to, passing another spring in 100 yards and climbing steeply up the bank behind the bay. The trail climbs nearly 100 feet above the lake, then begins to traverse the hillside. The trail stays high above the water and does not follow the shoreline route depicted on the 1954 series USGS.

Huge rock slabs have slumped from the steep slopes above the trail. Tall red spruce once covered the slopes of West Lake Mountain to the north. Stands of these softwoods lured loggers here at the turn of the century, but except for the absence of spruce, which are slowly returning, the scene along West Lake's northern shore is as wild as it was before the loggers came.

If you are interested in bushwhacks, watch at just over 1 mile for the place on the trail where each trunk in a cluster of beech is blazed, and there are three blazes on a maple. This spot is 150 yards east of an intermittent stream that in turn is about 150 yards east of a fairly significant stream that tumbles from the hillside above. This stream is not shown on the current USGS but it has several lovely little waterfalls, some within a short distance north of the trail. Dunham in *French Louie* called it Sucker Brook.

Take note of the blazed place—a roadway used to climb toward Twin Lakes from here. Trees in the roadway are over twelve feet tall—no one seems to go this way since fish have disappeared from those lakes. This route or a bushwhack starting near the stream is described in section 42 as a means of reaching the top of the cliffs on West Lake Mountain.

The yellow trail to Brooktrout heads downhill beyond the stream crossing and approaches a drying beaver marsh at 1.5 miles. Look to the north from the marsh and you can spot cliffs on the hillside above. A bushwhack toward magnetic north for 0.3 mile will take you behind them for a view across West Lake.

The trail is presently routed below the long sinuous dam of this beaver marsh. Beyond, it climbs to traverse the side hill again, circling above a headland. The trail drops between boulders, and at 1.9 miles a side path leads 150 feet down to a campsite at the western end of West Lake. This is a choice spot beneath boulders and ledges with a beautiful view east across chains of rocks that interrupt the lake. Pillsbury Mountain lies in the distance just south of east.

The yellow trail now pulls away from the lake heading north of east through a high valley, the divide between the Mohawk and St. Lawrence watersheds. Just beyond lakeshore you pass an enormous boulder or erratic. The trail in the draw is through a wet marshy area with hillsides both north and south. Then you see a small cirque ahead and climb up and over an arm of it. The trail continues through a spruce swamp beside a stream flowing toward Brooktrout Lake. You cross the stream three times. The effect of the glaciers is evident everywhere: Boulders have been plucked from the ledges above and tossed into the valley. You walk through a lovely ferny glen, then intersect the trail from the Moose River Plains, section 78. Just beyond, one of those boulders hangs over a fireplace by Brooktrout's lean-to. For more about the lake, see section 78.

42 West Lake Mountain Cliffs
Bushwhack, map VI

The bushwhack to West Lake Mountain's fabled cliffs is the most exciting adventure in the region. From lakeshore, either at West or South lake, the view of these cliffs is deceptive: they appear to be at the top of the ridge immediately north of the lake. They are actually a mile farther north on a second and 300-foot-higher ridge. The cliffs are much taller than they seem from lakeshore, rising over 300 feet almost to the top of the 3100-foot summit knob of West Lake Mountain.

The literature is full of references to climbing West Lake Mountain, and Dunham's biography of French Louie even has two photographs from the mountain. However, these pictures were taken from the lower mountain slopes just behind West Lake where there used to be several open ledges with views. With the exception of the western outcrop, these view spots no longer exist, so the best views are at the end of a more than challenging bushwhack that requires nearly a day's effort for hikers camped either at Brooktrout Lake or at West Lake.

From the intermittent stream on the north side of West Lake, just east of

the larger stream described in section 41, head toward magnetic north. The woods are mostly open hardwoods. Within ten minutes you cross the larger stream, which drains the high valley below the cliffs. The route is generally level until at 2650 feet in elevation, thirty minutes from the trail, you cross a second stream. Then your route takes you fairly steeply uphill until at 2950 feet in elevation you reach the top of the ridge. The route north is 0.7 mile long and takes about thirty-five minutes since the going has been remarkably easy walking thus far.

Now head east across the ridge for 400 yards, climbing to 3000 feet, then head southeast for another 400 yards. The summit of West Lake Mountain is fairly open with lush ferns beneath stands of white birches. Its many beech trees have claw marks from bears that climb to the top for the nuts. Turn briefly south and emerge on the top of the cliffs after a bushwhack of about an hour and ten minutes.

The cliffs, which range to the east for nearly half a mile are between three and four hundred feet tall..But, watch out! Their tops are rounded and you cannot safely see the bottom of the cliffs from the top. You can, instead, enjoy the view across West Lake to South and Mud lakes with Pillsbury in the distance. The view south is across densely forested rolling hills leading up to Spruce Lake Mountain.

You can walk east along the cliff tops, but back from the edge, for 0.5 mile, until you can descend to the northeast and circle around behind them. A compass course south will take you back to West Lake. The first part of the route is beneath stately hardwoods, free of underbrush, but it does take you across a steep ravine and through numerous hobblebush thickets.

If there is time, you might want to poke about beneath in the talus jumble beneath the cliffs where boulders, plucked from the cliff face by a glacier, have fallen, and, in one place at least, have created a cave. However, the fallen boulders make walking beneath the cliffs tedious and somewhat dangerous.

The route of the old woods road west of the mountain can serve as a bushwhack course to Twin Lakes, but most of the road is too overgrown to follow. A corduroy route follows the edge of the western pond, and there are open areas beside its outlet; but you will find the eastern pond is ringed with such thick spruce as to make it impenetrable. Also, the beaver dam on the outlet that was so large it impressed the mapmakers is no more. Neither are the fish for which the ponds were famous.

West and South Lakes from the cliffs on West Lake Mountain

Cedar Lakes

43 West Lake to Cedar Lakes Dam

6.65 miles, 3½ hours, 300-foot elevation change, map VI

This stretch of the Northville-Placid Trail has side trips to two lean-tos before reaching a third at the north end of Cedar Lakes, 0.2 mile short of the dam. This many-armed body of water is always referred to as Cedar Lakes (plural) even though the three lakes that comprise the cluster have been flooded into one lake since the current dam was built in 1904. With the water five feet lower as shown on the 1901 USGS, there were three distinct lakes: the northern or first lake stretched south to the narrows west of Good Luck Mountain. At that time, the arm known as Noisey Inlet was only a shallow marsh. The second lake, the middle one, stretched east to encompass Pillsbury Bay. The third lake, the southern one, had only a small connection with the middle lake where today a rocky peninsula and islands narrow the lake.

Trout fishing is excellent in the Cedars and a canoe is most desirable for anyone staying there any length of time. Many fishermen carry in inflatable rafts. Otter often chase the progeny of several pairs of nesting loons whose cries give campers sleepless nights. An osprey nests in a tall pine where the lake narrows.

From the site of headquarters at Big West or North Lake as West Lake was sometimes called, head west on the blue trail. Within ten minutes, at 0.25 mile, a long causeway of logs bridges a widening in the outlet stream of West Lake, but beaver flooding has put a good deal of the planking under water. It is apt to be a wet crossing.

The maturing red spruce forest seems tall and relatively undisturbed where the trail traverses a knoll. Here a hidden pathway branches right, southeast from the knoll. It leads to the shore of Mud Lake where canoes are often secreted. Beyond, the trail returns to the level of Mud Lake, reaching its shores at 0.75 mile.

The trail, occasionally muddy and wet, circles north around the lowlands that border Mud Lake. Ledges line the hills to the north and boulders plucked from these ledges by the glacier lie near the trail. Those peculiar holes in the trail are where the telephone poles that served Headquarters were removed. The marsh bordered with swamp maples that surrounds Mud Lake Inlet is visible through the trees at just short of 2 miles, and at 2 miles there is a bridge over Mud Creek. In the next mile, the trail winds over a low hill, making several sharp turns near the crest of the hill. Just short of 3 miles, there is a path right to Kings Pond, which has a handsome outlet and a little rock ledge that drops cleanly to the tiny pond.

Beyond the path, the trail crosses the outlet of Kings Pond and gradually takes on a northeasterly direction for a gentle downhill. At 3.75 miles the trail makes a left turn, and an unmarked trail heads straight ahead. You will not spot the yellow markers on this side trail until you have walked along it for a hundred feet or so. It leads toward the marshes at the head of Cedar Lakes, crosses part of those marshes in a very wet area, rounds a knoll in a spruce stand heading west, and descends, 0.5 mile from the blue trail, to a lovely bay of the lake. A lean-to, dubbed fishermen's lean-to, sits close to the shore. The twelve-minute walk to it is along a very pretty route, if you overlook the wet spots at the beginning.

The blue trail heads north through a deep spruce and balsam woods, approaching close to a very small bay on Cedar Lakes at 3.95 miles. Old timers dub this West Canada Bay. A nice campsite lies between the trail and shoreline. The trail remains muddy as it enters a much smaller, younger forest. Patches of tall, thin hardwoods, mostly maples, alternate with dense spruce pockets.

The trail begins a long uphill at 4.4 miles through stands of smaller beech and maples to a height-of-land at 5.1 miles that the current USGS designates as Cobble Hill. This is not the true Cobble Hill and certainly not the Cobble Hill French Louie visited. His Cobble Hill, which was so named on the 1901 USGS, is a sharp little knob 0.5 mile due north of Kings Pond and 0.5 mile due west of West Canada Bay on Cedar Lakes. Louie's cave is on this knob, and his hand hewn bunk is reportedly still in the cave. The old trail from West Canadas to Cedar Lakes was high on this hill, just below and southeast of the cliffs of its sharp summit knob.

During the gradual 0.6-mile descent toward the lakeshore from the height-of-land, the trail traverses a forest of small white and yellow birch, through which you can glimpse Beaver Pond to the northwest.

Within 100 yards of the channel between Beaver Pond and Cedar Lakes, the trail splits into three unmarked parts. The first, a left fork, leads 200 yards south of west to a spring. (The rest of this old road is totally overgrown, in fact, full of balsam ten feet tall or more.) Fifty feet farther, a right fork leads up to a lovely, windswept promontory over the Cedar Lakes with a good lean-to and a view across the north end of Cedar Lakes to Noisey Ridge with Pillsbury visible to the southwest.

The trail, straight, reaches, at 5.9 miles, a bridge over the channel, where again there are views of Pillsbury Mountain. Beaver Pond to the northwest is large and shallow—before the current dam it was mostly marshland.

Beyond the dam, the trail is atop a long causeway. To the north there is a tent site hidden by blowdown. It is close to the shore of Beaver Pond. Continue between walls of young balsam to a marked trail intersection at 6.05 miles. The way left, with yellow markers, leads to Lost Pond, section 45, and the road that separates the Moose River Plains from the West Canadas, section 61. The blue trail curves away from the lakeshore, heading generally east. After crossing an inlet stream, it approaches the site of Cedar River Headquarters where all that remains are one lean-to and three outhouses. The lean-to is at a lovely site in a field, 200 yards upstream from the dam. Robert Barton, an interior caretaker in the 1950s, planted a row of Cedar trees at lakeshore—the only ones that grow at these Cedar Lakes. To the east of the lean-to are the foundations from the headquarters building.

The trail approaches the dam, which used to be surmounted by a bridge. The bridge is out and may be replaced. Crossing the Cedar River below the dam is possible in low water, and two nice campsites are on the eastern shore of the long thin outlet. You would need to cross the river to complete the loop to Sled Harbor, section 44. The blue trail continues north from the dam to Cedar River Flow, section 51.

44 Cedar Lakes to Sled Harbor

5.5 miles, 3 hours, 520-foot elevation change, maps IV and VI

This section describes the 2.7-mile segment from Cedar Lakes dam to the intersection with the Pillsbury Lake Trail, which completes the 18-mile circuit through the West Canadas, or a 23.6-mile walk from Sled Harbor. The 2.8-mile segment from Sled Harbor to the Pillsbury Trail intersection is described in section 33. Because the bridge at the dam is out, you have to hop rocks to cross the river below the dam; hence, trying to complete the loop in high water may not be advisable.

On the east side of the Cedar River Dam, several paths meet the trail at various angles, and they could cause confusion, so watch for the yellow disks that mark this trail to the southeast around Noisey Ridge. The first mile is relatively level to gently downhill with much old corduroy and some wet spots. The next mile has more variety in terrain with moderate ups and downs, but one stretch of about 50 yards of wet muddy trail, a short respite, and another muddy stretch. Beyond the wet spots, you cross the first sizable brook and begin a dry, gently descent. From here on the wet spots have been improved by broad planking.

The forest changes from all hardwoods to include a mixture of evergreens. Dry stretches alternate with brook crossings and more planking. At about 1.5 miles, you pass a small clearing and find yourself in a beautiful evergreen corridor. At 1.9 miles this opens up into a broad grassy meadow through which flows Grassy Brook, which is crossed by a rustic, very solid, plank bridge. The meadow is bordered by beautiful evergreens, making you stop to imagine how lovely this would be in winter.

There follows another stretch of planking, then an open meadow with parts of the foundation of a long-gone building, IP's Camp 20. At the end of the meadow, there is another solid plank bridge, again over Stony Brook, at 2.3 miles. A short path to the left leads to a spring. The stone foundations of an old vehicular bridge lie to the left of the trail here. Beyond, the trail becomes wider as it climbs gently uphill to reach the intersection at 2.7 miles.

Note: For those who wish to push a canoe to the Cedar Lakes using a wheeled cart, the upper part of this route is level, but the muddy spots are quite difficult. The 2.8 miles between this trail and Sled Harbor are occasionally rocky and worn, though the grade is a fairly consistent and gently uphill for the most part. The 5.5 miles is longer than the approach from the Cedar River Flow, see section 51.

45 Cedar Lakes to Lost Pond
3 miles, 1½ hours, 200-foot elevation change, map VI

A yellow-marked trail heads north from the fork that is 0.15 mile north of the bridge over the channel between Beaver Pond and Cedar Lakes. The guide board points to Lost Pond (no mileage) and Otter Brook Bridge, 10 miles. The latter indicates the road that marks the boundary between the Moose River Plains and the West Canadas. Otter Brook Bridge is 8.7 miles from Cedar Lakes on this route.

The portion to Lost Pond was cut expressly as a trail from a series of logging roads, and it traces a rather circuitous route to reach the pond. From the intersection, the trail heads north for 0.2 mile to cross a small stream. Taking a more northwesterly course, the trail heads upgrade through a tall spruce swamp with a balsam understory. Beaver Pond is visible through the trees on the left. Beaver have dammed an inlet stream that you must cross at 0.4 mile. The trail is poor here.

The trail continues on a gentle uphill through mature mixed hardwoods, then becomes more steep as it heads west of north into a draw. It curves around the hillside reaching a height-of-land at 1 mile where it is following a fairly obvious old logging road. The trail gradually takes a westerly direction as it heads downhill through a young forest. Here you cross several small streams. Then at 1.6 miles, the trail turns north, downhill, leaving the logging road. It makes a very wet crossing through a huge marsh that beaver have flooded along the outlet of Lost Pond, which is the headwaters of Otter Brook. Some logs at 1.7 miles span the three- to four-foot-deep brook to make an improvised crossing, but it is apt to be a wet crossing. Beyond it, the trail heads uphill, angling back northeast, to reach an intersection at just short of 2.2 miles. The way left leads to the Otter Brook Trail, section 74, and the way right curves back southeast to reach the shore of Lost Pond in a grassy area on the northern shore. Several small bays surround the pond whose shores are often muddy. Nevertheless, it is a lovely, remote place.

Cedar River Road

CEDAR RIVER ROAD was first settled by hunters and fishermen. The 1870 Wallace's *Guide to the Adirondacks* tells of a new hotel with a capacity for sixty guests, built by W.D. Wakeley at Cedar River Falls. He advertised that he kept boats 14 miles distant in Indian Clearing, now called the Moose River Plains. That hotel burned by 1878 and a smaller version was rebuilt, only to burn again in 1884. This was rebuilt, sold to Finch-Pruyn & Co., burned, and was never rebuilt.

State land touches only parts of the north and south ends of Cedar River Road. Most of the points listed in the mileage section below are on private land, so you can not explore them. Still, you will enjoy naming these points of interest as you drive the road or walk its southern 6.7 miles, which are considered a part of the Northville-Placid Trail.

Driving along the road is pleasant. Glimpses of Cedar River are on your left near the beginning. At 9.8 miles you have views of towering cliffs nearby on the right, but the area is owned by the Cedar Valley Club and posted. At 11.3 miles, you cross the outlet of Wakely Pond. From here you can see Wakely Mountain and the tall tower on its western flank. The pond and the area around it have recently (1988) been purchased by the state from International Paper Company. Both fishing and paddling on Wakely Pond are pleasant.

At 12.0 miles the trail to Wakely Mountain, section 49, goes off to the right, northeast, marked by a DEC signpost. Continuing south, you reach, at 12.3 miles, both Wakely Dam and the eastern entrance to the Moose River Plains. A sign indicates you should register at the cabin to go into the plains or use the Wakely Dam Area, but there is currently no charge.

Mileages

0.0   Cedar River Road heads south from NY 28 and 30, west of Indian Lake Village

2.2   Road into Forest Preserve, reforestation area

4.4   Sprague Pond, section 46

5.6   Northville-Placid Trail turns west at McCanes, section 47

7.2   End of paved road

8.9　Hikers and hunters access to state land. A yellow arrow points to a yellow-marked trail that leads west for 0.4 mile to state land, along a log road that provides a right-of-way across posted Finch-Pruyn Paper Company land. The road continues into state land by a small brook, but it is not maintained beyond this point.

9.55　Lower Water Barrel Hill, views

9.9　Sugarloaf

10.5　Town Line Hill, falls in gorge on Cedar River to the east are on private and posted land

10.7　Upper Water Barrel Hill

11.3　Outlet of Wakely Pond. Land on both sides of the road from here to Wakely Dam are now owned by the state. While the previous owners had allowed public access, they permitted no camping or fires. Now you can camp here, near the pond and on sites near the river, as long as you are 150 feet from water.

12.0　Wakely Tower Trail

12.3　Headquarters, camping permitted, way left is Wakely Dam on Cedar River and Cedar River Flow; way right, west, registration booth for Moose River Plains Road

Turn west

13.6　Road south, with barrier, is Northville-Placid Trail

46　Sprague Pond

Path, short walk, camping, fishing
0.4 mile, 10 minutes, level, map IX

The path to Sprague Pond is short (under 0.4 mile) and smooth and better than most trails. It is not marked, but marking would be superfluous. The path starts behind a barrier on the north side of Cedar River Road, 4.4 miles from NY 28/30. It winds a little east of north, almost level, through a lovely forest.

The pond is a well-kept secret for all but natives who enjoy it. There are small rock islands and rocky peninsulas, all capped with evergreens. You almost always see loons in the pond. Carrying a canoe here is very easy and a must for camping and fishing. Some of the shoreline near the road shows signs of heavy camping use, but the rest seems untouched. Midweek you can have this half-mile-long pond all to yourself, and all for only a ten-minute walk.

47 Northville-Placid Trail to Stephens Pond

Hiking, camping, fishing, cross-country skiing
2.4 miles, 1 hour, 160-foot elevation change, map IX

The elevation change from Cedar River Road to Stephens Pond is so slight that this is an easy route for a weekend backpacking trip to the lean-to, an overnight fishing trip with an inflatable raft, or a cross-country ski trip. The pond is only 89 feet higher than the road.

The trailhead is on the right, northwest, side of the road 5.6 miles from NY 28/30 near a group of buildings labeled McCanes Houskeeping Cabins. The DEC guideboard beside the road indicates Lake Durant Campground is 5.3 miles on the blue-marked Northville-Placid Trail, Blue Mountain Lake is 6.7 miles.

Park off the road on the south side. The land is private and should be respected. A sign reminds hikers that owners permitted marking of this trail for the benefit of the public, but hunting, fishing, and camping are not permitted. Walk up the driveway to the left of the house and continue straight ahead with a woodshed on your left and a small shed on your right. Here you will see the wide, clear trail going northwest through an open maple grove.

In ten minutes you reach a long, wet area, some of which may require a detour. Waterproof boots are useful on this trail as there are a number of places that are swampy and almost impossible to avoid. Dampness has its rewards, however, as it makes you slow down and enjoy the forest and the extensive array of cinnamon fern and spinulose woodfern.

At 0.6 mile, the wood road forks; you will see a blue marker to your left here after about a fifteen minute walk. Five minutes farther along, at 0.8 mile, yellow blazes mark the beginning of state land. You reach a height-of-land at 2020 feet at 0.9 mile and begin a gradual descent.

Look sharply as you descend, for after thirty minutes, at 1.4 miles, there is a sign on the left indicating that the trail turns right along a narrow foot path that winds through a spruce and balsam thicket. This detour takes you over a drier section of the swamps. In winter you could go straight on the traditional trail, that is if the swamp is frozen enough to cross. A small brook flows east through the swamp, eventually flowing into Lake Durant near the campground. You cross this brook on two cedar logs and in five minutes are back on the main trail. If you are hiking the other way, from north to south, the main trail is blocked by two blowdowns at the point where the detour begins; a small trail sign also marks this spot.

The trail now rises slightly. Hiking is slow as there are numerous wet places to negotiate. After forty-five minutes, you reach a small brook that you can jump across, and shortly cross another even smaller brook. Both of these streams flow into a beaver meadow that you can see to the right through the trees. In fifty minutes, there is another muddy area with an old corduroy log base in spots. When these wet spots are frozen, the wide level trail is excellent for skiing.

In less than an hour you see Stephens Pond ahead as you come down a small hill. Reaching the level, you cross another stream and the main trail continues to a T and Cascade Pond, section 90. A sign directs you along a path to the newly reconstructed lean-to which has been relocated back from the shore at the southwestern end of the pond. Pickerel weed grows abundantly in the shallows near the lean-to. If the lean-to is occupied (as it is apt to be in summer), there are flat areas nearby on which to pitch your tent.

48   Wakely Dam and the Cedar River Flow
Picnicking, fishing, camping, canoeing, map V

The Cedar River entrance to the Moose River Recreation Area has become a very popular place. There are about ten sites with picnic tables and fire rings that you can drive to and four or five more that you reach in a short walk. In addition, there are a number of sites along the Cedar River Flow accessible by canoe or boat with a small outboard. The fishing is not exceptional, apparently, but the flow is stocked and speckled trout can be caught. The camping area is located along the Northville-Placid Trail and is convenient if you wish to climb Wakely Mountain for a view of the Moose River Plains from its fire tower.

There is a large open field near the entrance to the Plains and a place to launch car-top boats or canoes on the left, just above the dam. If you want to paddle up the flow to camp, you can easily transfer your gear from the car to the canoe and then park in an out of the way spot in the field. Car camping is permitted around the field and there are two or three more isolated spots you can drive to on the west side. Outhouses for campers are plentiful and clean.

You can also drive across the dam and camp to the right or left. Four campsites on the east shore of the flow can be reached by a short hike from the dam area. From this side of the flow you have a view up the water, with Payne Mountain rising across the way, and you have greater privacy. Land northeast of the dam is part of the large tract the state recently acquired from International Paper Company so that now not only is the public permitted here as it was before, but camping is also allowed. There is an improved gravel road leading north for 2 miles through the new land, which includes about 1.4 miles of the Cedar River.

In spring near the campground, painted trillium is common in the attractive woods that surround the water. The flow is actually a large lake, so a canoe is definitely needed to explore its various coves. The extreme upper end to the south is very shallow with water lilies and other water plants. You may see loons on the lake, and you will definitely hear them calling at night.

49 Wakely Mountain

Hiking, sweeping views from the fire tower
3.2 miles, 2 hours, 1500-foot vertical rise, map V

A steep but short climb to the top of 3744-foot Wakely Mountain, then up the sturdy steps of its fire tower, gives you a panoramic view of the many ponds and peaks in the vast, rolling sea of green of the Moose River Plains to the west. You can see peaks north along Long and Tupper lakes, many of the High Peaks, and the expanse of the Cedar River flow and its surrounding mountains to the south.

The beginning of the trail is on the parcel the state recently (1988) acquired from International Paper Company. In the winter of 1986-87 this land was logged extensively, disturbing forests along the access road and the trail on the lower slopes of the mountain. Nevertheless, this little-known mountain is well worth the hike, particularly if the tower is manned in summer when the observer can help you identify the distant peaks.

The marked trailhead begins 12 miles south from NY 28-30, 0.3 mile north of Cedar Gate. Turn right, northwest, up a logging road at the DEC sign that reads "Wakely Mtn Observatory 3.0 miles." The road is passable by car for 1.0 mile where there is a logging camp on the right at 2250 feet. Park off the dirt road or in one of the turnarounds before reaching the camp. It is not known, however, whether the state will keep the first mile of the road open, so it is possible that in the future you will have to walk from Cedar River Road to this point.

Continue walking up the logging road; you will see a high peak ahead at 310° magnetic. It appears higher than a peak to the left, which is Wakely, though its tower is not visible from this point. In five minutes you will cross a stream on a bridge. Two minutes beyond there is a large staging area for the logging operation with the usual clutter of jugs and cans, log ends, and oil spills. Just beyond, you are rewarded by the pretty brook on your left—in stark contrast with the heavily ravaged woods on the right.

The road follows the brook, winding uphill; there are no trail markers along the road. After walking for nearly 0.5 mile on a stretch of road running west, you will see the tower clearly ahead on the seemingly smaller peak. In just under twenty minutes, less than a mile, you cross the brook that drains the col between the tower and the peak on the right. You pass another staging area with extensive logging, then at about 2 miles and at 2600-foot elevation, you come to a small sign: "Wakely Mtn Tower 1.2 miles." This indicates the trail to the right. Straight ahead there is a large beaver pond with several dams and a large beaver house in the middle. Walk up the road for a hundred yards for a better look at the pond. Cloud reflections and dark grey-brown stumps in the still water make this a beautiful pond to photograph.

Back at the sign, start up the trail at 300°. It is a well-traveled, dry trail, with red markers going up a rocky ridge of beech and cherry. You soon climb fairly steeply and reach an area where both sides of the trail have been logged. It is surprising to see that a skidder has operated on such a steep hillside. However, from here on the woods are pure enjoyment.

In spring, trout lilies are in bloom and warblers call in the woods. After a twenty-five minute climb, at about 3200 feet, a sign guides you to the right. Short of 3700 feet, yellow arrows on a rock mark a survey point. An hour after leaving the logging road—it is a steep climb so you will need time to catch your breath—you reach the level summit. It is mostly tree-covered, and the thick balsam fir and spruce keep you from seeing the tower that is off to the left. To the right is an open area with a helicopter platform, which is used to supply the fire observer's cabin. On the summit you will find grey-cheeked thrushes, boreal chickadees, and black poll warblers, but it takes a keen eye to spot the saw whet owls that nest along the trail.

The tower is ninety-two feet tall, the tallest in the Adirondacks. You can climb it even though the observer is not on duty. Payne Mountain is to the southeast, and beyond stretches the Cedar River Flow. To the west you can see Fourth Lake beyond Lake Kora, with Sagamore Lake north of Kora. To the north of it you can see all of Raquette Lake with its 96-mile shoreline. If it is a clear day, you will be able to see other fire towers in the distance: Pillsbury Mountain tower to the south, Blue Mountain tower to the north beyond the helicopter pad, and Snowy Mountain to the east. There is a small observer cabin at the base of the tower and a picnic area. Be sure and bring your own water.

The trail is so steep that it is hard to make time going down, but you should be back at the logging road in about thirty-five minutes and back at your car in under an hour. The hike is a good introduction to many of the peaks and ponds in this guide.

50 Cedar River Flow to Lean-to on Northville-Placid Trail

Canoeing, map V

If you find the right channel through the weeds, and if you are not bucking a headwind, it only takes two hours to canoe from Wakely Dam to the "lean-to that hums" because of its location in the buggy field above the Cedar River. You can also reach the lean-to via the Northville-Placid Trail, section 51, but the canoe route eliminates that walk, something you will appreciate if you have a heavy pack. From the water you may spot grey jays and boreal chickadees.

From Wakely Dam you canoe 3 miles to the head of the flow and another nearly 1.5 miles through the twisting river channel to the lean-to. You can canoe upstream from the lean-to for another 0.5 mile, and if you pull through the shallows, there is another mile or more of flat water.

From Wakely Dam head south past the islands, then bend east around a spruce-covered peninsula. You see a small cliff on Payne Mountain to the west. Little Moose and Manbury are the huge mountains that begin to show in the southwest. Buck, Onion, and Lewey are visible in the southeast, while due south, Blue Ridge Mountain dominates the flow. It's cliffs and slides, section 29, are clearly defined below and to the east of the summit.

The east shore is a series of spruce-covered knolls with marshes between them. Just past halfway down the flow, rushes and reeds begin to appear in the water. They gradually grow thicker until you think you are standing in the midst of a prairie of waving grass not paddling in the Adirondacks. You can paddle almost everywhere through the reeds, but as they thicken, definite channels appear through them. Buell Brook, which drains a large tract purchased by the state in 1894, flows in from the east.

As the channels become more defined, take those that lead closest to the eastern shore. The main channel is here, and the place where it emerges from the shrub marshes at the head of the lake into the grassy channels is quite concealed. At this point, the channel is no more than 50 feet from the east shore in reeds and grasses. Beyond, the channel heads southwest, zigzagging through the oxbows. Shrubby plants and bushes fill the marsh, though there is still no solid ground beside the channel. As you progress upstream, these give way to alder swamps, and gradually to evergreen dominated forests. The transition from reeds through shrubs to deep woods is lovely. Still farther along, the outside curves of the oxbows are cut into deep sand banks. There is one particularly lovely campsite partway up the channel on a pine covered knoll. There is a road and a ford just as you see the lean-to ahead.

If you want to carry a canoe to the Cedar Lakes, the easiest way is to canoe this far, then hike the Northville-Placid Trail, section 51.

51 Northville-Placid Trail from Wakely Dam to the Cedar Lakes

Hiking, camping
10.1 miles, 5 hours, 350-foot elevation change, maps V and VI

It is possible to drive the first 1.25 miles west from Wakely Dam to the junction where the Northville-Placid Trail forks south. There is limited parking at this fork. The trail follows a gated road that leads across state land for the first 2.6 miles. Toward the end of this stretch, the trail swings close to the Cedar River Flow at Ice House Landing where there are several campsites near the water. At 2.4 miles, the trail pulls away from the flow and at 2.6 miles enters private and posted lands. At 3.8 miles, there is a road right, and a second at 4.0 miles, which leads to the private club at Little Moose Lake. Shortly beyond, the trail reenters state land at a barrier.

The only break in the scrubby forest appears at 4.45 miles, where the roadway-trail is through an open alder marsh. From a bridge over a stream in the marsh, there are views to the northeast as well as west to Little Moose and Manbury mountains. At 4.8 miles, a roadway, no longer open to vehicular traffic, forks left, east, leading to a ford across the Cedar River. Less than 100 yards beyond, a trail forks left, east, for 0.15 mile to the Cedar River Lean-to, section 50.

The blue trail heads south, past an area of old blowdowns, and through a

Looking at the Cedar River from the Lean-to that Hums

spruce swamp with a covered archway of spruce and balsam. At 5.6 miles, a bridge carries the trail over Lamphere Brook in the midst of marshes surrounding the Cedar River. There are views toward Onion Hill and Lewey Mountain.

The trail climbs gradually, and at 6 miles the red trail to Lewey Lake Campground forks right, east. See sections 31 and 53. The blue trail, still following an old roadway, climbs west around a shoulder of Lamphere Ridge. It begins with an uphill stretch, traverses a level where the trail is grown in with maples, then descends. There are rock ledges on the side of the ridge to your right. At one point you have a view up to cliffs on Blue Ridge Mountain to the southeast. Then the trail is close to a beaver meadow that surrounds the Cedar, and at 7.75 miles, the trail comes to the site of the old bridge over the Cedar. There is a campsite and a fire ring near the crossing.

The DEC has eliminated this and another bridge 0.35 mile downstream from the dam at Cedar Lakes and constructed a new trail that remains on the west side of the river. This trail no longer follows a roadbed, and it is over a series of ridges that drop to water level. The road makers went to the trouble of constructing the bridges so the trail could traverse the level route on the east shore.

A word about that east shore route: there are times when the Cedar can easily be forded here. The roadway was well built and climbed gradually about 160 feet in just under a mile as it circled around the lower slopes of Round Mountain. It then descended to cross Grassy Brook and approach the Cedar, which it recrossed just below a swampy area at the head of a lovely little gorge. Part of the roadway is through a beautiful hardwood forest. The roadway is still there, and with the exception of blowdowns, it is still a good trail. It is not too difficult to cross the Cedar again 1.5 miles south at the head of the gorge, and here rejoin the main trail. If water levels permit crossing, you might consider this route. People have used it to transport canoes with wheeled carts. The 5 miles between the Cedar River Lean-to, where you can easily pull your canoe out, and the dam is much easier than the 0.5 mile longer route that follows the new west shore trail.

From the crossing, you will need more than an hour and a half to reach the dam on the west shore trail. The route is pretty, but the walking is really rough. It begins at water level, and already the trail is filling in with witch hopple. For the first 0.4 mile it is level, at water level, then it climbs the first of many ridges. The descents are sharp, the valleys between ridges are short, and the roots of the spruce that shelter the trail make walking difficult. At just over 9 miles, 1.3 miles from the crossing, the trail cuts away from an oxbow in the river into a spruce swamp. Shortly you cross a stream, which the maps show incorrectly as the outlet of Beaver Pond.

The trail is briefly near the Cedar, as it winds through a deep, dark, mature spruce swamp with a carpet of sorrel, dryopteris, and clintonia. Again, the trail leaves the river and climbs noticeably. At 9.4 miles, there is a campsite with a fire ring near the trail. The new route rejoins the old at 9.75 miles. The last 0.35 mile is relatively level. If you are walking this route north from the Cedar River, ample arrows and signs point you to the new trail. Campsites exist on both sides of the river just south of the dam and the lean-to is only 0.2 mile south along the shore. Near the lean-to there are several good tent sites. From here, the chapter on the Heart of the West Canadas will guide you on.

52   Carry Pond and Squaw Brook Valley
Paths along woods roads, map V

Wade or paddle across the shallow ford on the Cedar River, 100 yards downstream from the lean-to, section 50. The roadway heads downhill

Cedar River near Colvin Brook Lean-to

from the Northville-Placid Trail to this ford just 50 feet short of the fork to the lean-to.

The roadway continues east of the ford, and since vehicles have used it through the summer of 1987, you cannot get lost following the first part of it. After a ten minute walk, 0.7 mile, watch for a faint path on the south side of the roadway with a yellow arrow. It leads along a fading roadway south for 250 yards to Carry Pond, a tiny and unexciting spot that used to have good fishing. Blowdowns along the route have recently been cleared.

If you continue on the main roadway east, then northeast, over relatively level terrain for about 2.5 miles from the ford, you reach a newly acquired parcel of state land. Shortly the camp here will be removed and all vehicular traffic east of the ford will cease. The roadway is in the valley of Little Squaw Brook, but never within sight of the brook.

The roadway peters out, but you can continue northeast up into the high valley that lies below the west slopes of Snowy Mountain. Squaw Brook drains north from this valley into Indian Lake and the high divide is now filled with a long chain of beaver meadows making exploring it very difficult.

53   Colvin Brook Lean-to

Camping, hiking
1 mile, 30 minutes, 200-foot elevation change, maps V and VI

This short red-marked trail connects the Northville-Placid Trail on the west with the Sucker Brook-Colvin Brook Trail on the east, section 31. The only thing missing is a bridge that would guarantee access to the lean-to that sits on the east side of the Cedar River. In low water, crossing on exposed rocks is easy; the rest of the time you can always wade.

This connector heads southeast from the Northville-Placid Trail, 6 miles south of the Moose River Plains Road, before that trail begins to climb the slopes of Lamphere Ridge. Note that the trail is not as shown on the 1950 series USGS. The route has many ups and downs but no significant elevation changes as it traverses the lower flanks of that ridge. The trail emerges from the woods 50 yards downstream from the lean-to that sits at the head of a chain of marshes along the Cedar. It is a lovely and rarely visited out of the way spot.

The Moose River Plains

THE MOOSE RIVER Plains was one of the Adirondacks' last frontiers. This vast region was visited only by sportsmen, hunters, and trappers until well into the 1900s. Logging pierced the fringes of the area, a few hotels or camps catered to sportsmen, but a great part of the area was untouched until after World War II. Then in a period of less than twenty years, part of the area was stripped of its forests—logged for pulp on a greater scale than almost anywhere else in the mountains.

The Moose River Plains is a broad glacial valley that stretches for several miles along the South Branch of the Moose. It was formed during the retreat of the last glacial sheets that covered the Adirondacks. Its sands are a combination of kame terraces, fluvial, and fluvial deltic deposits laid down after the glacier covering the Adirondacks melted, but before the ice in the Black River Valley melted, so that sand from the decaying ice in the Adirondack glacier, a little farther north, was trapped.

The glaciers were responsible for the number of boulders that dot the hillsides, and erratics are scattered everywhere. The glaciers also shaped the modern landscape by permitting the construction of a dense network of logging roads. The Plains roads were built with modern road graders and tractors that cleared rocks and filled the roadways with gravel from numerous borrow pits. These hard-packed surfaces are broad and flat, eroded in only a few places, and in the southern Plains are only now beginning to fill with brambles and small trees.

The South Branch of the Moose River rises in Little Moose Lake on the slopes north of Little Moose (elevation 3630 feet) and Manbury (elevation 3464 feet) mountains, which stand like sentinels guarding the eastern plains. Northeast of the Plains is a ridge of mountains that rises on its eastern end to Cellar (3200 feet) and Wakely (3744 feet) mountains. To the south, low mountains, the tallest of which is Kitty Cobble (3200 feet), rise above a high plateau that contains the interior of the West Canadas. To the west, the Plains narrow to the sites proposed for both the Higley and Panther dams. If these dams had been constructed, significant portions of the Plains would have been flooded. Here, the Moose River flows through the Adirondack League Club property, all of which is posted and off limits to the public. And, in the southwest, there are the low hills that rise around the Indian River, where great flat trails lead to distant ponds.

Gould Paper Company owned and logged most of Township 4 in the Totten and Crossfield Tract (the square that includes western portions of Otter Brook and the Moose River as well as Sly Pond and Little Moose Mountain), and in the Moose River Plains Tract, half of Township 4 (the region south of Squaw and Indian lakes and the part of the Wilderness Area around Falls Pond and Wolf and Deep lakes), and almost all of Township 5 (the westernmost rectangle of the Wilderness that includes Stink, Horn, and Balsam lakes and part of Ice Cave Mountain).

This Gould parcel of 51,000 acres in the southern Plains included all of seventeen lakes, seven miles of the Indian River, and four mountains. They began logging this area in the 1940s and continued logging until 1963. The land was purchased by the state in 1964 for an average sixteen dollars an acre, a veritable bargain in that an estimate prepared for the state valued it at over twenty-one dollars an acre. Butterworth, who prepared the estimate, was impressed by the "many streams and rivers that seem to wander aimlessly over this entire tract" and by the stands of virgin spruce that exceeded a hundred feet in height. Under terms of the sale, Gould was able to cut many of these stands.

The purchase price may seem advantageous to the state, but the paper company's logging was as heavy as any done anywhere in the state. Great patches appear to have been clearcut. Huge stands, logged in the last few years of their operation, are no more than thickets of arm-sized starts of maples and beech. Logging like this benefits game species and here it has enhanced the Plains' reputation for deer and bear.

Although you will meet few places with good forests in the southern Plains, the situation is much different to the north of the Gould parcel. Lots southwest of Beaver Lake, west of Mitchell Ponds, north of Indian and Squaw lakes, and along the Moose were purchased or acquired by the state at a tax sale in 1899. The center of the Plains, near the Moose and around Icehouse and Helldiver ponds, was purchased in 1895. So were lots to the west of Icehouse Pond. A few lots north of the Plains Road were purchased as early as 1891.

Wellington Alexander (Ira) Kenwell built a hotel for sportsmen on the Moose River in 1891. The lot where his hotel stood was acquired by the state in 1901. At that time there was a rough track leading to Kenwells from the east. This track, which could hardly be called a road, was the only route into the Plains.

Some of this area was logged for softwoods, which were floated down the Moose River, but the rest of the forest was untouched. Huge stands of pine remain at the outlet of Beaver Lake and along the trail to that lake. Along the Otter and the Moose, you can see stands of black spruce that were never cut.

In these areas you can see how the glaciers shaped not only the land but the forests as well. The sands and gravels of the glacial lake that became the Plains were eroded to form the modern streams. The sterile glacial soil and the high water table account for the stands of enormous black spruce, which were never considered commercially valuable at the turn of the century when their surroundings were logged. Although they are dwarfed by some of the towering pines, these stands of black spruce contain giants of their species, many reaching sixty feet or more, heights that are rare elsewhere.

The broad fields that mark the Plains are covered with low, pioneering shrubs and trees, blueberries, cherries, and spireas. They are gradually growing up with spruce. Heavy deer browse keeps most trees from growing as you can see when you pass the deer exclosure pens where the forest is quickly becoming established.

The state has recently acquired all of International Paper Company's large tract at the eastern end of the Plains. This includes the land north of the road surrounding Cellar Mountain. South of the road, IP leaseholders retain exclusive rights to a 1000-acre tract surrounding Little Moose Lake, but even this will revert to the state in ten years (1998). The rest of IP's holdings south of the road are now state land. While hunters will benefit greatly from this acquisition, only the future use of Little Moose Lake will be of interest to hikers and campers, for IP had already opened the most desirable parts of its land to the public.

In the areas of extensive and recent logging, the forest floor has a relatively limited understory of interesting plants. But, the pockets of old growth timber host a diverse flora, high points of which are described with the trails through these stands.

The Plains have been a hunter's paradise because the flat areas around the Moose are a great winter deeryard. The small trees and low forests permitted a larger deer concentration than is found in deep woods. So great was the population of deer that the old Conservation Department maintained exclosure pens to protect the land as well as feeding stations for deer.

The Plains is a vast region, so it is fortunate that so many of the logging roads, over forty miles, remain open to cars. These roads, as well as the game, account for the popularity of the area with sportsmen. A rather

devious technique was used to ensure that the Plains Road would remain open to vehicles, since incorporating it within the Forest Preserve might have meant the closing of the road. The state accepted a gift of 26.2 acres through the tract, under an easement that permits the state to accept as a gift any lands that provided public hunting, trapping, or fishing, provided that the lands or waters did not become subject to the limitations of the constitutional amendment that created the Forest Preserve. Hikers and sportsmen are pleased that the 1988 acquisition from International Paper Company was also done in such a way that the eastern end of the Plains Road through new tract will always remain open to the public.

Today, this main access plus another fifteen miles of road are open only from Memorial Day until the end of hunting season, but they are very well maintained. The 15-mile-an-hour speed limit, however, makes a trip from Cedar Gate to Indian Lake, for instance, take nearly an hour and a half.

Perhaps the most unusual feature of the Plains is the number of campsites designated along the roads, each with a pit privy, fire ring, and picnic table. There are almost 150 sites available to car campers, and many are lovely ones close to water. There is currently no fee for camping at these sites in the Plains.

Many more roads, over twenty-seven miles of them, have been marked as trails; curiously all the hiking trails are marked with a uniform yellow color. The flatness of these trails makes it possible to use wheeled carrying carts for canoes, so many of the interior ponds can be enjoyed by canoe.

Many more miles are designated as snowmobile trails, and since the Plains Road is not plowed in winter, it becomes a superhighway for snowmobiles, groomed daily by communities at either end. This attracts huge numbers of snowmobilers. Unlike many other areas, there could be a conflict if skiers tried to use the snowmobile trails.

In addition, many, many miles of good logging roads and skid tracks crisscross the area. Some are overgrown, especially in the north, but some in the south are relatively clear and easy to follow. This condition will remain for another decade, perhaps, so those roads with inviting destinations are mentioned in the text for the avid bushwhacker to explore. However, be cautioned that the maze can be confusing. The southwestern area that was logged last has relatively modest changes in topography, so navigating can be difficult.

There is something very special about the wildlife in the Plains. You will

Giant pines and tamaracks along Moose River Plains Road

see rabbits and foxes, deer and coyote (sometimes they are so noisy you cannot sleep), beaver and otter, and an occasional bear. Watch for hawks and owls, ducks and loons, warblers, thrushes, and boreal species. There are two reasons why birding is so good in the area: the ease of spotting birds along the roads and open fields and the numerous edges, contacts between different vegetative cover, such as forests, open fields, wetlands, and ponds, that encourage a diversity of birds.

A DEC booklet describes the special regulations that apply to hunting, fishing, and snowmobiling regulations. Camping is permitted only at designated sites along the road, but you can camp anywhere else as long as you are 150 feet from water. Permits are required for stays of three or more days. Campers, trailers, and other recreational vehicles are permitted in the area from Memorial Day to October 15, and four-wheel drive or two-wheel drive vehicles with chains are permitted up to the end of hunting season. No ATVs, motorcycles, or motorized bicycles are permitted on the Plains roads.

The Eastern Moose River Plains, Access from Cedar River Gate

Mileages

Plains Road West from Headquarters on the Cedar River at Wakely Dam

0.0   Registration booth
1.25 Northville-Placid Trail, left fork
1.5   Payne Brook
1.75 Road right
3.4   Road right, Cellar Pond
4.7   Road south, private
5.8   Road north to Cellar Brook
6.05 Spring, road north just to west
6.15 Cellar Brook
7.25 Bradley Brook
7.3   Road north, loop Bradley Brook
7.75 Silver Run on left, marshes right, picture stop with ledges
7.8   Loop Road, road along South Branch Moose heads east here to private land of Little Moose Club

9.7   Road south, sign: Moose River 0.1 mile, Sly Pond 6 miles
11.65 Road north, Lost Ponds and Snowmobile Trail, sign: Lost Ponds, 1 mile
12.1   Big Tamarack
12.85 Trail south, Helldiver Pond, 0.45 mile
13.65 T in the road, the way right, north leads to Limekiln Gate and Inlet, 12 miles

Note: Mileages on the sign post here for these destinations from west to east have slight discrepancies.

54 Cellar Pond

Path along old logging road, map V

Logging roads and the rusting remnants of old logging and hunting camps are prevalent in the Moose River Plains. This hike has some of these, plus a pretty destination pond at 3000-feet elevation and a pile of old horse-shoes and horseshoe nails.

Turn right on the unmarked dirt road 3.4 miles from the eastern registration booth (Cedar Gate). On your left, 0.2 miles up the road, there is a hunting camp labeled "Cellar Mountain Boys." At 0.45 mile the road is washed out, and you must leave your car here. The elevation is 2780 feet.

Start hiking uphill along the road. In two or three minutes it swings right. There are blowdowns and eroded gullies. This area was heavily logged a few years ago. After hiking for a little over 0.5 mile, you find that balsam fir is filling the roadbed. Soon after, 1.2 miles from the Plains Road, you swing to the left in a gradual loop and start downhill. The road forks and you bear right, keeping to the contour of the mountain. Continue on the level through young balsam, and you will come to a boggy area. Sphagnum, labrador tea, leather leaf, and sheep laurel have invaded the road right on the side of the mountain. A bog environment can be found in many different locations.

After a half an hour walk of 1.2 miles (1.7 from the Plains Road) you come to a clearing where you see the pond through a thick stand of twenty-year-old spruce trees on your left. In the clearing are the remains of a logging camp that dates back to the days when logs were skidded out of the woods with horses. On the edge of the clearing, toward the water, is a pile of old horseshoes and bent horseshoe nails.

You can reach the marshy shoreline of Cellar Pond by walking about thirty feet east of the clearing until you come to a small path leading down to the shore. At the narrow opening there is a view of Wakely Mountain to the northeast; its fire tower is out of sight behind the trees to the right. The shore is shallow—clumps of leather leaf and other shrubs form off-shore islands. Dead spars of young spruce rise from the shoreline and frame the hills beyond. There are no large rocks along this shore to swim from and the pond supports no fish.

When the state purchase is completed, you may camp near the pond. It is only 200 feet higher than where you left your car, and the walk back takes the same thirty minutes as the trip in.

55   Bradley Brook Loop
Path on an old logging road, map X

As you drive west on the Plains Road from Cedar Gate you cross Bradley Brook, which flows from the north at 7.25 miles. Just beyond, there is a dirt road to the right, which ends in a loop where there are three pleasant camping spots, numbers 16, 17, and 18. If you walk straight through #17, with Bradley Brook tumbling over rocks to your right, you will pick up a logging road that runs parallel to the brook. Following this road will lead you on a pleasant day hike past logging camp ruins, an old beaver meadow, and the company of Bradley Brook with its swift stream and cool, shaded banks.

The road is open and easy to follow although some evergreens are beginning to fill the road in places. After seven minutes, the road forks; keep right, going almost north with the brook downhill on your right. In twelve minutes the road swings away from the brook up a hill. In fifteen minutes a spur goes left; again keep right. A hundred yards beyond, you reach a height-of-land and start down. The road appears to lead straight into a beaver meadow with a small stream crossing it. Actually the road goes right through new red spruce and balsam fir growth before it gets to the meadow. You have to look hard to find the path—it is just after you pass a large rock on your right.

Make your way through the dense growth following the faint path until it becomes almost impassable and then turn left toward the outlet of the beaver meadow. You will hear Bradley Brook ahead before you go left. In ten feet you should be out of the spruce and pick up the road again where it crosses an old log bridge, which is still in good shape.

Across the bridge, the logging road forks, although the fork is hard to see because of young evergreens. The left fork goes around the west side of the beaver meadow; the right fork goes 100 feet toward Bradley Brook and then heads left, northwest. If you scout around the high ground in the clearing you will find the remains of a cabin and bunkhouse. Many rusted bed frames are clues to the former logging camp, which is shown on the 1954 USGS map.

You can follow the logging road that continues northwest (350° magnetic) from just beyond the camp. In about seven minutes you come to a corner marker with extensive pink blaze marks on trees. This is apparently the southeast corner of Lot 58. A pink-flagged hunter's trail leads north from this corner.

The 1954 USGS shows a trail going through this area and leading over to the stillwater on Sumner Stream. This route is believed to be the location of the Albany Road that was built for military use in 1812. Faint wheel ruts or fragments of built-up stream crossings can be found to mark an ancient passage, but if the Albany Road went through here, time seems to have completely obliterated it.

56 South Branch Moose River Trail

Hiking, mountain biking
3 miles, 1 hour, level, map X

A level road runs easterly parallel to the South Branch of the Moose, ending after 3 miles at the private land of the Little Moose Club. The trail begins at a turn south from the Plains Road, 7.8 miles from Cedar Gate. Drive 500 yards to a pleasant camping spot beside Silver Run. There is a barrier before the stream, but no bridge. You start the hike by wading the shallow stream, which is sixty feet wide at this point. The rocks are slippery so it helps to have a hiking staff for balance.

Across the stream, the weed-choked path cuts around to the right and follows the brook due south for a short way. It then swings easterly and starts climbing slightly. After a five minute walk, a path goes right to the Moose River. At 0.6 mile you cross a brook. The road is still fairly open with red spruce beginning to invade the way. At 1 mile you climb slightly and then level off, walking over bedrock. At 1.2 miles there is an open sandy area with a brook and a beaver meadow ahead. Just short of 2 miles you come to an inactive beaver pond. A large beaver house sits in the center, and there is a pleasant view of the pond and the long low ridge of hills to the north. These distant hills parallel the entire route but are only seen in a few sections. You continue on beside the flooded area and at 2.5 miles descend slightly to a very extensive beaver meadow system through which Butter Brook flows from east to west. A fairly large old bridge marks this crossing that may have been the place the Albany Road crossed so many years ago, though of course, no sign remains.

Continuing east you climb onto higher ground, and at about 3 miles you reach a mature forest with large beech and maple. Here a posted sign announces the boundary of the Little Moose Club, so you have to turn around and retrace your steps.

57   Crossover Trail, Moose River to Otter Brook

Hiking

DEC had kept this level, 3.5-mile route open for administrative purposes and it served as an alternate route to the lower Plains when the Moose River Bridge was out. Inexplicably, the bridge at the eastern end of the route has been removed; and without the Unit Management Plan for the region in place, it is difficult to predict whether or not it will be replaced with a footbridge at some point in the future. A short gravel spur heads south from the plains Road 9.7 miles from Cedar Gate to the bridge site. A sign indicates the trails south are closed, as does the sign at the western end of this route, 2.6 miles south of the T. You can easily hop rocks to cross the river in low water, but there is really little need to follow this route as it no longer invites the all terrain bicyclist; the description is included in the expectation that a bridge will be rebuilt.

From the northeastern end, the trail crosses the Moose River and follows it downstream in a southwesterly direction. The stream falls gradually in this section and could be canoed in high water. There is no forest here— only scrub alder and skimpy white birch, similar to growth after a duff-consuming forest fire. In 0.7 mile, the road forks, and you continue straight. (The left fork goes to Sly Pond, section 58.) Beyond the fork, you cross a weak bridge over a small, pretty brook that flows in from the left. After walking on the level for 1.4 miles, you begin to climb gradually. By now you are away from the river in an area that has been heavily logged; only scrub birch, alder, and poplar remain and no tree is larger than six inches in diameter. There are many stumps on the forest floor.

At just under 2 miles, you cross a height-of-land at 2120 feet and begin a slight descent. You have crossed the ridge line and land is now higher on your right than on your left. At 2.5 miles you cross a small brook flowing through a metal culvert and climb again, going 260° magnetic. There is a low rocky ledge on your left and a valley on your right. Here the road runs toward magnetic west through red spruce and some small maple.

In just over a hour's spirited walk you will see a yellow barrier ahead, 3.5 miles from the start. This is an easy if somewhat unexciting walk, but it is recommended for mountain bikes.

58 Sly Pond

Bushwhack

The removal of the bridge over the Moose River does not preclude the public from hiking to or camping at Sly Pond, though the closure of the trail and the fact that it is no longer maintained means the 5.1-mile route now has to be considered a bushwhack, and with a pack, a fairly difficult one. If you are adventurous and the water is low enough to ford the river, you can still reach this pond on the shoulder of Little Moose Mountain. The route however, has become increasingly overgrown. You can hike up and back in one day, and three hours might do for the climb to this gem of a pond.

The first 0.7 mile is the same as the trip of section 57. Going southwest parallel to the Moose River you reach the marked left trail to Sly Pond in about twelve minutes carrying a pack. A sign, with yellow markers, indicates Sly Pond is 5 miles away (it is less than that). For the next 1.2 miles you will be following the old road that went south toward Kenwells. After this, the trail follows a circuitous logging road that does not show on the 1954 series USGS map.

The trail at the beginning is open, grassy, and bordered by red spruce and balsam. As you go slightly uphill you can hear a tributary of the Moose River down to the right; the trail will follow the route of this brook for about 3 miles. The route is south, then southwest, climbing gradually, but steadily through a young forest that was heavily cut not too many years ago. At 1.9 miles, you reach a series of beaver meadows. The old road to Kenwells went across the stream at this point, but the beaver activity conceals the place. You can see distant peaks ahead. Across a small stream, you begin to climb, and at 2.4 miles you are on high ground with two summits ahead of you. The trail begins to swing to the northeast, passing an open gravel area. You circle the northern summit, crossing several streams and one wet area, which is hard to detour around. At 3.7 miles you cross a larger brook, with rocks big enough to hop over. The brook is certainly big enough to show on the USGS, but it does not. It may seem you have climbed higher, but you are only at 2200 feet.

You continue climbing, southeast now, and at 4 miles turn south with the views of the peak between you and Sly Pond. Here you enter an even more extensive series of beaver dams than below. You cross over one large dam but find the trail beyond has been completely blocked by trees felled by beaver. You must take to the woods for 50 feet. The beavers here are master builders and especially industrious; there are about ten terraces, several constructed up the narrow brook valley on your right. It is worth the hike to this point to see these impressive engineering feats. The trail follows that valley or draw toward the southeast, climbing steeply.

At about 4.5 miles you will find a stream flowing down the trail, and there is an open area with a fire ring. Hunters have camped here, and it appears to be the location of an old logging camp. Beyond this clearing, the trail climbs steeply up slippery moss and leaf-covered rock ledges. Here you see your first yellow trail marker! There is another level spot for camping, and this is the last place to pitch a tent until you reach the pond. You continue steeply and just short of 5 miles enter a col from which you descend to the pond through a spruce and balsam thicket.

The pond is a slight anticlimax as the thicket rings the shoreline, and there is only one, small, damp spot to pitch a tent. The pond is pretty, undoubtedly devoid of fish. Little Moose Mountain rises directly across—a frustrating view. The cliffs southeast and just below the summit of that mountain, which are visible from so many other spots, must have a fantastic view; but the spruce are so thick on the slopes that rise 750 feet above the pond that it is impossible to reach them, even if they are less than a mile from the pond!

The trip back is obviously faster than the climb up, but slippery rocks call for caution and wet areas must be detoured. It will take two and a half hours, which allows time to admire the skill of beavers one more time.

59   Lost Ponds and Lost Ponds Snowmobile Trail

Fishing, camping, hiking, bicycling, canoeing
0.7 mile, 20 minutes, level, maps VI and X

The entrance road leading to the wide foot trail to Lost Ponds is 11.65 miles west of Cedar Gate. You can drive north along the road for 0.3 mile to a metal barrier; there are several large camping sites before the barrier with space enough in each for several cars. Walk north past the gate and you will see Sumner Stream down a slight bank on your left. The trail to Lost Ponds bears right and follows a wide dirt roadway that is easy to walk. The ponds are popular with trout fishermen who either carry canoes or boats or push them to the pond using a wheeled carrier. You can also ride bicycles to a number of camping spots beside the road and near the pond.

After walking for ten minutes past the barrier, 0.4 mile, you start down a small hill and see a wooden bridge across Sumner Stream ahead of you. Part way down this hill smooth rock slabs lie diagonally in the roadbed. Turn right at the slabs and look for the almost hidden path to the Sumner Stream Stillwater. This narrow route passes through dense balsam fir, which screens the stillwater effectively. You reach the shore in a short minute walk. The pond is created by a dam on Sumner Stream, and you reach the pond near the driftwood choked outlet. The shore is wooded. There is no place to camp. A small fisherman's path follows the right, east, side of the pond but eventually disappears in blowdowns. A canoe could be launched here for a quiet paddle, but the pond is not fished extensively.

When you return to the roadway continue downhill over the bridge. This is a change of trail location from the 1954 USGS map. Climb a small hill beyond the bridge and then turn sharp left where a small sign and arrow indicate a trail. Another logging road, see below, continues straight up the small hill. Follow the road to the left, and in a few minutes, you will see the western pond. Circle around the south side to a camping spot located up on the bank from the pond. There is a table, fire ring, and pit privy. Below you, the clear water laps a pretty rock-ribbed shoreline that is sparsely forested on the opposite shores. A sign at the put-in alerts you to the fact these are brook trout waters and that you cannot use fish as bait. It is a popular fishing pond. The logging road continues on a ways going north but does not provide additional pond access and eventually vanishes in the woods.

Returning from the western pond to the trail sign, you can go left, northwest, up a hill on an open logging road that runs between the two waters. This road was used in the logging operation that cleared the blowdowns from the hurricane that struck the area in November 1950. Shortly the road swings north and starts downhill. The western pond is on your left, but access at this point is marshy. Half a mile from its beginning, this logging road forks. The left fork will lead you in six minutes to a very scenic bay of the western pond. It is a secluded spot for a picnic beside the quiet, shallow waters. Black ducks can often be found here.

If you turn right at the fork, instead of going to the bay, the logging road runs northeast up a low hill between Sumner Stream and Pine Grove Creek. The roadbed is being invaded by red spruce and balsam fir, but the path is still clear and makes a nice walk. Five minutes from the fork you cross a wet area, and you can see how the road was built up from borrow pits along the sides. Blueberries are plentiful. At an elevation of 2120 feet, the logging road starts down the northeast side of the hill and becomes harder to follow. This area has not been as heavily logged as other parts of the Plains, and large beech and maple create a nice hardwood forest on each side of the road.

This route has been marked as a snowmobile trail, but it has not been cleared in some time. From the ridge, you can retrace your steps to your car in an hour and a quarter. The extension beyond the ponds does not really lead anywhere, but it is a nice, easy walk.

60   Sumner Stream

Canoeing, map VIII

With all the places to canoe in the Plains, it might seem silly to talk of canoeing a stream as small as Sumner, but it is fun. If there has been enough rain, you can canoe the 2 mile distance to the bridge on the Limekiln Road, 0.2 mile north of the T, or continue on for 1.3 miles to the Moose just downstream of the Carry, section 72. Both stretches are elongated by the winding, twisting stream, which makes its way between alders in the marshes that surround the stream.

You can put in on the Lost Ponds Road or 0.5 mile west of that road where there is a sort of pull-off bulldozed into the bank on the north side of the road. Push through a fringe of trees and after 100 feet of meadow reach Sumner Stream.

For the next 2 miles to the culvert, Sumner meanders tightly through a beaver meadow sunk below the level of the Plains. The channel is narrow but deep enough. There are occasional beaver dams.

Below the road culvert, Sumner has some shallows and is more crowded with alders. At the junction with the South Branch a massive beaver dam blocks the outlet, diverting the brook through the alders.

61 Helldiver Pond
Stroll, nature study, canoeing
0.25 mile, 5 minutes, level, map VIII

Helldiver, which bears a name often given to grebes, is among the more intereseting of the ponds in the Plains, mostly because the shores have such a variety of plants. In fact, you can experience almost all of this variety in the short path that leads to the pond.

Turn from the Plains Road 0.8 mile east of the T and drive for 0.2 mile to a turnaround. You may find this access road flooded, so park and walk. There are campsites along the access road. The trail, marked yellow, heads south from the turnaround through a dense red spruce stand. It is so dense that few plants dot the lush carpet of needles, only an occasional clump of dryopteris or gold thread or shining clubmoss or clintonia. The last 100 yards or so of trail is a narrow corduroy path through the bog plants that border the pond. You can find pale and sheep laurel, bog rosemary, and labrador tea. Tall tamarack and black spruce border the pond. You may spot such boreal birds as the grey jay, Lincoln sparrow, black-backed woodpecker, and boreal chickadee.

The level of the pond is above what it has been in years past, but when it is a bit lower, stands of cranberries emerge from the sphagnum carpet, which is also home to sundew and other bog plants. This is a good place to explore by canoe, and the carry is short, though rough and occasionally wet.

The Northern Moose River Plains, Access from Limekiln Gate

Mileages
Road North from T to Limekiln Gate

Sign at T: Red River 4, Limekiln Gate 8.85, Rock Dam 9

0.0   T
0.2   Sumner Stream
0.35 Benedict Brook
0.4   Mitchell Ponds Trailhead
1.0   Trail behind campsite to Bear Pond Tract
2.5   Spring
2.9   End of loop road, snowmobile trail to Bear Pond Tract is 0.4 mile from south end of loop, 0.8 mile from north end of loop
3.3   Snowmobile trail to south to Mitchell Ponds
3.7   North end of Loop Road
3.8   Red River
3.85 Road to Rock Dam
5.4   Snowmobile trail to Limekiln Lake
7.3   View of Fawn Lake (road)
8.5   Limekiln Lake entrance

Limekiln Gate to the T

0.0   Limekiln Gate
1.2   View of Fawn Lake (road)
3.1   Snowmobile Trail to Limekiln Lake
4.65 Road to Rock Dam
      Mileages on Road to Rock Dam from turnout near Red River crossing
      2.75 Whites Pond Trailhead
      3.75 Trail to Rock Dam
      4.4   Turnaround and barrier at Adirondack League Club Property
4.7   Red River

4.8   Beginning of Loop
        Loop is 1.2 miles long and the Snowmobile trail to Bear Pond Tract (road barrier) is 0.8 mile from the north end of loop, 0.4 mile from south end.
5.2   Beginning of Snowmobile Trail to Mitchell Ponds
5.6   End of Loop
6.0   Spring
7.5   Trail behind Campsite to Bear Pond Tract. This snowmobile trail is a dead-end route leading to the tract but not Bear Pond. Blowdowns that blocked the trail during the summer of 1987 have been cleared, but this still does not offer the hiker an exciting destination.
7.75 Giant double pine tree on side of road
8.1   Mitchell Ponds Trailhead
8.15 Benedict Brook. (Historical note: According to Adirondack historian Warder Cadbury, this stream was named for Farrand N. Benedict, who started coming through the Adirondacks in the 1830s and probably knew more about the general terrain than anybody for the next twenty years. He owned most of Township 40 and a good bit else at one time and was a partner of Marshall Shedd for whom the present Sagamore Lake was originally named.)
8.3   Sumner Stream
8.5   T Straight to Brooktrout, Indian etc.; left, east to Cedar River Gate and Indian Lake Village

62   Limekiln Lake

Campground, cross-country skiing
14 miles in many loops, relatively level, map VII

In the early 1970s, the Town of Inlet received a large federal grant to build and improve trails in the area. A 14-mile system was constructed, and maps for the dense network of trails south of Inlet are available from the Town of Inlet Ski Center on South Shore Road.

The local ranger designed part of this system at the outlet of Limekiln Lake to include the 1.5-mile, Old Dam Self-guiding Nature Trail, which is accessible via the campground in summer. The snowmobile trail system is shown on map VII because the ski trails cross it in many places, and it is so little used by snowmobiles it has become part of the ski network. The roads in Limekiln Campground are mechanically groomed with a track set and

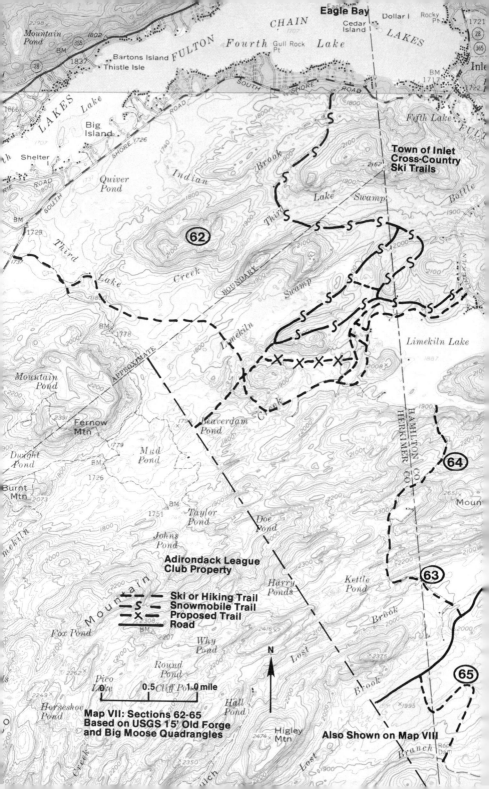

Eagle Bay

CHAIN · · LAKES

FULTON Fourth Lake Gull Rock Pt

Dollar I Rocky Pt

Bartons Island Thistle Isle

Mountain Pond

Big Island

Fifth Lake

Quiver Pond

Indian Brook

Town of Inlet Cross-Country Ski Trails

Shelter

(62)

Third Lake

Creek

BOUNDARY

Lake Swamp

Swamp

Limekiln Lake

Mountain Pond

APPROXIMATE

Limekiln

Creek

Beaverdam Pond

Fernow Mtn

Dwight Pond

Mud Pond

Burnt Mtn

Taylor Pond

Doe Pond

Adirondack League Club Property

(64)

(63)

Johns Pond

Harry Ponds

Kettle Pond

Brook

S ═══ Ski or Hiking Trail
S ═══ Snowmobile Trail
X ═══ Proposed Trail
═══ Road

Mountain

Fox Pond

Why Pond

Lost

Pico Lake

Round Pond

Cliff Pond

N

Horseshoe Pond

Hall Pond

**Map VII: Sections 62-65
Based on USGS 15' Old Forge
and Big Moose Quadrangles**

Higley Mtn

(65)

Also Shown on Map VIII

Lost

Branch

0.5   1.0 mile

are good for beginning skiers. The trails leading from the campground are classed as intermediate. A new ski trail from the campground to the snowmobile trail to Limekiln Creek has been proposed and will probably be built in the next year, making a shorter loop than is now possible.

The ski network has three trailheads: Limekiln Lake Road access is 1 mile south of NY 28 on Limekiln Road. Limekiln Lake Campground entrance is 1.8 miles south of NY 28 on the same road. The Third Lake Access is 0.3 mile from the west end of Petrie Road or 5.5 miles from NY 28 on South Shore Road. There is limited parking at all three sites.

If you start at the entrance to Limekiln Campground, you follow the groomed and set track on the left side of the road with the snowmobile trail on the right for 0.6 mile. At 0.6 mile, site #2 in the campground, turn left. At 1 mile you reach the campground beach and the intersection with the Limekiln Road Trail. Go straight through the picnic area and lower loops of the campground roads to the leach field where at 2 miles you find the start of the Nature Trail Loop. If you wish to go no farther, there are three loops in the campground that take you back to the beach area.

Follow the Nature Trail on the north side of Limekiln Creek where at 2.5 miles you reach the site of one of the old dams that was last used in 1948 in the last run of logs down the Moose River. As you cross the creek, the outlet of the lake, on two bridges, you see another area that was flooded to your right. To stay on the Nature Trail Loop, keep left to return to the leach field in 0.7 mile more.

If you turn right, you cross the area you viewed from the bridge. The trail follows along a series of falls, then crosses the outlet again. At 4 miles the trail intersects a snowmobile trail. Take a right on the trail for about 200 feet, and then back left on the ski trail. If you continued on the ski trail, it would take you back to the campground loop in 2 miles.

Following the ski trail, continuing west of north, you cross a stream called Limekiln Swamp and pass a large clearing on your left. Logs were stock piled here and dumped into the stream that carried them to the Moose River. You reach an intersection at 4.5 miles. The way straight leads 3.4 miles to Third Lake, and you might want to have a car spotted at that trailhead if you plan to make the through trip from Limekiln Campground. The way right leads back to Limekiln Road following an old log road at first, then through some thick spruce and back into open hardwoods. You pass a small pond, called West Pond, on your right at the head of Limekiln Swamp. Skiing gradually uphill through open hardwoods you intersect at 6.1 miles a trail that leads right, back to the campground. At 6.6 miles you reach the main groomed Town of Inlet Snowmobile

Trail. Bear right on it for 500 feet and then left back on the ski trail. At 7.0 miles you intersect the Town of Inlet Cross-country Ski System where you bear right. Passing two more intersections, you leave the Inlet System at 7.6 miles and bear right. At 7.8 miles you are back on Limekiln Road where you bear right again and head 0.8 mile uphill to the campground entrance.

The map obtained from the Town of Inlet shows the trails maintained by the town. These offer a great variety of loops and circuits of varying lengths. With the connection to the trails from the campground, there are enough miles of trails for many days of adventures.

63 Whites Pond from Rock Dam Road

Hiking, camping
1.9 miles, 45 minutes, 300-foot elevation change, maps VII and VIII

Two trails approach Whites Pond, this one from the south, and one from the north at Limekiln Lake where the trailhead can be reached only by canoe, section 64. The pond is a pretty one, nestled in low hills, with a beaver dam at its outlet. Use this route to reach the pond, or continue on to Limekiln Lake for a longer walk.

The trail with yellow markers follows a handsome old logging road through mixed forest with balsam and spruce on both sides of an eight-foot passageway. The way is level for 0.5 mile to a small stream crossing, and at 0.6 mile, the trail climbs to a second level where the trail turns to the southwest. Shortly, there is a steep rise to another level stretch where at 1.2 miles there is a small marshy-bordered pond to the left of the trail. You are heading generally north now.

Another rise follows, then a downhill to cross a small flowing creek at about 1.5 miles. Here you step on rocks to cross below where the stream flows over a vertical ten-foot slab.

The trail no longer appears to be following a logging road as it leads through hardwoods. At 1.8 miles there is a small pond to the left of the trail and at 1.9 miles you reach the outlet of Whites Pond. The USGS shows a trail leading around the east side to a cabin site on the island, and in places there is a path heading along this side, but it just disappears.

Whites Pond

64 Whites Pond from Limekiln Lake

Hiking, camping
1.6 miles, 35 minutes, 500-foot elevation change, map VII

The trailhead is due south of the state campground just to the west of the little southeastern bay. The trail starts up a fairly steep grade where rock in the trail is moss covered and slippery. After 0.3 mile, the grade eases, but you continue uphill and generally south to a high ridge. There is a large flat topped rock that makes a good place to stop and picnic. You walk across the ridge that is pretty and open, then head southwest toward the pond. The trail follows along the north side of a small hill, and there are views toward the pond that improve as you descend toward the outlet. At 1.6 miles, you reach the outlet and the guide board directing you on toward Rock Dam Road.

65   Red River, Rock Dam, and the Moose River

Hiking, swimming, canoeing, camping
1.8 miles, 40 minutes, 160-foot elevation change, maps VII and VIII

Most routes this long in the Plains are still reasonable canoe carries, mostly because it is so easy to use wheeled carrying carts. However, this route, which leads to the foot of the longest stillwater on the Moose, see section 71, is not such an easy carry. Only part of the time is the road following old roads, and part is wet and difficult to walk, much of the time.

From the trailhead, 3.9 miles south of the bridge over the Red River, the trail, only a narrow footpath, heads downhill to a sphagnum bog. It curves east through the bog and at 0.8 mile intersects a roadway from the north. The trail turns right to follow this roadway through boggy spots and wet places, through a dense spruce stand with a thick carpet of sorrel beneath. The route continues gently downhill, reaching the confluence of the Red River with the Moose. Both rivers flow over a low rock dam, and there is a campsite on a spruce-covered knoll nearby.

Canoeing the Moose from the Carry to Rock Dam is described in section 71. From Rock Dam you can also canoe upstream on the Red River, though there are small rapids and shallows between Rock Dam and the longest stretch of the stillwater. Red River is a very narrow stream that widens into a large flow just to the west of Mitchell Ponds.

66   Bear Pond Tract

Hiking, nature walk
2.3 miles, 1¹/₃ hours, 200-foot vertical rise, map X

The Bear Pond Tract consists of 1100 acres purchased by the state in 1985 with a thirty-five-year reservation that permits the owners to continue to use an 11-acre site during that period. However, the nicest part of the tract is Bear Pond itself, which is approached, but not quite reached, by a DEC snowmobile trail. A second route to the tract along Benedict Brook has recently been cleared by DEC, but it does not lead to the pond. The best route begins from the loop from the Limekiln Road and is 0.8 mile southeast along that loop. The trail, marked as a snowmobile trail, begins from a barrier behind the campsite at that point.

The trail begins as an old roadway, and you will walk for ten minutes before you see your first orange marker. You start uphill through thickening maple starts shortly after the marker. The roadway becomes covered with a canopy of hardwoods. The trail splits, but the way right heads south and ends. Stay to the left, where a three-inch maple has been slashed and some spruce have been cropped; you will see another marker. The trail is still on a logging road headed northeast, but there are several blowdowns. After about 1.5 miles, the roadway and trail ends.

A herd path continues to a marsh. Go across the inlet and stay on the high ground north of the old beaver pond. You will come to the remains of the Miller Camp in a clearing. There is a blazed path leading from the east end of the clearing, past a five-log-high, tin-roofed outbuilding, to the shore of the pond. This short trail from the clearing is in thick balsam and spruce and has several blowdowns. It crosses the old state line boundary. It is not over ten minutes from the end of the trail to the pond. At Bear Pond you will find a lean-to on the north shore, just off the skid road used during the recent logging.

The last part of the trip to Bear Pond is not easy, but well worth the effort, for you will be delighted when you see the bog. Tamarack surround the pond. The pitcher plants are so thick you cannot walk out on the bog without trampling them. There is open water, but the boggy shores are the most delightful part.

67 Mitchell Ponds and Cliffs

Hiking, camping, canoeing, exploring, fishing
3 miles, 1½ hours, relatively level except for 200-foot climb to cliffs, map VIII

Mitchell Ponds are a spectacular destination. The 2-mile walk to the first pond is along a roadway that is so level that people regularly push canoes to the pond using a wheeled cart. The road sides have a greater variety of interesting plants than any other trail in the Plains. The cliffs offer a short, easy bushwhack to a spectacular view of the ponds. And, like many of the region's ponds, Mitchell had a resident trapper, Robert West, who used an old logging camp in the clearing east of the pond.

The roadway begins in a field of bottled gentian with an alder swamp to the south. In 180 yards you reach a barrier. Yellow markers, only a few scattered ones, mark the trail that generally follows the valley at the base of a steep mountain to the north. That mountain is typical of the long, east-west trending ridges that are found in this part of the Plains. The forest of yellow birch and maple with scattered black cherry was obviously disturbed, but it is maturing. There are occasional glimpses of the marshes to the south. You cross a small stream on an old bridge, then another on a new bridge.

Watch the trail sides for at about 1.1 miles. You begin to see rattlesnake and dissected fern, *Botrychium Virginianum and dissectum,* and at 1.3 miles there is a steep bank to the right lushly covered with maidenhair fern. There is a small stream now to the left of the trail that climbs through a small draw at 1.4 miles. Marsh opens out to the south again and the roadway is level as it approaches a large field, the site of West Camp, at 1.8 miles. The roadway circles through the field and at its western end, a sign directs you to the right for the continuing trail. Before you turn that way, continue on the trail/roadway toward the first pond. It turns left over a small knoll beyond the field and reaches a campsite with picnic table at the head of the pond at 2 miles.

What a view from here! The cliffs that range behind the second pond seem suspended above the far end of this pond.

The marked yellow trail heads briefly north across a wet area with a little bridge, and follows a roadway for 100 feet, before heading west on a narrow path. (The roadway heads uphill and intersects the Plains Road; it is a designated snowmobile trail, section 69.)

The narrow track follows the north bank of the pond, there is a lovely rock for a picnic partway along, then a shallows with water lilies at the far end of this first pond. A narrow, very wet peninsula separates the two ponds. Along the shore of the pond and the peninsula you will see purple fringed orchis and in the shallows the tiny purple bladderwort. The trail is just high enough to stay dry as it traverses the 200 yards that separates the ponds. The trail is even narrower as it continues beside the second pond. The forest is dark with balsam and spruce and huge boulders line the lower slopes of the steep hillside to the north.

The trail climbs over a small knoll and officially ends at a natural rock dam in a draw at the outlet of the pond, which is incorrectly shown on the 1954 series USGS. You can hop across these rocks and climb to a pine-covered knoll to the south. It has a very nice campsite. The knoll

Mitchell Ponds from the cliffs

overlooks the narrow outlet arm of the second pond. Paths lead around the arm, but disappear, though they reappear on the south side, and it is possible, with a little bushwhacking, to use them to circle both ponds.

Any approach you take to the cliffs will be steep. If you return over the small knoll to the corner of the pond, you can find the easiest place to start up toward the cliffs. Angle to the right for the closest cliff, which is but 150 feet above the pond, and climb around behind it. You really have to work to get behind the cliffs either to the east or west of this point. The views over the ponds are lovely and from the western, higher cliff top you can look west along the outlet valley toward the Red River. The mountainous ridge continues west to a last knobby cone that rises above a third pond in the chain, just upstream from the confluence of the outlet with the Red River.

At the head of the second pond, lying against the west shore of the peninsula, are a number of huge pine logs. You can use them as a way of walking along the wet peninsula. A short, weak beaver dam connects the southern end of the peninsula with the south shore where you will find the shore-side path. The barely-visible eastern end of that path is 70 yards from the campsite at the head of the lake, right where the trail makes a turn to the north.

68 Moose River Cliffs on Mitchell Ponds Mountain

Bushwhack, map VIII

From the huge, new bridge over the Moose River you can look north of west to Mitchell Ponds Mountain. The cliffs range east and west just below the summit. They are over 300 feet tall at their tallest and their top is 450 feet above the valley of the Moose. From them you can look south across Beaver Lake, southeast to the hills that lead up to the plateau of the West Canadas, east to Icehouse and Helldiver ponds, and southwest along the South Branch of the Moose with Stink Lake Mountain to its south and Higley Mountain to its north. The view is beyond the Plains to the Adirondack League Club property.

A mile-long bushwhack from the first Mitchell Pond takes you up a series of shelves to the long summit ridge, which wears a thick crown of

almost impenetrable small spruce. Along most of the cliff tops there is no place to stand to enjoy the view, for the spruce crowd right up to the vertical face. Along a 200-yard stretch near the very highest point, however, there is a small ledge from which you can safely enjoy the view.

You can either cross the peninsula and the beaver dam or walk around the eastern end of the first pond on the faint path. From the south shore, take a compass heading toward magnetic south. The climb is fairly steep in places, and you cross five, very faint, old logging roads before you reach the summit. Above the third, there is a steep slope that ends in a flat, wet area. The climb takes the better part of an hour, the return about thirty-five minutes. Soaring hawks will share your perch above the Plains.

69 Mitchell Ponds from the North
Hiking
1.5 miles, 40 minutes, 200-foot elevation change, maps VIII and X

A snowmobile trail approaches the head of the first Mitchell Pond from the north. It makes a delightful alternate to the level route described in section 67, and with two cars, it offers a loop to the ponds. The trail begins 3.3 miles north of the T, 5.2 miles south of Limekiln Gate, where a dirt road heads south. It is marked only with a silver disk. A road just north of it leads only to a campsite.

You walk southwest for 0.25 mile to reach a sign prohibiting motorized vehicles except for snowmobiles. At the beginning of the trail, weeds can be shoulder high, but after you break through them, the trail is quite beautiful. Shortly, you cross a new snowmobile bridge, then a second, where huge pines shelter the trail and bottled gentian border it. You climb gently, curving east to a height-of-land at 1.1 miles, where you start downhill. Then the going gets steeper, and you cross a third new bridge. Just beyond it you can see Mitchell Ponds if you look to your right, west. At 1.5 miles you intersect the trail that leads to the far end of the second pond.

In summer, you will undoubtedly see loons at the ponds; in autumn, the views from this trail improve as you descend toward the pond.

Southern Moose River Plains

Mileages along Road South from T

Note mileages at sign at T pointing south differ from those given below. Sign at T: 0.45 Icehouse, 1.2 Moose River, 3 Otter Brook, 3.5 Beaver Lake, 6.5 Squaw Lake, 8 Indian Lake, 12 Horn Lake

0.0	T
0.25	Big Tamarack
0.7	Trail west, Carry to Moose River, 0.4 mile
0.9	Trail east, Icehouse Pond, 0.3 mile
1.3	Bridge over Moose River
1.3 +	Trail west to Beaver Ponds, 2.25 miles
1.7	Campsite near Otter Brook, area of large pines on Otter Brook
2.6	Trail east, left, Sign: Cedar River Road, 3.5 miles; Sly Pond, 7 miles
2.85	Spring
3.3	Campsite, old road east from behind campsite to Kenwells
3.4	Otter Brook
3.4 +	Trail east along boundary road between Moose River Plains Area and the West Canada Lakes Wilderness, side trail to Lost Pond
3.45	Sign as road angles west: 3.1 Falls Pond, 4.1 Squaw Lake, 4.4 Deep Lake, 4.9 Muskrat Pond, 5.8 Indian Lake, 6.9 Brooktrout Lake, 11 Balsam Lake, 12.5 Stink Lake, 13.5 Horn Lake
4.45	Trailhead for West Canada Lakes Wilderness. Sign at trailhead: 2.1 Falls Pond, 3.4 Deep Lake, 3.4 Wolf Lake, 5.9 Brooktrout Lake, 6.4 West Lake (Note: Sign at Brooktrout gives mileage to West Lake as 0.65 mile)
6.35	Enormous beaver dam beside road, thicket of flooded and dead spruce to south
6.8	Squaw Lake Trail to north, right, 0.45 mile
7.7	Campsites near marshes, Muskrat Creek crossing
8.0	Muskrat Pond, trail south, left, 0.1 mile
8.8	Trail north, right, Indian Lake, 0.2 mile
8.85	Barrier and campsite

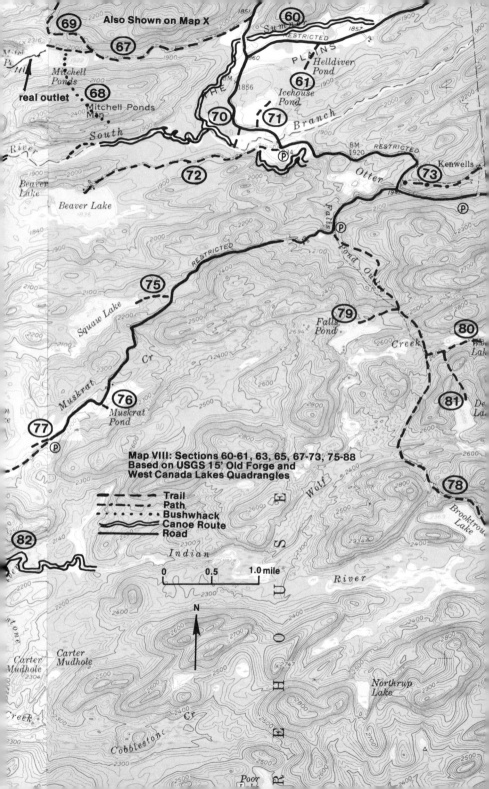

Also Shown on Map X

⑥⑨ ⑥⑦

Main Pull x 2316

real outlet

Mitchell Ponds 2100

⑥⑧

Mitchell Ponds Mtn

South

River

Beaver Lake 1840

Beaver Lake 1836

⑦⑤

Squaw Lake

Cr

Muskrat

⑦⑦

Ⓟ

⑦⑥

Muskrat Pond

⑧②

PLAINS

⑥⓪

RESTRICTED 1857

1851

THE Su... Branch 1900

1860

BM 1856

⑦⓪ ⑦①

⑥① Helldiver Pond

Icehouse Pond

1900

Branch

BM 1920 RESTRICTED

Ⓟ

⑦② 2000

RESTRICTED 1900

2100

2200

Otter

Falls Pond Ou

Ⓟ

⑦③ Kenwells

Ⓟ

⑦⑨ Falls Pond 2694

Creek

⑧⓪

⑧①

⑦⑧ Brooktrout Lake

**Map VIII: Sections 60-61, 63, 65, 67-73, 75-88
Based on USGS 15' Old Forge and
West Canada Lakes Quadrangles**

- – – – Trail
· · · · Path
· · · · · Bushwhack
～～～ Canoe Route
———— Road

Indian

H U D S O N

Wolf 2714 x

River

0   0.5   1.0 mile

N

Carter Mudhole 2304

Carter Mudhole

Northrup Lake

Cr

Cobblestone Cr

Poor

Outlet of Mitchell Pond

70 The Carry and Moose River Stillwaters
Canoeing, fishing
0.4 mile, 8 minutes, level, map VIII

A short, yellow-marked trail begins behind a campsite 0.7 mile south of the T and leads to the head of the Stillwater on the Moose River. It is a narrow path, filling with weeds and brambles, but it offers an easy way to carry your canoe to the river, hence the trail's name. The trail leads past a deer exclosure to fields beside the river. Wellington Alexander Kenwell built a house nearby to serve as a hotel for visiting hunters and fishermen, but only his water pump remains.

Below the last rapids to the right of the trail, there are 1.5 miles of deep stillwater winding between high grassy banks with towering spruce and occasional pines. At the first left bend, Sumner Brook joins from the north. Later bends are a succession of blind side channels that can be confusing for those coming back upriver. The long line of cliffs near the crest of Mitchell Ponds Mountain, section 69, soon dominates the view.

After coasting along the side of the mountain, you see boulders ahead in the river, the start of the rapids nearly 2 miles from the Carry.

The Stillwater ends at the remains of a wooden dam or bridge, which you have to lift over in low water. In the pool just beyond, on the right shore, is the start of an old path that runs about 0.3 mile past the shallowest part of the rapids, but not past all the shallows. The path climbs the small hill, levels off, and then descends to the river bank that it follows, gradually becoming fainter, until it peters out halfway down the rapids.

The river here has about 0.6 mile of continuous wide, shallow rock garden rapids, Class 2 at first, but getting easier. Then comes a shallow, but calm pool for 0.3 mile, and another 0.3 mile of shallow Class 1 rapids ends just below the mouth of the Indian River. In the summer, these rapids are all too shallow and require that you mix wading with paddling. Walking a boat through the rapids either up or down is not hard.

Below the Indian River the South Branch is flat, slow, and rather shallow, 1 to 3 feet deep, with some sandbars to avoid. The scenery is good, especially views back of Mitchell Ponds Mountain. This 2-mile stillwater ends at Rock Dam, where the trail, section 65, leads uphill to the road from Red River. This portage is difficult enough that it is almost easier to go back upriver to the start. Note that below Rock Dam, there is another mile of river on state land, but the rapids are steeper making it hard to return upriver. Below, the river flows into the posted lands of the Adirondack League Club.

71 Icehouse Pond

Camping, fishing, canoeing
0.45 mile, 8 minutes, level, map VIII

Most of this short yellow-marked trail traverses the open fields filled with meadowsweet and cherries that are so typical of the Plains. The fields are scattered with spruce and balsam and aspen. A few large pine dot the wooded border of the pond whose shores are mostly filled with spruce and very tall pines. There is a picnic table and fire ring near the end of the trail that follows an abandoned roadway. Because the roadway is so level, carrying or wheeling a canoe to the pond is an easy matter.

Icehouse Pond is a classic kettle bog, the result of a melting block of ice at the end of the last glacial period. Commercial hunters from Piseco were said to have used its ice to preserve fish, hence its name.

72 Beaver Lake

Hiking, camping, fishing
2.3 miles, 1 hour, relatively level, map VIII

Just south of the bridge over the Moose River, a roadway forks right, west, 0.2 mile to a parking area and a barrier beside the fairly new, large bridge over Otter Brook.

A part of the Plains that includes the confluence of the streams as well as areas west of Beaver Lake have always been state land. The water table is relatively high in the sandy, gravelly soil that underlies this portion of the Plains and is thus able to support lush stands of black spruce. You will recognize it by its short needles that are blue-green, often with a whitish tinge. The needles are more dense than red spruce and the trees themselves are more dense than the red spruce. The trees you see are very old and fully mature.

Otter Brook meets the Moose River in an alder marsh. The trail, which heads generally west, passes meadows filled with flowers and butterflies, then starts uphill into deep woods. You pass through a stand of huge yellow birch, a dense spruce grove, and a tall mixed forest of spruce, maple, and yellow birch. There are a few enormous white pines beside the trail with a rich understory of lycopodia, golden thread, bunchberry, and sorrel. A few huge white pines line the trail along with stumps and logs from fallen giants.

You approach the lake through a meadow that makes a good camping area. This land was once the private preserve of the Chapin family who built an elegant home here in 1904. The lake is named for its shape, which resembles a short-tailed beaver.

The trail is so easy you can wheel a canoe along it and thus explore the dam and marshes at the outlet and the stand of virgin pines downstream, a stand of some of the tallest pines in the Plains. The huge beaver house in the west inlet is a condominium—nesting loons have shared the top as a nesting spot for the past twenty years.

While you are at the trailhead with a canoe, you might want to explore a bit of the canoeable stretches of the Otter. South of the bridge there is a slack, deep channel curving through marshes for 0.5 mile. The hills close in and a shallow rapid on a bend is visible ahead. The canoeable channel appears to end. You can walk your canoe up the two shallow rapids beneath a bank of tall spruce and a rocky bluff. The stillwater continues for another 0.5 mile, meandering through an even prettier area. Just past another shallow riffle, the canoeable portion of Otter Brook ends in a pool at the foot of a long chain of rapids.

73 Kenwells

Path, hiking, camping, fishing
1 mile, 30 minutes, 100-foot elevation change, maps VI and VIII

This old roadway is designated a path only because it has no official DEC markers; it is an obvious trail in every respect. The roadway leads east for 1 mile along the north shore of Otter Brook to the site of Gerald Kenwell's place. He was Wellington's son and had a guest house there for thirty sportsmen until the late 1950s.

The path begins from the cluster of campsites north of the bridge over Otter Brook and 3.3 miles south of the T. It heads due east up a hardwood hill, then descends gradually below a small hill that is faced with lovely rock cliffs and ledges. The eroded upthrust ledge, some of it moss-covered, forms an imposing backdrop to the young yellow birch and maple that grow at its base. The cliffs grace the left side of your walk for 0.3 mile.

At 0.6 mile, the roadway comes quite close to the brook, where small rapids drop noisily into quiet pools. The stream has trout that will rise to a fly if you are carrying a fly rod.

The path then climbs again, still beneath those handsome ledges, heading northeast. You come to an open, but weed and bramble choked clearing facing a stillwater on the brook. Just beyond, up a slight rise, the road appears to end in the field where the house stood.

The field is worth a few minutes exploration, for it contains several old saws and pieces of machinery, including an old donkey engine, a water-cooled gasoline engine, the kind sold by Sears and Roebuck in the early 1900s. Its function in the camp is not clear—although it could turn pulleys, its speed was too slow to generate electricity.

The entire route is handsome, well worth the walk, whether you are fishing, exploring, or just strolling. You can camp in the clearing, a secluded spot, and if the weather should turn bad, you are near enough to your car to return in under half an hour.

74 Otter Brook Trail to Lost Pond

Hiking, camping, riding mountain bikes
7 miles, 3 hours, 550-foot elevation change, map VI

The Otter Brook Trail follows an abandoned roadway that marks the

border of the West Canadas Lakes Wilderness to the south and the Moose River Plains to the north. Otter Brook Road turns east from the Plains Road, immediately south of the bridge over Otter Brook. You can drive 0.5 mile to a barrier and the trailhead.

The first 3.7 miles of trail to Otter Brook are so level and hard packed that you can easily ride a mountain bike along this stretch, in fact, a bike can be used all the way to the turnoff to Lost Pond. The trail to Lost Pond or to Beaver Pond in the West Canada Lakes Wilderness forks south at 6 miles. The roadway continues east, curving around the massif of Little Moose and Manbury mountains to reach the private lands of the Little Moose Lake Club 2.8 miles beyond the turnoff for Lost Pond.

Starting from the barrier at the parking area, the road-trail east is straight and slopes gently uphill for 2 miles to the wide old bridge over Jimmy Creek. Between this bridge and Otter Creek, there is another creek crossing, with a bridge. At 3.5 miles, the road curves north, and at 3.7 miles you reach Otter Creek, where there is no bridge. You can wade across, but the water can be knee deep with a fair current.

The trail or roadway, which is still quite open and easy to follow, heads uphill, gradually, and leads to a campsite. The forest is very young, obviously recovering from heavy logging. Stumps are scattered throughout the area, but the young forest probably accounts for the fact there are so few blowdowns on the roadway.

Within 0.5 mile of the crossing, there is another creek, this time with a bridge that is broken in two, but there is no problem walking through the shallow creek. There is a distinct forest change here. Deep ferns lie beneath the trees, and spruce stands edge the road. The next creek crossing has a bridge in good condition. Just beyond there is a hole on the left side along with iron skis from a skidder. From here you can see the cliffs on Little Moose Mountain. Among the remnants of an old logging camp nearby you can find a harness and a cast iron stove. There is a clearing just down the road, at 4.9 miles, where a camp is marked by a wooden wagon and barrels. The road turns right, south, then east again, where you spot one of the few yellow disks marking this route.

At 6 miles, you reach a sign at a fork, indicating a turn left to Lost Pond, 1 mile, and Cedar Lakes Trail, 2.2 miles. A log skidder lies to the left of the sign. Signs also indicate that no motorized vehicles are permitted in this Wilderness Area. The trail south also follows an old logging road with a creek to the east, which you soon cross. At 6.2 miles there is a second intersection, and the sign indicating Lost Pond points southeast. This too

Lost Pond northwest of Cedar Lakes

is a wide, open logging road, but it is quite wet throughout this area, and you may have to leave the trail to avoid the water. Small trees and balsam border the trail. The right fork here is the trail connecting Lost Pond and the Cedar Lakes Trail near Beaver Pond and is described in section 40.

At 6.9 miles you can see the pond. The trail turns south and you reach the shore of this lovely hidden pond, coming out to the bay through high grass. Grassy fields alternate with mud patches full of deer tracks along the shore. A profusion of labrador tea edges the forest border.

If you go straight ahead, east, along the Otter Brook Road instead of turning south to Lost Pond, you will find that the roadway has a number of downed trees and the forest is more mature. For quite a distance, a marsh lies off to your left, then a canopy of hardwoods covers the track. About 1 mile from the turnoff you reach a clearing from which you can see the lower slopes of Manbury Mountain. At 1.5 miles, there is a marsh on your right, south. The stream that drains the marsh widens into a small pond.

Beyond, the trail turns to a northeasterly direction. From a beaver dam in the marsh to the left of the trail you can spot the cliffs on Manbury Mountain. The trail continues northeast, then northerly to the private land boundary.

75 Squaw Lake

Hiking, camping, canoeing
0.45 mile, 10 minutes, 80-foot elevation change, map VIII

Beaver, Squaw, and Indian lakes are the three largest and the most attractive of all the Plains' lakes. Their popularity seems to correspond to the distance you have to walk to them, and Squaw is midway on the list. The drive to it, 15.3 miles from Limekiln Gate, is very long, but except in midweek, you will likely find people here.

Township 4, which includes these lakes, was surveyed in 1823 by Duncan McMartin, Jr., a distant relative of mine. His map with lot numbers shows Indian and Squaw lakes with their names reversed.

The yellow-marked trail descends along a tiny gorge with hemlock and spruce, a handsome place with boulders strewn beside the trail. The trail is steep and muddy, probably too rough for a wheeled cart, but short enough to carry a canoe, and you should have a canoe here. The trail reaches the easternmost bay of the lake, then turns north to cross a spruce-covered

Muskrat Pond

bank to a large campsite. From here you have a view down the 0.8-mile lake, past several small islands and rock ledges crowned with enormous pines along the north shore.

Other campsites can be reached by canoe and the lake has a number of hidden bays to explore. Loons and osprey nest along the north shore.

76 Muskrat Pond

Nature walk
100 yards, map VIII

Tall, straight stumps of giant spruce and pines give a decaying feeling to the long thin marsh called Muskrat Pond. Just a few years ago it was a drying marsh; beaver have changed that and today it is quite a body of water. You might enjoy sitting along its northern shore, looking at reflections and watching for birds. It is a two-minute walk downhill from the road.

In 1956 a fire started at the east end of Muskrat Pond, burned west, jumped Indian Lake, and continued half way along Indian Lake Mountain before being contained.

77 Indian Lake

Hiking, camping
0.2 mile, 3 minutes, level, map VIII

You can hardly consider it a hike to Indian Lake, and the trail, though muddy near the lake, invites a canoe carry. The trail is so short that this is a very popular lake, in spite of the lack of fish. It is a very pretty lake, shaped like a large boot, with the southern foot part bordered with marshes and spruce swamps. Indian Lake Mountain rises steeply to the west, and the leg of the boot points northeast past bays and tiny islands to the outlet.

There is an official campsite with outhouse and fireplace to the east of the end of the trail, and with a canoe you can seek out more secluded spots along the shore. You will find loons and a new osprey nest on the east shore—though you wonder how long they will stay now that the lake is devoid of fish.

The West Canadas from the North

Access from the southwestern Moose River Plains

THE PREVIOUS CHAPTER introduces you to the Plains, the road through the Plains, and mileages along the road. Two trailheads on that road give access to the inner recesses of the West Canada Lakes Wilderness Area. Most of these trails were logging roads in the Gould Paper Company lands and these forests were the last logged by that company, with the area along the trail toward Brooktrout Lake and toward Horn Lake logged as recently as 1963.

Gould Paper Company at Lyons Falls bought pulp wood from the Honnedaga tract of the Adirondack League Club in the 1920s. Gould opened roads to the north and west in the 1930s, all the way to Stink Lake Mountain. Roads and tracks were pushed from Honnedaga Lake to Jones and Horn Lakes and almost to the edge of the Moose River Plains. The emphasis of their logging operations shifted to the Plains just after World War II, and they logged all of the Plains and the plateau that reaches toward what is now the northern plateau of the West Canada Lakes Wilderness in the next two decades, logging for a second time apparently the lands around Horn Lake, Ice Caves Mountain, and toward Jones Lake.

Brooktrout Lake Trailhead

The trailhead is 18.5 miles from Cedar River Gate and 13.0 miles from Limekiln. There is parking for a number of cars, and roadside campsites are located nearby.

78 Brooktrout Lake

Hiking, camping
5.9 miles, 2¹/₂ hours, 600-foot elevation change, maps VI and VIII

Brooktrout Lake is the westernmost of the cluster of lakes that comprise the heart of the West Canada Lakes, but in many ways it differs from those lakes. The high plateau of the West Canadas is the birthplace of three separate drainage systems, and while West Canada Lake flows south through West Canada Creek to the Mohawk and the Cedar Lakes flow north to join the Hudson, Brooktrout Lake, just 0.65 mile from West Canada Lake, drains west then north through the Indian River to the South Branch of the Moose to the Black and thus to the St. Lawrence River.

This beautiful, remote lake has an almost sinister aspect. The final approaches to the lake are beautiful. Both trails (see section 41 for the trail from West Canada Lake) merge near a handsome lean-to sheltered by the slant-rock face of an erratic almost as large as the lean-to. A short path leads west to the shore where chains of boulders allow you to walk along the shore and view the protecting ring of steep hills that circle all but a small portion of the southeastern shore. But then you notice the eerie clarity of the water, its crystal blue transparency, and the algal mat that lines the bottom in the shallows. This is a lake with no fish, and there have been no fish there for years. At 2369 feet above sea level, this lake was one of the earliest Adirondack lakes affected by acid depositions. The loss of living things creates a silence that overwhelms the restful quiet of this wilderness spot.

The first two-thirds of the way to the pond is along a logging road that is so gradual and open that you sail along it. It starts beside flows created by an enormous beaver dam on Falls Pond Outlet in a very scrubby forest. Fresh beaver work on a little tributary stream almost floods the trail at 0.4 mile, then the trail heads gently uphill on the east side of a big valley. The terrain is unbelievably rocky, with huge piles from the road clearing lining the way.

A steeper climb brings the trail back near Falls Pond Outlet, at 1 mile, and there is a campsite in the woods between the trail and the stream. At 1.4 miles a good bridge takes you across a stream that is not shown on the USGS, and at 1.6 miles, almost hidden to the right of the trail is the guidepost for the trail to Falls Pond, section 79. A small cairn in the middle of the trail marks the spot. After a slight rise, the trail heads southeast, then curves through a long, level area of glacial sand exposed by the road and bordered with spruce and balsam. The trail descends from an old gravel pit with open rock to cross a stream flowing into a little pond to the right, west of the trail. You cross another small knoll, then descend to a huge hikers' bridge over Wolf Creek. (Notice the small, but handsome rock gorge below the bridge.) The way so far has been so easy that you can reach the bridge in forty-five minutes without a pack, making the distance seem shorter than the given 2.4 miles.

Just beyond the bridge there is an open field with bare rock slabs poking through the thin soil. A sign in the field points straight ahead to Brooktrout Lake, 3.5 miles, and West Lake, 4 miles. Notice that the trails for Wolf Lake and Deep Lake, sections 80 and 81, begin to the east, left, side of this field.

The trail continues southerly up a hillside on exposed slabs like a paved highway. The trail swings to the southwest, with boardwalks to transport you over a wet meadow. At 2.8 miles the trail heads almost west beside a drying beaver flow, the meadow of which is filled with bog wool and bottled gentian. Stay left where the trail is flooded.

The trail continues southwest leaving the meadow. There is a short, steep downhill where the road is muddy and strewn with rocks, then the trail heads briefly up toward the east of south. Another downgrade leads to a second marsh, this one with open water to reflect the bottled gentian. Here the trail detours left away from the marsh on the right with a big erratic on the left. The route is still west of south, and the trail is marshy with stretches of stringers traversing the wet spots. The trail, roadway, is still descending along the side of a hill, when you notice a marked change in the forest cover. Here at about 3.6 miles, you leave the logged lands and reach forests that have scarcely been touched by loggers.

Tall spruce line the trail, and you round a spruce-covered knoll to make a moderate descent to reach the outlet of Deep Lake. Use the boulders to cross this pretty stream. In 200 yards, beyond a decrepit bridge over a small tributary stream, the trail turns southeast to follow the valley of the tributary up a beautiful hillside.

You are no longer on a visible roadway, but the narrow trail is still marred with mud wallows. The trail turns southerly and at 4.3 miles reaches a height-of-land. There is a sharp drop to a ledge and you see the first of the huge erratics that line the hillside north of Brooktrout Lake. At 4.7 miles you descend to the edge of the hill and can see the lake through the trees. The walk so far is a brisk two hours, but there remains a twenty-

Wolf Creek

minute descent over nearly a mile before you reach the lake. The narrow pathway winds down and easterly, below huge erratics, circling high above the three-quarter-mile-long lake, before finally descending past a campsite near the trail at 5.7 miles. One more sharp descent brings you to the trail junction within site of the lean-to.

The return takes about equal time, but those with packs need another hour or two in each direction. Be sure to continue east to West Lake for this is the handsomest hike in the West Canadas.

79 Falls Pond

Hiking, camping
2.2 miles, 50 minutes, 440-foot elevation change, maps VI and VIII

It is especially dismal walking the heavily logged section of the Brooktrout Lake Trail to the fork to Falls Pond when you realize that the area about 1 mile north of Falls Pond Outlet near the Otter Brook Valley was once French Louie's sugarbush, one of the finest stands of tall, straight maples. His sugarbush was still standing in 1952 when Dunham described how Louie made sugar, but this was part of the land logged by the Gould Paper Company shortly after that.

Falls is the largest and prettiest of the three ponds reached from the Brooktrout Lake Trail. Little rock islands dot its northern bays, and there are campsites beneath its spruce covered northeastern slopes.

Walk the Brooktrout Trail of section 80 for nearly 1.8 miles to the marked intersection and turn right, west. The trail begins level at the edge of a deep drop to the north. You descend gradually, then turn south along a flooded section of the outlet. The trail crosses a natural rock dam on the outlet, then winds through a dense spruce thicket to a rocky promontory on a small peninsula. You reach this spot, 0.4 mile from the main trail, within ten minutes.

A herd path continues back from the north shore 150 yards to a campsite with views of the rock islands. The pond is not too far from the trailhead to carry an inflatable raft or wheel a canoe.

80 Wolf Lake

Hiking
3.4 miles, 1¼ hours, 500-foot elevation change, maps VI and VIII

At present the walk to Wolf Lake is a wet but handsome trek beside huge beaver marshes that surround Wolf Creek, with the lake itself almost an impossible destination because of the flooding. Take the Brooktrout Lake Trail for 2.4 miles to the field as described in section 78 and turn left, still following logging roads. In 200 yards, the trail forks and you take the left fork again.

The wide grassy path leads uphill into a wet, muddy level, where the trail is filled with sphagnum and lined with handsome lycopodia and young spruce and tamarack. You reach the enormous beaver dam over Wolf Creek 0.3 mile from the intersection, and pick your way west along the flooded trail. Ledges border the long beaver flow on the north. The dense spruce stand beside the trail offers little incentive to bushwhack through it to keep dry. Rock ledges border the flow on the north, a backdrop for the stumps that dot the flow.

Where the trail rises, it is handsome and dry through young stands of balsam and spruce, but where it is wet it becomes impossible to pass, so you may have to turn back about 0.8 mile from the intersection, just short of the lake, which is now drying, with shrubs around the edges and less water than the flows downstream along the outlet creek.

81 Deep Lake

Hiking
3.4 miles, 1½ hours, 700-foot elevation change, maps VI and VIII

Deep Lake is deep and fairly attractive, but from the way the narrow path to it is overgrown, it appears to be infrequently visited. Its elevation, 2588 feet, and the resulting lack of fish may explain that.

The trail follows the Brooktrout Trail as far as the field at 2.4 miles where the trail turns left. At 200 yards take the right fork, a logging road that heads southeast uphill through a draw. For the first 0.5 mile the trail follows the roadway, turning from southeast to south, and winding along the west side of a little draw. At the last rise, the woods change, and you enter forests that have not been cut recently.

The trail crosses a wet saddle on a level traverse with a high hill to the right. There are few markers. Watch as the trail makes a series of short descents, for just as you would expect it to continue straight, south, it makes a sharp bend to the left, heading briefly north of east. This point is not well marked, and several herd paths lead away from the bend in the wrong direction; many hikers have been confused here. The trail descends to cross a little stream and begins to follow it south to the lake. Within 50 feet it recrosses the stream and continues along its western bank to the lake.

Beaver have raised the level of the lake and flooded the labrador tea and pitcher plants that border it, and there is hardly a flat place along the spruce-covered northern shore to camp. There have been no fish in this lake for twenty years.

Trailhead near Indian Lake at the Western End of the Plains Road

82 Indian River Stillwaters

Hiking, canoeing, fishing
4.4 miles of trail, 1½ hours, 200-foot elevation change, map VIII

Only the most ambitious individuals will wheel canoes along the logging roads that lead to several points on the Indian River, but the rewards of exploring its stillwaters are great. For the rest, these easy trails over well-constructed logging roads lead to an area recently designated as part of the West Canada Lakes Wilderness. There are quiet spots along the river to enjoy, and this trunk trail gives access to three other lakes and the western border of the Wilderness.

This Indian River, one of three in Hamilton County, begins as the outlet of Brooktrout Lake. It picks up the outlet of Northrup Lake and Wolf Creek, which has already added the outlet of Deep Lake, before flowing west through a chain of stillwaters.

The trail heads west from the end of the Plains Road, and from it you can see Indian Lake through the trees to the north. At 0.5 mile, a marsh stretches north of the trail, overshadowed by Indian Lake Mountain. At 0.7 mile you cross a low ridge and start downhill. A pretty beaver pond lies north of the trail, and beyond it a narrow drying marsh filled with bog wool stretches beside the trail. The old Linn tractor corduroy road can be seen in the marsh, where trains of logs were pulled to the Moose River before the last log drive in 1948.

Rock ledges begin to line the slopes north of the trail at 1.2 miles where it begins to descend. The descent quickens, and fern-covered slopes drop away from the trail to the south. At 2.2 miles you reach a small field. The way left leads across a small stream to an overlook on an oxbow in the Indian River.

A logging road, fairly overgrown, heads south then east through a small field into woods. It can be used to make easier the 0.6-mile carry to the Second Stillwater, where there is a good mile of canoeing, a short stretch of rapids, and another mile or more of flat water stretching upriver to the east.

The trail continues beside the river for 150 yards to a second left turn. This one leads past a fireplace and campsite to a washed-out bridge on the Indian. The only way to cross the river here is to wear sneakers and wade, unless someone has left a boat nearby. It is fairly deep, and the current can be strong. The road across from the bridge can be followed as it winds south past Yale Brook Falls, section 88.

The main trail continues northwest beside the river for 0.2 mile, then swings north past a gravel pit. The roadway continues north, making a gentle descent of 100 feet. Tall spruce that line the Indian River alert you to the next approach to the river. Here, too, at 4.2 miles, the bridge is out, and the crossing may also be difficult. Rocks from the dam's cribbing are fairly close to the surface, so that in low water you can hop across without getting wet. Otherwise the river is deep here. You may spot a boat secreted in the woods nearby. Courtesy demands that you return it to its hiding place if you borrow it to make the crossing.

A path leads south beside the river, and it is just a couple hundred yards to the head of the First Stillwater. From here there is nearly 2 miles of flat canoeable water.

83 Balsam Lake

Hiking
5 miles, 2 hours, 200-foot elevation change, map VIII

This is the western continuation of the 4.2 mile trail to the Indian River crossing. Allow extra time for that crossing. The roadway continues generally west, gradually beginning to fill in with tall grasses and small balsam. The way is level through larger spruce and balsam, with two old roads forking left before the fork to Horn Lake, 0.6 mile from the crossing. In another 250 yards watch for the fork right, north, to Balsam Lake. It is somewhat concealed at the edge of a grassy widening of the trail. A narrow footpath leads along the lake's right shore, into a dense spruce thicket with many blowdowns, where it disappears. There do not seem to be any camping sites along the lake, which is nevertheless a handsome, long, thin lake stretching northeast for 0.4 mile.

84 Stink Lake

Hiking, camping, fishing
6.9 miles, 2²/₃ hours, 220-foot elevation change, map VIII

Stink Lake used to have a good reputation for fishing. It supposedly got its name from a catch of trout abandoned by a novice sportsman, whom French Louie was guiding. Old beaver work once raised the level of the lake several feet above its current height, so a flat and muddy shoreline is now visible.

From the crossing of the Indian River, section 82, at 4.2 miles, continue west past the fork to Balsam Lake, at 4.9 miles. The flat road takes on an endless quality. You are following Balsam Lake Outlet, and there is one opening in the horizon over the outlet that lets you view Stink Lake Mountain and its small cliffs. At 5.7 miles the trail passes the site of an old

Vly between Stink and Balsam lakes

camp, near the 1953-foot benchmark. An unmarked roadway forks north here and from the site there is a lovely view to the east along the outlet of Balsam Lake. You will shortly discover this view is as pleasing as that across Stink Lake.

The trail continues generally west, and level, part of the time beside an esker topped with tall spruce. At 6.4 miles, you reach a marked fork north. This narrower route with a canopy of trees leads in 0.5 mile to the outlet of Stink Lake. There is a campsite on a knoll near the outlet. A roadway continues across the outlet, heading east over a knoll. It leads around to the northeast, paralleling Stink Lake Mountain, before it swings south to the 1953 benchmark. From its northernmost bend, an orange-flagged route heads north through a draw in the mountain, then east of north to Rock Dam. This route was used extensively by hunters when the Moose River Bridge was out.

85 The Western Boundary
Map VIII

Usually only hunters and fishermen venture farther west on the trunk trail than the fork to Stink Lake. Hunters expect the rich herds from Adirondack League Club property to venture into this wilderness. The trail arcs north, then approaches marshy fields where at 0.8 mile from the turn to Stink Lake, 7.2 miles from the Indian Lake Trailhead, a trail forks southwest through the marshes known as Cahan's Farm. This southern trail parallels Natural Hatchery Brook almost all of which lies on League Club property. Shortly beyond this fork on the main trail, there is a barrier blocking access to League Club property.

86   Horn Lake

Hiking, fishing, camping
7.8 miles, 3 hours, 650-foot elevation change, map VIII

Horn is about as inaccessible as a wilderness lake can be as attested to by its nesting loons. It once had a population of native trout that the DEC attempted to protect for breeding. Formerly, fishing was prohibited here. It is now permitted, though this fact is not reflected in the brochure describing the Moose River Plains. Fishing must be good, for there are signs that fishermen have wheeled canoes or boats the entire 7.8-mile distance to its shores.

Start by walking the 4.2 miles to the Indian River, and after you cross it, head west for 0.6 mile. Here the trail to Horn turns left, also following a logging road that served some of the most recent Gould Paper Company operations. Since there are several old logging roads heading south from the main trunk trail, you should watch carefully for this one, which has a partially concealed sign high in a tree to the side of the trail, near the turn.

There are infrequent yellow markers along the side trail to Horn Lake, barely enough to keep you on the correct logging road, for the trail intersects many other roadways. The markers are so few, this almost ranks as an unmarked path.

The way is narrow, growing in with brambles and maples. The forest is uniformly small hardwoods, and the terrain is relatively featureless, all of which make the 3-mile walk from the trunk trail boring and not entirely obvious. (The guide board says 2.7 miles, but it is short by at least 0.3 mile.)

On the bright side, the road that the trail follows was well built and provides easy walking. The road heads generally southwest, rising slightly, then more gradually. Almost all the walk is a long, gentle traverse, climbing 350 feet. Shortly after leaving the trunk trail, you enter a small field. Head through it to the southwest, keeping right. (Another, fainter road forks left in the field.) At 1.4 miles you again keep right in another very small field where a faint roadway forks left. Beyond, the trail appears to be at the edge of a valley that drops off to your left.

At 1.7 miles, there is a marsh on your left and a very small knob with rock ledges on your right. Just short of 2 miles, the trail turns south, left, in a field. (There is a well-built roadway heading up to the right. It can be followed for over 4 miles as it traverses the northern flanks of Ice Cave Mountain before reaching Adirondack League Club property. It is interesting to note that the first tractor used for logging pulled logs over this ridge in 1914.)

Within 100 feet, the trail to Horn, the left fork, enters a sand flat where even mosses have failed to colonize. Head sharply left as you enter the field, then drop down to cross an unbridged stream at 2.1 miles. This fair-sized stream flows from your right and is not shown on the 1950 series USGS. In fact, that series even shows the outlet of Horn improperly, adding to the confusion in this area. The unnamed stream flows from the flanks of Ice Cave Mountain. Horn Lake Outlet flows from a bay to the east of the one shown on the map. The two streams approach each other just to the east of this trail crossing, but they flow independently, about a quarter mile apart, all the way to their separate confluences with the Indian River.

Beyond the stream crossing, walk 100 feet to a field and turn sharply right. A faint road continues straight but there are markers here to reassure you of your course. The trail crosses a field where brambles and maples have almost filled the roadway. Suddenly lots of markers, old yellow Conservation Department ones, vintage 1968, line the trail. At 2.6 miles, the roadway you are following appears to go straight. The trail makes a right angle turn to the left, to head east of south; watch for a marker high in a dying beech to alert you to this turn. Very shortly you will see the lake through the trees.

Modern campers have stopped here at shoreline, at the site of an old camp. Some fishermen have routinely shortened the walk by bushwhacking from the first approach to the Indian River directly to Horn Lake's southern shore. This is not an easy trek, but it shortens the trip by 4 miles, one way.

87 Monument, Mountain, and Snyder Lakes
Bushwhack, map VIII

Horn Lake is in the center of the remote square of state land, Township 5, that is bordered on three sides by Adirondack League Club property. That square has some of the most inaccessible parts of the West Canada Lakes Wilderness, and there are a half dozen small lakes farther south and much harder to reach than Horn Lake. For those who like challenging bushwhacks, this one, described by Paul Sirtoli and Jay O'Hern, takes you to three of the lakes. Nestled between Ice Caves Mountain and the North Branch of the Black River to the northwest and the Middle Branch of the Black River to the south, Monument, Mountain, and Snyder lakes are wild and pristine, hemmed in by bogs, thick stands of spiked spruce, and rugged terrain.

To begin the bushwhack, walk the Indian River Trail to the crossing immediately south of the oxbow, section 84. Cross the river where the bridge is out to the south side and continue on the unmarked trail that twenty-five years ago was a major logging road. Now it is a glorified foot trail, although at places, the gravel road bed is most evident. Be careful, as minor roads do intersect the path, but generally, your route parallels the Indian River in a southeasterly direction.

You meet a sizable stream about thirty minutes down the path. It is not shown on the USGS but the Vs on the map indicate at least an intermittent drainage. From this point, take a compass heading southwesterly toward Mountain Lake. Except for some blowdown, bushwhacking is fairly easy, over rolling and gently rising terrain. The region was logged as shown by a rotting stumps, some discarded timber, and the fast fading minor skid rows that were etched by heavy machinery. The small fir, beech, maple, and cherry saplings are punctuated with an occasional huge yellow birch or spruce. The undergrowth is thick with witch hopple at times. The shores of the lakes are dense with low spruce and balsam.

Though each lake is different, the lakes all have dark green algal mats, they are crystal clear, and they appear to be shallow. Mountain Lake has several spots where you can sit on rocks near the shore, watching the dragon flies that are at the top of the food chain in this acidified lake. Most of the shoreline, though, is bog, with blueberry bushes dotting the marshy surface.

To reach Monument Lake, head in a west-southwesterly direction. It takes an hour to cover the hilly terrain between the lakes, and you may need to navigate around a marsh. Monument has the most rocks of the three lakes; there is a small rock island and the northern boggy shore is broken with massive, low rock slabs.

Snyder lies twenty minutes south of Monument, though the going is rough because of spruce stands and thick undergrowth as well as wet areas to bushwhack around. To return you can head northeasterly toward the Indian River. If you camp at the river, then this circuit can be done in a long day's bushwhack.

Yale Creek Falls

88 Yale Brook Falls
Bushwhack, map VIII

The route to Yale Brook Falls is called a bushwhack only because no markers delineate the sequence of logging roads that lead to the falls. The route is clear and generally obvious, though filling in. At the second clearing, 2.2 miles west of Indian Lake, section 84, where the bridge is out, you need to figure a way to cross the stream. Sometimes there is a boat nearby; if the weather has been relatively dry, you can don sneakers and wade across the knee-high water.

From here it is 4 miles to the falls, and the principal route leads there. However, there are several branching logging roads, some of which you may not even notice. Nevertheless, check your compass frequently to be sure the direction you are taking keeps you on the main road.

The logging road heads south from the crossing (0.0 mile); it is filling with spruce and balsam, some knee-high, others head-high. In places there is a wide track—the roadway continually changes from wide open to thickly grown and narrow. The roadway curves to southeast, and at about 0.5 mile you may see a roadway forking right, southwest. The road now climbs, and another not obvious road forks left, due east, at 0.8 mile. At 1 mile you cross a fair-size stream, one of many that are not shown on the current USGS.

Just beyond there is a large clearing, but the roadway is obvious. It keeps a fairly level contour as it circles east around the hillside. In one place the road is filled in with young spruce and maples and beech; near the 1.6-mile mark the route is so scoured that it looks as if it were recently cleared. You enter a large clearing, heading just west of south, and at 1.8 miles cross a stream with a huge culvert and a bridge of logs two feet in diameter. Another road to the southwest is definitely becoming overgrown, and even your route, which is now more easterly, is quite filled with young trees. Large rocks line the left side of the trail. At 2.3 miles you see a small creek to the right of the trail; you cross it a little farther along.

The road turns southwest at 2.5 miles and generally keeps that direction all the way to the falls. The falls lie to the right of the trail, and the roadway dips to cross the brook and continues southwest. You can not see all of the falls at once; it is a series of cascades that curve right and left over the rocks.

The Northern Tier

WILLIAM H. H. MURRAY visited Raquette Lake in the 1860s. There were only a few settlers there until 1874 when William West Durant built two cottages on its shores. He and others developed the summer resort at Raquette Lake and along the waterway west from Blue Mountain Lake. Visitors came from the railroad at North Creek by stage, then by steamer, and ultimately a short railroad along this watery course. Durant built Camp Pine Knot on Raquette Lake for his own family, but later (1895) sold it to Hollis P. Huntington. Durant built Camp Uncas on Mohegan Lake in 1890 and sold it in 1805 to J. Pierpont Morgan. In 1893, Durant built hunting lodges on both Shedd and Sumner lakes. Sumner Lake became Lake Kora and Shedd Lake became Sagamore, which was sold in 1901 to Alfred G. Vanderbilt.

In 1898 a group of these wealthy vacationers, including many with estates on Raquette Lake, joined together to build an extension of the railroad from Clearwater, now Carter, on the New York Central to Raquette Lake. Thus it was not until this century that there was any need for an improved road from Blue Mountain west to Raquette Lake. This makes NY 28 one of the more recent Adirondack roads and it helps account for the fact that the Blue Ridge Wilderness Area to the south was so little touched by development. The lack of lakes in the Wilderness Area, compared with the very attractive lakes farther west and north, explains the rest.

While few trails penetrate that Wilderness, the sale of the lands surrounding two of the great camps has recently opened to the public many new trails, which will become increasingly attractive as the forests recover from the logging done just before their sale to the state a little more than a decade ago.

Lycopodia on the Buck Creek Trail

Blue Mountain from Sawyer Mountain

89 Sawyer Mountain

Hiking, picnicking, snowshoeing
1.1 mile, 1 hour, 800-foot vertical rise, map IX

The views from the two rocky openings near the summit of this small mountain are intimate and pleasant, not sweeping and panoramic, but well worth the climb up a gradual, well-marked trail. The trailhead is on the west side of the NY 28 and 30 between Indian Lake and Blue Mountain Lake. It is 4.5 miles north of Indian Lake. There is an official parking area, with a DEC sign. Frequent yellow discs show the route.

You start hiking in a westerly direction through an open hardwood forest. The trail starts very gradually and swings around to the northwest and up onto a small ridge. From the ridge you swing west, drop into a small col, and then continue to climb gradually. There are a lot of dead beech trees in the woods and many beech nuts, but no signs of bear claws on the trees. Pileated woodpeckers thrive on the dead snags, and the large elliptical cavities in the trunks, with large chip piles below on the ground, are proof of their industrious probing for insects.

Near the summit, the trail leads to a rocky outcrop. Pause here and look north for a striking view of some of the High Peaks: the three summits on the horizon are Algonquin on the left, the mass of Marcy on the right, with the smaller cone of Colden between them. In an hour, longer on snowshoes, you reach a summit knob that has no view. The trail goes right, west, and slightly downhill to a rock outcrop. From here the Cedar River Valley stretches west and southwest with the slopes of Panther Mountain forming one wall of the valley, Metcalf and Wakely mountains the other. Walk down the rock about ten feet and look to the right, and the familiar open rock areas on Blue Mountain appear. You can see the fire tower on both Blue and Wakely mountains. The two small ponds of the Blue Ridge Wilderness Area, Stephens and Cascade, nestle in the dense woods below you. With a map you can visualize the route of the Northville-Placid Trail as it climbs from Cedar River, past Stephens Pond and goes on to the east of Blue Mountain.

The return to your car takes but a half an hour. This is a nice family trip as small children will have no difficulty in negotiating the trail.

90 Rock Pond, Cascade, and Stephens Ponds

Marked trail, hiking, camping, cross-country skiing
3.1 miles blue Northville-Placid Trail, 3.8 miles red trail, 400-foot elevation change, map IX

This blue trail is a continuation of the Northville-Placid Trail from Cedar River Road to Stephens Pond, section 47, and leads to the state campground at the eastern end of Lake Durant. The red trail is a spur that passes Cascade and Rock ponds and ends at the western end of Lake Durant. A shuttle car can be left at any of the three trailheads so that the trip can be hiked or skied in one direction.

From the lean-to at Stephens Pond, walk west for 200 feet to the main blue-marked trail. Turn right, north and continue along the level for 0.1 mile. The trail begins to climb gradually, gaining over one hundred feet in altitude before turning northwest at 0.4 mile. The trail is wide and clear and can be skied easily in either direction. You descend slightly and reach a T at 0.6 mile. The guide board gives mileages to distant points on the Northville-Placid Trail as well as to "Stevens Pond," which is misspelled.

A right turn here, northeast, leads in 2.5 miles to the Lake Durant Campground. The trail is generally downhill in a northeasterly direction. The woods for the most part are large mature hardwoods and a joy to walk and ski through. From an altitude of 2160 feet at the T, the clear trail is easy to negotiate. At 1.4 miles, 0.8 mile from the T, there is a steep downhill in what is becoming a gully with considerable erosion. It is easy to hike, but on skis you should be cautious as there is limited space to stop.

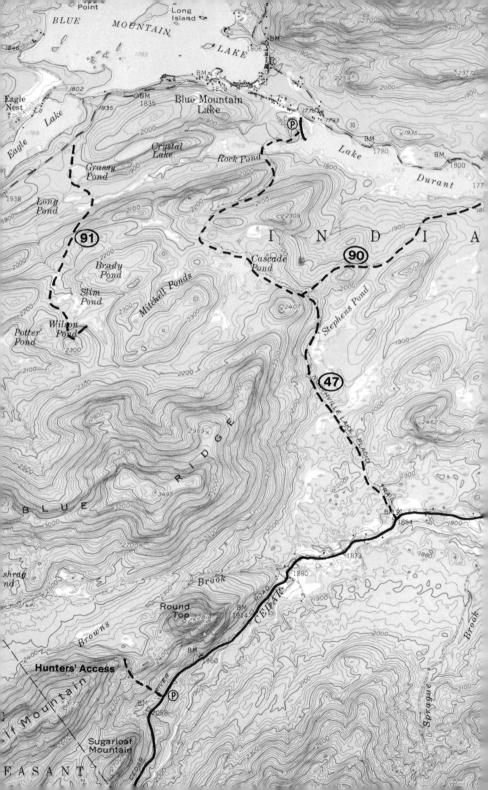

Map IX: Sections 46-47, 89-91
Based on USGS 15' Blue
Mountain Lake Quadrangle

N

| 0 | 0.5 | 1.0 mile |

Trail
Path
Road

At the end of this drop (1.7 miles), you enter an evergreen grove in a swampy area, and the trail swings more to the east, again in hardwoods. For skiers, this is a long, gentle downhill. It is easy to cross the next gully, which has a brook; there is a steep but short hill on the other side. Shortly after, at 2.8 miles, you reach campsites and turn right to follow the campground road. It crosses a large brook, the outlet of Stephens Pond, and there is a marvelous view of Blue Mountain just before the bridge. After passing the campground administrative buildings and the beach, the road swings left over a bridge crossing the outlet of Lake Durant, Rock River. Continue straight, behind the ranger's house and through an open field on a tack northwest toward Blue Mountain. This route takes you to the marked trailhead on NY 28/30 where there is parking on both sides of the road and the turnouts are plowed in winter. This trailhead is about 3 miles east of Blue Mountain Lake village.

An alternate, and longer, way to get to NY 28/30 from the T is to follow the red-marked trail via Cascade Pond. (The third variation would be to start at the campground, ski to the T, and make a loop back to NY 28/30.) From the T, 0.6 mile, ski west to the pond over a trail that is wide and easy to negotiate until the very end. You head northwest through open forest from the T, and if you are skiing, you will see the pond in fifteen minutes from the T, at about 1.2 miles. You ski parallel to the pond for another ten minutes, reaching a short, sharp drop at 1.6 miles, which takes you to the outlet of the pond with a sharp turn left at the bottom, so ski carefully. The outlet of Cascade Pond, which flows northeast into Durant, is steep and rocky. You can easily cross the outlet in summer on logs and rocks. In winter it is more difficult; you have to remove your skis. Do not cross on the flat ice near the outlet as it does not freeze deeply because of moving water. The lean-to beside the outlet is on a beautiful point of land. Looking southwest across the pond you can see the long spine of Blue Ridge Mountain.

The red-marked trail continues on west on the level for fifteen minutes, then, at 2.1 miles turns sharply northeast and climbs gradually. You reach a height-of-land in another ten minutes, 2.4 miles. The trail descends steeply through a depression between two low hills. This is a long downhill run in a northeasterly direction. At 3.4 miles the trail bears left, contouring around the hill and heading north to cross on a bridge between the narrow western finger of Lake Durant and the water on the left called Rock Pond.

Across the bridge, the trail heads northeast through evergreens, coming out on a marked spur off Durant Road. This spur goes to the lake where boats can be launched, and where there is a grassy area and several

View across Wilson Pond to Blue Ridge Mountain

camping spots. You reach this trailhead by driving west from the trailhead by the Lake Durant Campground for just over 2 miles, then turning left, west, on Lake Durant Road for 200 yards to a dirt road on the left, south.

Cascade and Stephens ponds, each with a lean-to and distant mountain vistas, are easy to reach for camping and cross-country skiing. Portions of the trail are wet and rocky so wait for adequate snow-cover before trying skis. By using two cars, you can try various combinations of routes, and the area is so inviting you will want to revisit it often.

91 Grassy and Wilson Ponds

Hiking, camping, fishing, snowshoeing
2.9 miles, 1½ hours, 460-foot vertical rise, map IX

Wilson is a tiny pond tucked between hills at the foot of massive Blue Ridge Mountain. The trail to this surprisingly delightful destination not only passes Grassy Pond, it traverses a number of different and handsome forest types.

The trailhead is 2.8 miles west of Blue Mountain Lake on NY 28, where a marked turnout on the south side of the road provides ample parking. The first 100 yards of trail are on private land where no camping or fires are permitted. The red marked trail begins with a slight rise, then continues south and relatively level through a young hemlock, spruce, and balsam forest. You cross a path just before reaching state land, but continue straight, and within just a few minutes begin to see Grassy Pond through the trees on your left. This is a deep, rich, ferny woods with bunchberries and yellow bead lily, *Clintonia*.

At 0.5 mile, a ten-minute walk, you find a short path leading to the grassy, shrubby shore of the appropriately named pond. Continuing on the red trail, you quickly cross the outlet on logs. Tall evergreens shelter the trail as it winds southeast, then turns southwest around the side of a small hill. Down on your left you see the marshes that surround the outlet of Long Pond. You head south to hop across rocks below an ancient beaver dam on that stream.

Continue southeast across another ridge, past a wonderfully large glacial erratic capped with ferns, then down to the marshes that surround the outlet of Wilson Pond. These marshes stretch for nearly two miles north-northeast to Rock Pond. As you approach them, you see the slopes of the ridge you are about to climb. From the marsh you have a view of Blue Mountain. At 0.9 mile, the trail cuts straight across the marsh to the stream where a log is all that remains of a bridge. The marsh, as well as the crossing, can be wet underfoot. Across the stream, a sign points left to a spring. Turn southwest along the edge of the marsh on corduroy. Shortly the trail ducks into the woods and begins a long traverse up the ridge through a beautiful maple woods.

The traverse lasts for about fifteen minutes, 0.5 mile, then the trail winds southeast, then southwest, climbing around small knolls for another 0.4 mile. Watch as steep slopes develop on your right, northwest, and you begin to hear the outlet, for a small path forks left to a marsh along the outlet stream. The trail heads west across the outlet at 1.8 miles on a three log bridge, then climbs a knoll covered with tall spruce and balsam, thick stands of young spruce, and paper birch.

The stream flows through marshes most of the way to Wilson Pond. A widening of the stream is called Slim Pond. The trail makes nearly a mile-long, wide arc to the west of the stream to avoid all the marshes and in the process describes such a tortuous route over so many knolls that it takes more than a half hour to walk this stretch. After crossing five rocky ridges, the trail heads east and steeply down with small cliffs to the left of the trail. You cross an intermittent stream within sight of marshes again, then cross the outlet stream.

The narrow trail winds through dense thickets for 350 yards to a lean-to on the north shore of the narrow outlet bay. A path leads 50 feet to a lovely rocky promontory on that bay. From here or from vantages farther east on the shoreline, you look across a rocky promontory capped with evergreens to the massive, trackless, and densely wooded slopes of Blue Ridge Mountain.

92 Secret Falls
Path

A thin sheet of water plunges over horizontal ledges for thirty feet to create a charming waterfall on the edge of the mountain south of Raquette Lake. The stream is a small tributary of Death Brook, and the walk is so short almost anyone can visit the falls for a picnic.

A roadway with a barrier heads south from NY 28, 10 miles west of Blue Mountain, 3.6 miles east of Sagamore Road. It leads in five minutes to a flooded area; a path circles right around it. Continue south for another 100 yards on the roadway to the falls. It is possible that stone was quarried from the rock face here. Paths lead to the top of the falls along both left and right sides. Behind the falls, the path continues southeast to the valley east of Estelle Mountain; it serves hunters headed for the interior of the Blue Ridge Wilderness Area and Slim and Bear ponds.

The marsh along Death Brook, which lies to the northeast of the roadway, is a good place for birds but not an easy spot to reach. The best you can do is approach the southern shore of the marsh.

93 South Inlet

Canoeing, map X

Driving east on NY 28 from Blue Mountain Lake for 11 miles brings you to Raquette Lake. Soon after you see it on the right, north, side of the road you reach a bridge over the South Inlet of the lake. The embayment is about 2 miles long and makes an excellent canoe trip to see water-loving plants and shrubs, and to have a picnic and a cool swim at the end of the inlet.

Park beside the road on the east side of the bridge; it is an easy 100-foot carry down to the water. Bring your binoculars as waterfowl are common, including the colorful wood ducks. And, before you start, you may want to explore the small knoll to the south of the road and east of the inlet where there is a native stand of red pine.

Depending on the season of the year, you will see white water lilies, pitcher plants, pickerel weed, pink asters, labrador tea, bog rosemary, and sheep laurel along the inlet. You must paddle slowly along the edge and search out the plants. After a mile paddle upstream, the shoreline changes; shrubs and labrador tea give way to grasses and a different group of flowers. Here swamp candles, bur-reed, and more asters are plentiful. The bay ends at a delightful spot where a small waterfall cascades in the brook that flows from Sagamore Lake. The stream is clean and cool and makes a nice place for a swim on a hot day. There is place to camp beside the brook if you want to make an overnight outing of the trip.

Motorboats may enter this inlet from Raquette Lake, but it is narrow and shallow, so few do. It is best suited for canoeing.

94 Cascades on South Inlet

Picnicking, walking
Two trails, each 1.5 miles long, 40 minutes, 100-foot elevation change, map X

Almost all of the lands of the huge Sagamore estate owned by Alfred G. Vanderbilt now belong to the state. The complex of buildings of this great camp are now a conference center and posted to all but guests at Sagamore. However, many trails on the former estate are available to the

Secret Falls between Blue Mountain and Raquette Lake

Cascades on South Inlet

public. Among them are two trails from Sagamore Road south of Raquette Lake to the Cascades, the lovely small waterfall on South Inlet. These are the carriage roads once used by Vanderbilt to carry guests from the South Inlet where they were driven in a motor launch from the Raquette Lake Railroad Station.

The two trails are as different as day and night, or more aptly, wet and dry. The trails lie on either side of South Inlet, which is just over 3 miles from NY 28. Both routes are delightful, and it is best to walk both of them, crossing over the stream above the Cascades to make a loop. *However, this is only possible in low water, so do not attempt it otherwise.*

The eastern trail starts through a field of raspberries with a campsite, then descends to follow the stream quite closely. You are never out of earshot of it and seldom out of sight of it. The forest, like all in the area, has been heavily logged in recent years, and small spruce and balsam crowd the roadway. At 0.4 mile, there is a dam on the Inlet and a power house below the dam. Be careful if you approach it because the sluice for the intake is a rock-lined trench concealed in high weeds. Downstream the Inlet enters a deep gorge; the trail, often very wet and muddy, is on a spruce covered bank above the stream. A track to the right leads directly to Sagamore. The trail crosses a small stream, passes another brick powerhouse, and then curves with the stream as it descends to the quiet water of South Inlet. Here, the trail emerges beneath large white cedars beneath the Cascades. Pinxters line the shoreline here at the end of the canoeable water on South Inlet.

The western trail, 0.1 mile north of the bridge over South Inlet follows a hardwood ridge, farther from the stream, occasionally within earshot of it, but almost never within sight of the Inlet. Several logging roads fork from the main route, but red flags should keep you on the correct course, which is a sinuous route, curving to match the stream. Just beyond the big hook in the trail, the trail changes from west to north and descends to an open field. The roadway cuts down across the field to waters edge, above the Cascades. A narrow path leads downstream to several vantage points from which to view them.

95 Sagamore Lake

Hiking, fishing, cross-country skiing
3.3 miles, 1 1/4 hours, relatively level, map X

When William West Durant built the camp complex on Sagamore Lake, the lake was known as Shedd Lake. He sold it to Alfred G. Vanderbilt. Later, Syracuse University acquired the buildings and the lake. They logged the land around the lake before selling it to the state in 1972. Sagamore Institute bought the buildings and a small piece of property surrounding them and offers tours, conferences, and outings throughout the year.

The Institute uses the logging road that circles the lake as a ski trail in winter, and the traditional direction for skiers is clockwise around this large body of water. All but the southwestern end of the 3.5-mile trail that circles the lake is on state land; however, the portion that is owned by Sagamore prevents the public from making the circuit. You can however, ski (it is an excellent ski route) or walk almost all the way around and return to the starting point, a small parking area with a Wilderness sign, immediately north of the bridge over the outlet. This bridge is barred to all but Sagamore guests and staff.

The land around Sagamore was fairly heavily logged in the late 1970s and the forest reflects this disturbance. The road heads north for 0.5 mile to a fork left that once connected with the Cascades Trail. A second fork left leads to an old pasture. Gentle ups and downs lead west; at 1.4 miles there is an iron cross to the north of the trail. It marks the spot where a tree fell across the trail, killing the carriage driver, but sparing the Vanderbilt children.

The roadway curves southeast, and at 1.7 miles a logging road forks left; it is one of many you see on route. This one heads northeast to cross East Inlet, then circles around marshes back to Lost Brook in the vicinity of several waterfalls. The roadway, now almost invisible in spite of the fact that it was cleared little more than three decades ago, now heads north of east past Aluminum Pond, and onto the Cedar River Road. In the late 1800s and the early 1900s, this was the principal route used by workmen coming to Sagamore and Uncas from Indian Lake. Today its route is a challenging bushwhack along which several hikers have been lost at various times.

Beyond the fork, the Sagamore circuit road dips, and at 1.9 miles crosses the inlet, a fairly large stream with the combined waters of East Inlet and Lost Brook that drain a large part of the western Blue Ridge Wilderness. It is this large flow that gives Sagamore its sixty-two-day flow-through rate, helping keep the acidity low. As a result, even though the lake is over 1900 feet in elevation, it remains an excellent fishing lake, with brook and lake trout and small mouth bass. It is, however, a special trophy lake, and no live bait is allowed.

Beyond the inlet there is a second bridge over a small stream, then the trail crosses a balsam ridge and enters a spruce bog. Other roads fork left, but the trail continues curving around the shoreline, finally getting close enough so that at 2.7 miles you can see the lake. You will have to turn around just beyond an intermittent stream with a little marsh, for shortly you reach the Sagamore property. Sagamore Lake's shoreline of cedars is cropped about five feet above the surface of the water—the limit that deer browse. Many deer are attracted to the lake in winter since the Institute feeds them.

96 Mohegan Lake

Hiking, camping, fishing
2.8 miles, 1 hour, relatively level, map X

If you turn right 0.5 mile south of the bridge over South Inlet, following the directions for tours, and then turn right again, opposite where the tours begin, you enter a large public parking area for those who wish to use the public lands surrounding Sagamore Lake and Lake Mohegan. The tours of Sagamore give you a wonderful feeling for the great camp days, and the community of workers that surrounded the homes of the rich.

Return to the main road from the parking area and turn right. In 0.2 mile you reach a barred gate, and there is limited parking nearby, so it is best to walk from the public parking area. Starting from the gate, at 0.0 mile, keep right, the way left leads to the posted lands of Camp Kilkare on Lake Kora, which was originally called Sumner Pond.

The road traverses a high ridge from which you can see Raquette Lake in winter. At 0.55 mile you pass a house; opposite is a roadway that leads south up a small hill with a broad view to the northwest. The views are best as a winter snowshoe trek. At 1.5 miles you reach a fork, the way left leads to the remaining private inholding on Lake Mohegan, which was once the summer home of J. P. Morgan called "Uncas." The way right, the Uncas Road, leads immediately to another barrier.

The continuing road is now access for the Bear Pond Tract, which was recently acquired by the state with a reservation that permits the club to use eleven acres and their buildings for thirty-five years. They currently have use of the road, which traverses state land. The public can walk the road and use most of the Bear Pond Tract, see sections 66 and 97. Just beyond the barrier, there is a field to the north of the trail, the site of a farm that served the Morgan complex. It is in a lovely high valley with views, a good place for a picnic, and its apple trees attract large numbers of deer.

The road continues west through heavily logged lands. Raspberries line the open route. At 2 miles, 0.5 mile from the second barrier, watch for yellow ribbons tied to a tree and a faint roadway heading south. It leads 0.2 mile to a pine covered, wind-swept knoll to the east of the outlet of Lake Mohegan, a nice place to picnic or camp. Mohegan is also a good fishing lake with brook and lake trout and smallmouth bass.

The outlet is quite pretty, but you can find an even prettier spot along the outlet stream. At just short of 2 miles, the roadway makes a big curve to the south in a field. A faint track, part of the Uncas Road, continues west for 0.2 miles to a washed-out bridge over the outlet. Only four huge, slippery, moss-covered logs remain. The bridge is in a small hemlock gorge, and there are small cascades both up and downstream from it.

If you continue south on the open logging road, you cross the outlet on a new bridge. This area was logged within the last decade. The road makes a big arc through the logged lands, heading back to the western shore of Lake Mohegan at 2.8 miles.

Map X: Sections 55-60, 66-67, 69,
93-99, 159, 164-168, 170
Based on USGS 15' Raquette Lake,
Big Moose, Old Forge and
West Canada Lakes Quadrangles

Trail
Path
Bushwhack
Canoe Route
Road
Shelter

0   0.5   1.0 mile

N

Also Shown on Map VI

97   Bear Pond Tract

Path, map X

The 1100-acre Bear Pond Tract was purchased by the state in 1987 for just under $120 an acre. The Bear Pond Club retains rights to eleven acres and two buildings for thirty-five years. The path described here is an open route, recently used as a logging road and the principal access to the Bear Pond Club buildings. From here to the pond, the path follows less distinct logging roads. From the approach to the shore of Lake Mohegan at 2.8 miles, section 98, continue south. The road passes the marshes south of the lake, and begins to climb. At 3.2 miles, a roadway forks right, see section 99.

The roadway straight ahead is through less disturbed forests for a while, but you will notice how heavily the Bear Pond Tract was logged as soon as you reach its boundary. There are innumerable confusing logging roads on the tract. To find the pond, watch closely as you approach the buildings at 4.7 miles. Just about the time you can first see them, a logging road climbs the ridge to the northwest, and continues in a southwesterly direction along a level terrace for another 1.8 miles to Bear Pond. Use a compass here to make sure you are on the right route. There is a lean-to with a dirt floor at the northern end of the pond. The pond has boggy shores, filled with pitcher plants.

For directions on reaching the pond from the south, see section 66. The two routes can be combined for a long and difficult through walk.

98   The Uncas Road South from Seventh Lake Inlet

Cross-country skiing, hiking
2.5 miles of snowmobile trail, 1 hour, 360-foot elevation change, plus paths along logging roads to connect with Sagamore, maps X and XV

This marked snowmobile trail is so seldom used in winter that you can safely ski it. Sagamore takes groups along it from the lake, past Mohegan, to a new crossover route and down to NY 28 for an all day ski outing. Because the route is downhill this way, it is described in the westerly direction, ending at a trailhead opposite Eighth Lake Campground, 4.8 miles west of Sagamore Road, 5.5 miles east of Limekiln Road near Sixth Lake.

Follow section 96 from Sagamore for 2.8 miles plus 0.4 mile on the Bear Pond Road, then head northwest, uphill. This part is unmarked, but the logging road is most obvious. The track quickly climbs to a height-of-land at 3.6 miles. Here at 2260 feet, 240 feet above Mohegan Lake, there are through-the-trees winter views of the lake. The roadway now begins a long, gentle downhill. There are some blowdowns, but at just 4 miles you reach a forest that has not been logged recently. For the next mile you are in one of the better forests in this part of the Adirondacks, making it pleasant walking even in summer. The dense spruce swamp has a lovely understory of gold thread and woodferns, *dryopteris spp.,* and bunchberry. The track zigzags through the swamp, crosses an old bridge, and reaches an intersection with the Uncas Road at 5 miles.

If you turn right, in 100 yards you are at the four log remains of the bridge described in section 98. If the bridge were passable, you could have reached this point from Sagamore in 2.2 miles, not the 5 miles required in the long detour south.

If you turn left at the intersection, you cross an unnamed stream in 100 feet and climb up 100 yards to reach the snowmobile trail, which is marked along this portion of the Uncas Road west to NY 28.

The trail now follows a very wide roadway, gently uphill to the north. The forest is more mature and a very pleasant mixture of maple and yellow birch that forms a tall, cathedral-like canopy over the route. At 5.7 miles the road reaches a height-of-land and turns west. There are lovely views to a marsh and a tear-drop pond that lie to the north of the trail. The route is now either level, or downhill, and 6.5 miles the hillside slopes steeply to the north to Seventh Lake Inlet. Look back northeast at the huge pines that dot the ridge on the north side of the inlet. There is a culvert over a stream, then the descent quickens.

In autumn, the cathedral of maples and birch has a brilliantly covered ceiling. You hear the inlet, then descend to cross it on a bridge that is washing out, but still holding. The barrier and NY 28 are 0.15 mile away.

99   Buck Creek Trail

Snowmobile trail, cross-country skiing, hiking
4.2 miles, 2 hours, 400-foot elevation change, map X

Like other snowmobile trails near Sagamore, this one is not heavily used and is suitable for skiing. However, it has not been cleared in recent years, and if this is not done soon, it will become too overgrown for travel in either winter or summer. This route connects with the Uncas Road, section 100, and with it makes a great loop. The route also connects to routes that lead to Sagamore, section 98.

The trailhead is opposite the Seventh Lake Fishing Access site, 6.8 miles west of Sagamore, 3.5 miles east of Limekiln Road near Sixth Lake, and 2 miles west of Uncas Road along NY 28 if you are planning the loop.

Almost all of the route is through logged forests, and the beginning is clear and open, but filling in. There are erratics beside the trail and a stream that has chosen to run down the trail as it begins to rise. The stream has worn the trail to bedrock. You climb gradually until, at 0.9 mile, you cross a small stream. The trail continues to climb through a walled corridor of young spruce, and another stream joins the trail, which turns from west to southerly. At 1.5 miles, the trail makes a sharp turn to the left—an unused road continues straight ahead. It led toward the headwaters of the Red River.

The trail arcs to the east and climbs a bit more, then levels out in a long grassy stretch. At 1.9 miles you see the beginning of a huge marsh that stretches out to the south of the trail. You follow along its edge for 0.5 mile, and much of this stretch can be wet. You are rewarded with views of the marsh and a variety of wetland plants, including labrador tea, many, many kinds of clubmosses, *lycopodia spp.*, and even sundew in the sphagnum that is filling the trail. Toward the eastern end of the marsh, there is a large beaver dam and a flooded area. A path leads north around it.

As you leave the marsh, headed downhill and southeast, you cross to a watershed that drains to the east. Several tiny beaver dams have been built right across the trail, creating small ponds. Circle them through the spruce and pick up the roadway, which now drains the ponds. There is a veritable bog right in the trail. It is slow and wet walking through a spruce walled corridor, downhill. The water finally drains into its former stream to your right, and the trail continues beside the stream all the way to the Uncas Road. The trail arcs northeast and at 3.2 miles reaches a dry open field where the stream is in a drying beaver marsh below. It is a lovely place for a picnic with lichens, mosses, and lycopodia.

The trail continues northeast, crosses a stream on a washed out bridge, and continues on a relatively level course through a spruce-walled corridor. A washed-out bridge carries the trail over the stream at 4.1 miles, and at 4.2 miles you intersect the Uncas Road.

Ha-de-ron-dah
Wilderness Area

WEST OF OLD Forge lies one of the Adirondack Park's smaller wilderness areas, Ha-de-ron-dah. It's 26,600 acres are bounded by NY 28 on the south, the Independence River Wild Forest Area on the west and north, and private lands on the east. Lacking the dynamics of high mountains or canoeable waters found in other areas, it comes into its own by virtue of its subtlety. Rolling hills, peaceful streams, secluded ponds, and a rich forest give the visitor a feeling of remoteness and solitude.

The powerful Iroquois nation claimed northern New York as their *couchsachraga*, meaning "beaver hunting ground." Occasionally, Algonquin tribes to the north would chance an expedition into the region. If the Iroquois caught these trespassers, they were harassed, tortured, and, most likely, killed. Many times their forays were unproductive, and during harsh seasons, they were forced to eat bark and shoots from young trees and bushes. It was after observing this survival tactic that their Iroquois tormentors derisively referred to the hapless Algonquins as *ha-de-ron-dah*, meaning, "bark eaters." It was this phrase that the white explorers corrupted into Adirondack.

At the close of the American Revolution, shrewd speculators purchased large tracts of land in this region with the intent of reselling parcels at highly inflated prices. Many unsuspecting buyers faced bitter disappointment when they found out that their land could not support colonization or agriculture. In 1797 John Brown, a revolutionary war activist and successful Rhode Island businessman, sent his son-in-law, John Francis, to New York City to conclude a shipping deal. The well-meaning Francis was woefully inept in his mission and, falling victim to a group of slick land agents, returned home with a questionable title to 210,000 acres of land lying between the Black River valley and the Fulton Chain of Lakes. Determined to make the best of the situation, Brown had surveyors divide the tract into eight townships and a few hardy families trekked in over the Remsen Road to begin clearing and developing the land in the area of present-day Thendara. A dam was built at the outlet of First Lake and a sawmill and grist mill went into operation.

After John Brown's death in 1803, interest in the tract declined, and it wasn't until 1811 that another son-in-law, Charles Frederick Herreshoff, became interested in development possibilities. Under his direction, the Brown's Tract Road was cut from Moose River Settlement, east of Boonville, to the old clearings near the mills. The discovery of iron led to the construction of a forge for its processing. A modest manor house was built in which Herreshoff stayed to supervise operations. The ore was of poor quality however, and the mine frequently flooded. Hopes for high profits never materialized; and in the face of repeated failures, Herreshoff shot himself, ashamed to face his family.

Once again, silence descended upon Brown's Tract and many of the improvements fell into ruin. For years woodsmen travelling to the region gave their destination as "the old forge." One of these men was Nathaniel Foster, a veteran sharpshooter of the War of 1812. Nat was highly skilled in woodcraft and had earned the respect and admiration of many people. In 1832, at the age of sixty-five, after many years of wandering through the mountains, he settled into the Herreshoff manor with his wife. Also living on the tract at the time was Drid, an Indian whose jealous and violent character was in direct contrast to Nat's humble ways. He made repeated threats against Foster's life and was eventually shot as he paddled past a point on First Lake where Nat lay in ambush. After serving a one-year jail sentence, reluctantly imposed by a sympathetic court, Nat retired to Ava, New York.

In 1837, Otis Arnold left his farm in Boonville and, with his wife and six children, made his way over the Brown's Tract Road to settle in the manor. Life on the tract agreed with the Arnolds and six more children were born. They were able to amply provide for themselves by hunting and farming. Travelers passing through the area soon learned that they could count on the hospitality of the Arnolds for a good meal and comfortable lodging. From these modest beginnings, the inn-keeping industry arose and the direction for the region's future was set.

Industries dependent on forest products flourished and many acres of mighty hemlocks were dropped around Moose River Settlement to support the tanneries. Each spring saw enormous drives of saw and pulp logs head off to mills far down the Moose River. Unmarketable slash from these operations littered the forest floor, and when the Adirondack Division of the New York Central Railroad penetrated the area, many fires were started by stray sparks from the locomotives. In 1903, a devastating fire destroyed 25,000 acres of woodlands, the effects of which can still be seen.

Today, a well-structured trail system gives access to most of the major

Middle Settlement Creek where the Browns Tract Trail crosses

features in the Ha-de-ron-dah Wilderness Area. Easy grades make it possible to ski many of the trails, especially the Brown's Tract Trail, section 101, and the Big Otter Trail, section 112. These two routes serve as the main thoroughfares from which most of the other trails begin or end. According to the Unit Management Plan, trails north of the Big Otter Trail will only be cleared every five years. Users of these "reduced maintenance" trails can experience a deeper sense of wilderness and solitude but should be prepared for a more rugged route.

100 The Scusa Access Trail

Hiking access
0.6 mile, 20 minutes, one steep pitch, otherwise relatively level, map XI

A large New York State Department of Transportation parking area is located on the southeast side of NY 28, 3 miles south of the railroad overpass at Thendara. The Scusa Access Trail begins on the opposite side of the highway just north of the turnout, on an extension of state land. This is the main point of entry and the most direct route to trails in the

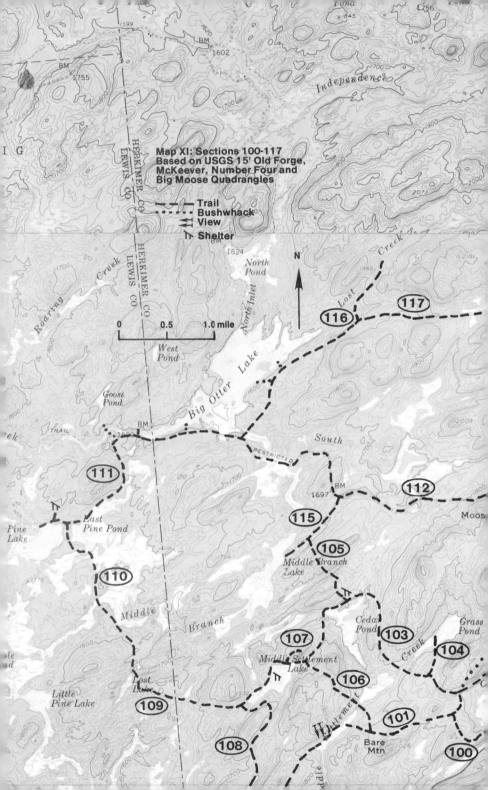

Map XI: Sections 100-117
Based on USGS 15' Old Forge,
McKeever, Number Four and
Big Moose Quadrangles

Trail
Bushwhack
View
Shelter

N

0   0.5   1.0 mile

southern portion of Ha-de-ron-dah, and it is marked with red DEC markers.

From the highway, the trail crosses the outlet of the Okara Lakes on a wooden bridge and comes to a register and a large wooden map of the trail system. What follows may be the steepest section of trail in the region, but it is short, and at the top of the knoll, there is bare rock where you can catch your breath or study the smoky quartz underfoot. The trail continues on through tall hardwoods and ends at a well-marked junction with Brown's Tract Trail, section 101.

To the east of the trail, there is a large heron rookery, which can be located by the noise and smell in June and July.

101 Brown's Tract Trail

Hiking, cross-country skiing
5.8 miles, 2³⁄₄ hours, easy grades, map XI

Brown's Tract Road was built in 1811 as the major route into the Brown's Tract. Though it ran through some of the most desolate forest known and its condition was always questionable, it served travelers for over three quarters of a century before it was overshadowed by rail and steamboat service. It led past Herreshoff Manor, which gradually fell into disrepair and was burned before the turn of the century. The site is now occupied by a large sandpit across the highway from the Thendara train station.

Brown's Tract Trail follows the original eastern half of the road except for a detour around private holdings along the Okara Lakes. Parts of it near both ends are in poor shape, but the middle stretch provides good hiking and skiing. To reach its eastern end, turn off NY 28 onto a road directly across from the Mountain View Motel, 0.4 mile south of the train station. Turn left immediately onto another road and follow it 0.3 mile to a point just beyond a house on the right. Parking here may interfere with local traffic and access to camps, so it is not recommended. The road is not plowed past this point in winter, and you need permission to park here in summer.

Ahead on the left is another camp and across from it on the north side of the road is an old trail sign. The trail, marked with yellow DEC markers, officially begins here and follows the road for about 1.4 miles. Yellow paint blazes marking the state land boundary line the north edge of the road for most of the way. The trail ascends moderately, then levels off after ten minutes and begins a gradual descent passing old tote roads. Swinging to the right, you cross a stream and begin a slight ascent. After thirty minutes, the trail swings back to the left and descends to a wet, overgrown section. Markers are hard to spot here and the trail is poorly defined. State land blazes cross to the left, the trail detours right and climbs above the roadway to a register near a maintained road that serves the camps and homes around the Okara Lakes. It is possible to begin hiking from here, and there is room on the shoulder to park.

From the register, the trail angles to the right and again becomes hard to distinguish as it descends to a wet area where it crosses Rock Pond outlet. The condition of the trail begins to improve as it rises away from the stream and follows along the base of a ridge. Less than thirty minutes from the Okara Lakes register, you reach a junction at 2.5 miles where the red-marked trail to Cedar Pond, section 103, heads off to the right.

The Brown's Tract Trail becomes quite enjoyable as it turns left and crosses a wet area on a new plank bridge. Having avoided the private lands around the Okara Lakes, the trail intercepts the Brown's Tract Road and swings right to follow its route. Less than five minutes and 0.3 mile later, the red-marked Scusa Access Trail, section 100, enters from the left. You continue straight on Brown's Tract Trail. For the next half hour you travel through tall hardwoods over rolling terrain that novice skiers will find pleasing.

At 3.8 miles, you reach another junction. Here the blue-marked trail to Middle Settlement Lake, section 106, heads north. From this point to its end, annual maintenance of the Brown's Tract Trail has been postponed due to denial of public access from Copper Lake Road. It can, however, be followed with little difficulty.

In ten minutes, the trail crosses the wetland of Middle Settlement Creek on the remains of an old beaver dam. On the opposite side of the creek, the trail turns left at a clearing and follows along the wetland to its end. You pass through an area of lush ferns and tall black cherry trees, evidence that the 1903 fire swept through this section.

Markers become scarce at times, and the trail gets rough with grown-in spots and wet areas as it begins a steady descent. A junction with the yellow-marked trail to Middle Settlement Lake, section 108, is at 5.6 miles, less than one hour from the previous junction. After dropping to cross a small stream, the trail rises up to the Copper Lake Road and the end of state land. NY 28 is just over a mile to the southeast, but the area property owners have in recent years denied access along the road to the general public. This is one of the areas under consideration for state acquisition.

102   Lookouts Accessible from the Brown's Tract Trail

Easy bushwhacks, views, map XI

From four points north of the Brown's Tract Trail, you can easily climb to open areas on hilltops or along ridges where the rewards are expansive views. It is likely that the fires of 1903 left these areas barren, and their exposure has slowed their recovery. Since the approaches are all through open hardwoods, winter ascents by snowshoe are enjoyable.

(A) The easternmost lookout is on a small hill less than 0.5 mile from the east end of the trail. The state land boundary meets the trail between the small house on the north side and the old trail sign. It may not be well-marked so stay a respectable distance from the house. You will want to parallel the boundary on a bearing of about 20° magnetic, which will take you shortly to a steep-sided gully. The exposed rock on the opposite side marks the base of the hill you want to ascend. Cross the gully and, swinging to the left, climb above the rocks, following the ridge line to the summit. Your main view is to the east where the mountains lining the Fulton Chain valley rise beyond the village of Old Forge, the most noticeable being McCauley with its ski slopes. Looking northwest, the expanse of Moose River Mountain can be seen past small wetlands.

(B) After the first rise of the eastern end of Brown's Tract Trail has leveled off, less than fifteen minutes from the old sign, turn right off the trail and begin ascending the shoulder of a hill. Swinging west, you should be able to follow a ridge to the large, open area on its summit. There are views in several directions of nearby ridges and distant mountains.

(C) A steep shoulder of Moose River Mountain extends down toward the Okara Lakes. There are a few exposed ledges that allow unrestricted views ranging from the hills on the south to the distant mountains in the east. East of the junction where the Cedar Pond trail meets the Brown's Tract Trail, you will notice the base of the ridge; this is a good spot to begin your ascent. Hike northeast along the top of the steep shoulder, and you will come to several small open ledges in a span of 1.5 miles. It is easy to spend an afternoon on the ridge, and you can return the same way or drop down to Rock Pond and follow the wetlands along its outlet back to the trail.

(D) Look for a large white pine on the left side of the trail, five minutes after crossing Middle Settlement Creek. Turn right off the trail here, and a twenty-minute ascent will bring you to the top of a rocky ledge with views of the hills in the Black River Wild Forest Area to the south and McCauley Mountain to the east.

View from ridge north of Okara Lakes, Old Forge in the distance

103 Cedar Pond Trail

Hiking, lean-to, fishing
3.1 miles, 1½ hours, easy grades, map XI

With its brushy shoreline and dense stands of conifers, Cedar Pond is an unlikely destination for swimming or fishing. It is, however, a good location to observe the plants, animals, and birds that inhabit this type of wetland community. The old, decaying lean-to which stood at the trail junction has been removed and will not be replaced.

The trail has red DEC markers and begins on the Brown's Tract Trail 0.3 mile east of the Scusa Access Trail junction. There are a few annoying wet spots, but the hiking is easy as the trail generally follows contours through a mostly hardwood forest. At 0.5 mile, the yellow-marked trail to Grass Pond, section 104, heads off to the right. A gradual descent brings you to Grass Pond outlet, which you can easily cross on stones. You cross several small streams and can then see Cedar Pond basin through the trees to the left. Dropping into a low area, the fragrances of balsam and spruce fill the air. An old spring hole lies to the right edge of the trail, just before the junction where the red markers end. The trail to Middle Branch Lake, section 105, turns right while the trail to Middle Settlement Lake, section 107, continues ahead.

104 Grass Pond

Hiking, campsites
1.9 miles, 1 hour, easy grades, map XI

The trail to Grass Pond turns to the right 0.5 mile along the red-marked trail to Cedar Pond. A single, narrow sign on the left side of the trail points the way, but it is not easy to see, so you might miss the junction. Yellow DEC markers lead 0.5 mile over a rise, then steadily descend to a campsite on the edge of the pond's brushy outlet. As you walk through the leatherleaf and sheep laurel toward the pond, you see signs of past and present beaver activity, tracks of racoons and otters, and waterlilies in abundance.

105 Middle Branch Lake

Hiking, camping, lean-to, swimming, fishing
4.4 miles, 2¼ hours, moderate grades, map XI

From the junction near Cedar Pond, two trails with yellow DEC markers begin. You head southwest to Middle Settlement Lake, section 107. To get to Middle Branch Lake, follow the one heading north. The trail is very wet for about 150 feet, but soon improves as it ascends away from the junction. After ten minutes, you reach a height-of-land. Then the trail descends to a wet area and as the descent becomes steeper, about a five minute walk, you cross a stream on old rotted planks. After a few more ups and downs and a tiny stream crossing, you soon come to a junction. The yellow-marked trail continues on another 0.7 mile to the Big Otter Trail, section 115. Turn left and follow red DEC markers along a high rib of land for 0.3 mile. There is a campsite on the trail just before it drops to the edge of Middle Branch Lake where the lean-to stands. This is a newer lean-to which replaced the one destroyed by fire in 1981. Its privy is in good shape. A narrow path leads to rocks at the water's edge from which you can swim or enjoy the view down this attractive lake. You may find it is a quieter alternative to the more popular Middle Settlement Lake.

An unmarked path to the right leads in 100 yards to a campsite with a boat, then continues on to the northern tip of the lake. Another path heads south along the edge, crossing a wet area and coming to a campsite in 0.3 mile. Nesting loons may disturb your sleep.

106 Middle Settlement Lake from the Brown's Tract Trail

Hiking, lean-to, camping, swimming, fishing, lookout
3.2 miles, 1½ hours, easy grades, map XI

Middle Settlement Lake is undeniably the most popular spot in the Ha-de-ron-dah Wilderness Area. It offers hikers just about everything they seek in backwoods adventure. The lean-to and privy are in good shape and campsites can be found nearby. Large slabs of rock allow good access to the water for fishing and swimming. There is even a small lookout twenty minutes away. This is an excellent choice for first-time backpackers. Once they see the area's beauty and hear the loons' nocturnal voicings, they will surely want to return.

The most direct route uses a combination of four trails beginning at the Scusa Access trailhead. Turn left at the junction with the Brown's Tract Trail and follow it for 0.9 mile to the junction with the blue-marked trail to Middle Settlement Lake as described in previous sections. Follow the blue trail as it heads northeast, crossing a stream and coming to a low area in just over ten minutes. The wetland to your right is at a bend on the Grass Pond outlet as it makes its way to Cedar Pond and not Middle Settlement Creek, as the 1958 USGS topographic map of McKeever implies.

The trail now begins a moderate climb over the shoulder of a hill, leveling off in ten minutes. A steady descent takes you past a stream and into a valley at the upper end of Middle Settlement Lake where the trail ends at a junction. This is a most scenic area. In front of you lies a jumble of boulders, some quite large, that have broken away from the steep rock wall behind them. One large slab resting on some smaller boulders forms a cave of sorts and over the years, people have filled in gaps with other stones to create a cozy shelter.

At the junction, the yellow-marked trail from Cedar Pond, section 107, comes in on the right. You should turn left and follow its continuation west along the north shore of the lake. The trail used to go through the flooded edge of the lake, but it now turns right, ducking between boulders on a drier route. As you start to rise away from the water's edge, a trail with red DEC markers turns right and leads 0.15 mile to a lookout from the top of the rock wall. This junction is marked with a narrow sign and is easy to miss. A brisk five-minute climb brings you out on a ledge with a view southwest over the lake. It is a good spot to have lunch or sunbathe.

Continuing west on the yellow-marked trail, notice the tall pines on your left. A path leads 50 feet to a campsite beneath them where slabs of rock afford good swimming. As you near the lean-to, you may see the traces of an old trail that followed a wet route nearer the water. The privy soon appears on your right and ahead is the lean-to, perched on a rocky bluff above the water. A path to the left leads to sloping rocks and good swimming.

The trail continues beyond the lean-to, passes a few other campsites, then drops to cross the multi-dammed outlet on an old beaver dam. It then climbs above the level of the lake to a junction 0.5 mile from the lean-to. The blue-marked trail to the right leads to Lost Lake, section 109, while the yellow-marked trail continues on to the Brown's Tract Trail and Copper Lake Road, section 108.

107 Middle Settlement Lake from Cedar Pond

Link trail offering loop options
0.9 mile between junctions, 25 minutes, easy grades, map XI

At the junction near Cedar Pond, this yellow-marked trail passes behind a large rock and heads southwest, crossing Cedar Pond Outlet, which is aflame with cardinal flowers in late July. The small bridge that was once here is gone, and there are plans to replace it with a more permanent structure, but for now, you must cross on stones and logs. The trail is wet for a few feet, then dries as it begins to climb through a draw. Descending from the draw, you come to the boulder-filled valley and trail junction at the northeast end of Middle Settlement Lake, section 106.

108 Middle Settlement Lake from Copper Lake Road

Hiking
2.4 miles, 1¼ hours, moderate grades, map XI

Since public access is currently prohibited from Copper Lake Road, annual maintenance of this trail has been postponed, and its future depends on whether or not land or an easement for access can be aquired as called for in the Unit Management Plan. It is, however, still well marked and in fair shape. It begins on the Brown's Tract Trail, section 101, 0.2 mile from the road.

Following yellow DEC markers, the trail steadily ascends away from the junction through a scenic hardwood forest with large rocks lying about. Wet areas, grown-in sections, and occasional blowdown slow your pace. In fifteen minutes you descend to cross an attractive, but wet little vly. An old road coming in from the left meets the trail about 150 feet beyond the vly. Old trail signs direct you to the right, paralleling the vly before turning north toward the lake. The trail continues over pleasant, rolling terrain, crossing a stream in twenty minutes. Rising over the shoulder of a hill, you begin a steady descent to the edge of Middle Settlement Lake's lower bay where there is a campsite. From here, the trail works its way clockwise around the bay to a junction with the blue-marked trail to Lost Lake, section 109. The lean-to is another 0.5 mile up the yellow-marked trail and is described in detail in section 106.

109 Lost Lake

Hiking
5.1 miles (from Scusa Access), 2¾ hours, relatively level, map XI

The trail to Lost Lake has a very wild character since it does not receive as much use as other trails in the area. It passes through varying terrain and certain sections have always been subject to flooding. To make maintenance duties more difficult, an extensive section of trail was blocked by a massive blowdown in 1986. The trail may be cleared by 1988, but the flooding is still unpredictable. These obstacles should not deter you from visiting this small lake, however, for it is a very scenic spot with its high banks of bare rock.

From the junction at the west end of Middle Settlement Lake, follow blue DEC markers as the trail passes through a rocky landscape. Ravens may be seen or heard near the jagged rock outcroppings to the north. The mixed forest becomes more dense as you drop to pass a small swamp. In twenty minutes, you come to the blowdown. As of this writing (1987), a herd path angles off to the right, by-passing the worst of the tangle, but the going is still rough. The path then swings left into the middle of the area to pick up the trail that has been cleared the rest of the way.

Just past the blowdown, the first of two wet areas is encountered. You must either cross on top of the beaver dam to the right or test your agility on the rocks and logs to the left. Both ways are quite difficult. The trail beyond has been rerouted to the left to avoid a flooded area, but it is so wet, you might wonder how the old route could be worse! Fortunately, you are soon on dry ground as you climb up to cross the Herkimer-Lewis county line marked by a sign on the left. Too soon, you come to the second wet area, but it is not as bad as the first. Again, you detour to the left on a new section of trail to avoid the worst. Hopefully your discomfort has not distracted you away from appreciating the thick black spruce and sphagnum-covered ground.

Finally, ten minutes later, you come to Lost Lake. You have covered less than 1.5 miles from the last junction, but it may have taken over an hour. You will want to relax, refresh and take in the beauty of your surroundings, and the best place to do that is from the top of the rocky hump to the left. Leave the trail and follow along the shoreline to the left, scrambling up the shoulder of the rock. From its top you look straight down the outlet. Huge slabs of bare rock line the opposite bank and, below, boggy plants interrupt the surface.

While at the lake, you should visit its outlet. The trail crosses at the base of an old beaver dam, one of three that break the water's flow before it tumbles over rock slabs and off into the woods.

110 East Pine Pond and Pine Lake

Hiking, lean-to, camping, fishing
7.4 miles (from Scusa Access), 5 hours, 2.3 miles from Lost Lake, easy grades, map XI

On the western edge of Ha-de-ron-dah, near East Pine Pond and Pine Lake, you can see evidence of the sandy glacial outwash plain that typifies

Lost Lake

so much of the neighboring topography of the Independence River Wild Forest Area. Sand-tolerant pines are more common; low, boggy basins and small eskers appear in the woods. The blue-marked trail from Lost Lake is quite interesting, winding its way through varied forest types and between wetlands. With all the diversions encountered on the series of trails that take you from your car to this area, it is easy to spend five hours making the journey.

Leaving Lost Lake, section 109, the rolling trail passes an old beaver dam on the left at a stream crossing. After contouring around a hill to the west, you will notice the hardwoods getting thinner as the forest floor becomes grassy. After twenty-five minutes, the basin of Middle Branch Creek is visible through the trees to the right. The trail crosses a brushy area where club mosses cover the ground, then climbs a bank overlooking the extensive wetlands of Middle Branch Creek. A steep drop brings you to an elaborate wood and steel bridge spanning the creek.

Open hardwoods continue to dominate the landscape for the next fifteen minutes, then the forest character abruptly changes. Dense spruce and balsam with a few pines intermixed lead you to a small wet area crossed by an old boardwalk. Tunneling through the evergreens on the opposite side, the trail pitches up onto an esker revealing East Pine Pond on the other side. A herd path leads right a short distance, allowing wider views of the pond. Its low, grass and shrub shoreline and floating plants would seem to be ideal moose habitat.

Dropping off the esker, the trail crosses the outlet on a second wood and steel bridge. Scotch pine grow in the sandy soil beyond the bridge, and as you enter the tall woods again, take time to notice the large poplars. East Pine Pond reappears briefly on your right and soon, Pine Lake is visible to the left. A faint path leads along its southeastern edge through pines and gray birches to a campsite. The blue-marked trail ends just ahead at a junction with an old road that has red DEC markers. It is on the border of the wilderness area and also has snowmobile trail markers. Turning left, you follow along the north edge of the lake, passing a campsite on the left. In three minutes, a yellow-marked trail turns right and leads 500 feet to a lean-to and privy, both in fair shape. The area is open enough to allow a few tents and a path leads away 100 feet to a stream. The red-marked trail continues ahead for another three minutes to a junction where it turns southwest. A yellow-marked trail stays with the snowmobile trail and leads 2.8 miles to Partridgeville Road. These routes are in the Independence River Wild Forest Area and are described in *Discover the Southwestern Adirondacks*.

Big Otter Lake

111 Big Otter Lake from Pine Lake

Hiking, camping, fishing
1.6 miles (between junctions), 45 minutes, relatively level, map XI

You can follow the red-marked snowmobile trail along the boundary east and north to Big Otter Lake where it connects with the Big Otter Trail. ATVs occasionally stray off the jeep road north of Otter Creek onto the trail, but their impact has been minimal . . . so far.

Leaving the unmarked junction with the trail to Lost Lake, the wide, red-marked trail rises into an evergreen dominated woods with large poplars to the right. East Pine Pond can be seen once again before the trail swings away to the north, contouring around a hill to the west. The forest type changes to open hardwoods and many boulders lie strewn about to your left. Within thirty minutes you will see signs indicating that the trail turns right. An unmarked path curves left and follows an old road 0.1 mile to a foot bridge over Otter Creek. Just over ten minutes later, you reach a junction at the extreme western end of Big Otter Lake where a heavy duty steel and wood bridge crosses its outlet. Across the bridge is the jeep road; the blue-marked trail heading east leads to the Big Otter Trail, section 112.

112   The Big Otter Trail to Big Otter Lake

Old road, trail, hiking, cross-country skiing, camping,
swimming, fishing, picnicking, waterfall
7.8 miles, 3½ hours, easy grades, map XI

In the 1930s the Civilian Conservation Corps built a road from Thendara to Big Otter Lake for fire protection. Today, it exists as a wide, well-maintained foot trail that is occasionally used by horseback riders. It passes over several easy ups and downs through a mostly hardwood forest, descending at times to evergreen lowlands. In addition to blue DEC markers, it has yellow ski trail markers and is classified as a novice ski trail.

To reach the trailhead, turn north off NY 28 onto Tower Road, immediately south of the railroad underpass at Thendara. Follow the road 0.4 mile to a parking area. There is a barrier across the road with a register and large wooden map of the area just beyond. This is private land.

The trail ascends from the register along a short section that is also part of the Town of Webb snowmobile trail system. Skiers should be alert to oncoming machines, especially on their way out. After 400 feet, the snowmobile trail goes straight and the Big Otter Trail swings left, snaking its way up to a level stretch through recently timbered lands. In less than ten minutes, a gate across the trail marks the state land boundary. Moderate descents take you down to the wetlands of Indian Brook, which you cross in a grassy, open area, 1 mile from the trailhead. The large pile of sand and gravel to the right is an esker, a deposit of glacial runoff ten thousand years old.

Beyond the esker, the trail reenters the woods and in ten minutes passes the junction with the yellow-marked trail to Little Simon Pond and East Pond, section 113. You now begin an easy ascent up the shoulder of Moose River Mountain that ends 0.8 mile later at a wide, level section of trail. An abandoned trail turns left and leads 0.5 mile to a clearing where the fire tower once stood. It was removed in 1977 and maintenance on the trail discontinued. There is no view now.

The Big Otter Trail works its way around and down the mountain in a series of descents broken by occasional even sections. A major stream is crossed, and just off the trail to the right is a campsite. Another campsite can be found at a clearing on the right a few minutes past the stream. The appearance of spruce and balsam stands tell you that you have entered the lowlands of the South Inlet. For the next twenty minutes, there is little elevation change until a short drop brings you to the junction of the yellow-marked trail to Middle Branch Lake, section 115. The trail swings to the north and moderately ascends a small hill. Gradually descending the opposite side, you swing west and reenter the spruce dominated lowlands.

At a point 6 miles in, after a little over two hours of hiking, you enter an extensive open area where South Inlet comes close to the trail. This is a most scenic spot and you will want to pause to take pictures and do some birding. As you emerge from the woods, there is another small esker to your left. Woodpeckers, cedar waxwings, jays, and chickadees are just some of the birds seen darting between the tall spruces and tamaracks lining the grassy old roadway. Ahead, a large wetland on the south drains under the trail into dense alders around the inlet. Depending on beaver activity, flooding can occur, but the way is usually passable.

Beyond the open area, the trail rises into hardwoods. About 150 feet in, look for a faint path that turns off to the right. It may be hard to follow, but a five-minute bushwhack to the northeast will take you to a beautiful waterfall on the South Inlet, less than 0.1 mile away. The water cascades over ledges and boulders for a total drop of about seven feet into a wide, deep pool. You can take pictures and have lunch from nearby rocks.

Back on the trail, at a junction less than ten minutes past the open area, the red-marked trail to Lost Creek, section 116, heads north. In another fifteen minutes, you will pass an old beaver dam on the left with dead standing timber behind it. Not far ahead on the right, a path leads 200 feet to a flat, open area on the shore of Big Otter Lake. The area is quite close to the water where impact can be serious, so visitors should make an effort to protect it.

The trail soon narrows, crosses a wet area and in ten minutes, ends at a junction near the Big Otter Lake outlet. The red-marked trail from East Pine Pond and Pine Lake, section 110, comes in ahead to the left and continues across the bridge over the outlet.

113 Little Simon Pond and East Pond

Hiking, camping, picnicking, swimming
4.3 miles, 2¼ hours, moderate grades, map XI

At a junction 1.5 miles along the Big Otter Trail, section 112, a trail marked with yellow DEC markers heads north. This narrow trail is a delightful wilderness route with many interesting changes in scenery and terrain. After winding through an open hardwood section, you come to a

broad wetland along a branch of South Inlet. A short wet stretch is followed by a long plank walkway that allows an easy crossing through the alder-choked waters. Several species of birds, from hummingbirds to great blue herons, can be found in this diverse area.

The trail rises away from the wetland, goes over the shoulder of a small hill, then drops to a very muddy spot at the edge of another wet area. Here, the trail crosses a second branch of South Inlet on large rocks. Reentering the woods, you come to a bend in ten minutes where a path ahead follows a faint old road north. The trail turns left and in another ten minutes, crosses a scenic vly that abounds in blueberries in July. Moving on, you see another vly through the trees to your left.

As you near Little Simon Pond you begin to see blowdown, caused by high winds in November of 1988. The trail has been cleared, but you may be disappointed to find that the inviting rock slabs and two small campsites on the knoll to the right of the outlet are now covered with fallen timber and are inaccessible. The beaver-dammed outlet retains its beauty, however, with water tumbling away over a series of rocky steps. This peaceful spot, less than two hours and 3.5 miles in, is a worthy destination in itself.

The trail crosses the outlet of Little Simon Pond on a plank bridge, travels along its western edge, then crosses an inlet—your parting view of the pond. For the next ten minutes, a steady, moderate ascent takes you through tall hardwoods on a hillside. The dense understory creates an especially wild feeling. After a short, level stretch, you descend to a junction where the blue-marked link trail, section 117, comes in from the west. Continuing ahead on the yellow-marked trail, a swampy bay of East Pond is visible through the trees to the left. Another junction is reached in 5 minutes, this one leading along a red-marked trail to Blackfoot Pond, section 114. After crossing a stream, you pass a clearing on the right where you could pitch a tent. Insulators and cable on a fallen tree are evidence of a logging camp that once operated in the area. Not far away is the clearing once occupied by a lean-to that burned down in the late 1970s. Old privy parts and a junk pile lie off in the trees to the left. The trail winds on a few more feet, ending at the brushy edge of the pond. A small, exposed rock provides a limited perch for relaxing and enjoying a view down the pond toward the outlet. Swimming is possible from the rock, but the bottom is mucky. Most of the pond's remaining shoreline is brushy and areas of dead standing timber add a deep woods mystery to the scene.

Waterfall on South Inlet near flooded area on Big Otter Truck Trail

114 Blackfoot Pond and the Mica Mine

Hiking, camping
1 mile, 25 minutes from junction near East Pond, 100-foot elevation change, map XI

From the last junction on the yellow-marked trail, just before the East Pond campsites, the red-marked trail to Blackfoot Pond climbs northeast through a draw. It parallels a stream on your left and in some sections, the route of an old logging road is evident. After reaching a height-of-land, the trail dips to cross a muddy inlet within sight of the pond. A brushy, swampy shoreline makes exploration difficult, but enhances the pond's wild character.

The trail goes beyond the inlet for a short distance. After five minutes, it passes, on the left, a rock outcrop with deposits of mica. This mineral is easily separated into thin, translucent layers and in the past was used for windows in stoves and lanterns. Past the mine, the markers end at the site of old logging camp where rusted pieces of hardware lie scattered.

115 Middle Branch Lake from Big Otter Trail

Hiking, camping, swimming, fishing
5.9 miles, 2¼ hours from parking area, map XI

Walk 0.3 mile from spur to the lean-to on Middle Branch Lake, then follow the yellow-marked trail of section 105 that passes the lake and ends 0.7 mile to the north at a junction on the Big Otter Trail, 4.9 miles from the Tower Road trailhead, section 112. This narrow, easy segment not only allows access to the lake from the north, but also provides a link for extended loop hikes. It traverses relatively even terrain through a mostly hardwood forest with one major stream crossing.

116 Lost Creek

Hiking, camping, swimming, fishing
8.4 miles, 3½ hours, relatively level, map XI

At a junction about 6.5 miles along the Big Otter Trail, not far beyond the marshes where South Inlet comes close to the trail, section 112, the red-marked trail heads northeast for 1.9 miles, ending in the vicinity of Lost

Creek. The trail was marked, cut out, and brushed in 1987. You cross several seasonal streams with little difficulty, but they can be quite muddy.

From the junction, you quickly come to the South Inlet where there is a new bridge, installed in the fall of 1987. The previous bridge washed out several years ago, and until the reconstruction, the crossing of the inlet was difficult if not sometimes impossible. Once on the other side, you must negotiate a very wet section. After fifteen minutes, Big Otter Lake is visible through the trees. A fishermen's path leads to a campsite near the shore, but it is hard to find if you are unfamiliar with the area. Bushwhacking is always possible, but it may bring you out at an undesirable spot, so keep a watchful eye. About thirty minutes past the inlet, another faint path leads to a large campsite near the boggy northeast edge of the lake. Whoever has been using this site has been careful not to spoil the area, setting a good example for those who follow.

Another fifteen minutes takes you through a few muddy spots to the junction where the link trail to East Pond, section 117, turns off to the right. The Lost Creek Trail drops down to the East Pond Outlet, which you can easily cross on rocks during times of average water levels. As you climb the steep pitch up the opposite bank, it is evident from the contours that you are following the route of an old logging road. Markers become increasingly rare and in 15 minutes, disappear altogether. By following the old road, you will end up in a large clearing on the edge of Lost Creek. This was the site of an old logging camp, and a little exploration may yield some interesting artifacts.

117 East Pond-Lost Creek Link Trail

Hiking
2.1 miles, 1 hour, easy grades, map XI

From its junction with the East Pond Trail, section 113 , this trail follows blue DEC markers to a junction on the Lost Creek Trail, section 116. It was almost completely clear of blowdown in 1987, but since it is designated a "minimal maintenance" trail, conditions may be uncertain in the next few years. The eastern half is well marked and fairly well defined as it parallels within sight of the multi-dammed extension of the East Pond Outlet. In twenty minutes, it drops to a wet area near the end of the extension where spruces dominate. The trail continues to follow the outlet closely for a few more minutes, then moves farther away. Several grown-in sections and fewer markers present difficulties along the western half as it gradually descends to the junction.

From Old Forge to Eagle Bay

FROM ITS BEGINNINGS as an obscure wilderness outpost, the village of Old Forge has grown into a major resort community. Lying at the foot of the Fulton Chain of Lakes, it is the western terminus of the popular Adirondack canoe system. The surrounding tracts of Forest Preserve lands are highly prized by hunters, trappers, and anglers. In winter, McCauley Mountain offers both downhill and cross-country skiing, while snowmobilers can find miles of groomed trails along the Town of Webb Trail System.

During the first half of the nineteenth century, woodsmen who used the area built lean-tos along the streams and lakes, occupying them as squatters. Even the builders of the first permanent camps and inns were largely conducting their business on the lands of others. For many of the title holders, however, it was a way for their land to be developed at little expense to themselves. Under this system, the area prospered and famous establishments such as the Forge House and the Bald Mountain House arose, catering to the affluent as well as the unknown. Today, many camps, public and private, in addition to primary and secondary homes, line the shores of most of the lakes.

118 The North Branch of the Moose River
Canoeing
11 miles, map XII

Between Rondaxe Lake, and its confluence with the Middle Branch at Old Forge, the North Branch of the Moose River twists and contorts, folding back upon itself in a series of oxbows that almost double the distance between those points if measured in a straight line. Though the banks along this waterway are privately owned, it has long been a traditional route for the public to paddle. Outfitters in Old Forge rent canoes and

Fourth Lake from Vista Trail

equipment and offer a shuttle service between endpoints, allowing many people to enjoy an easy through trip, aided by the gentle current. A few low beaver dams and one short carry are the only interruptions you will encounter, but you should allow four hours to fully enjoy your surroundings. The best time to begin your trip is at dawn. Not only will you avoid the midday flotillas, but you will be on the river at a time when wildlife activity is highest.

To get to the upper end of the route, turn left off NY 28 onto Rondaxe Road, 4.5 miles north of the tourist information center in Old Forge. In 1.3 miles, the old bed of the Raquette Lake Railway comes in from the right and parallels Rondaxe Road. North Rondaxe Road turns right in another 0.2 mile and you should take it for 0.5 mile to a bridge over the North Branch. Cross the bridge and park on the shoulder of the road; a path on the upstream side of the bridge leads to the water. This is the customary put-in point for the trip, and since the land is private, proper respect will keep it open to the public. The dam at Rondaxe Lake's outlet is 0.3 mile upstream.

Turning downstream, the river meanders between forested banks, passing under an iron bridge at 0.9 mile. The trees slowly recede from the water's edge, shrubs grow thick along the banks and an occasional sandbar invites you to stop and stretch your legs. A large wetland follows where tall grasses provide cover and nesting areas for a variety of birds. Occasionally, the grasses part to reveal a path used by an animal for access to the water. Deer feed in the shallows and great blue herons probe through the weeds for fish and frogs. As you round each bend, you may surprise muskrats, beavers, otters, and ducks swimming along the bank.

Well past the halfway point, after 7.5 miles, the river nears the abandoned tracks of the Adirondack Division Railroad up on the right bank. A short distance ahead, you will pass through a narrow section with high banks where a sawmill once operated. This spot was known as Moulin, and you can still see some of the old concrete work that supported the mill. The river continues to parallel the railroad in its own sinuous way until it reaches Indian Rapids near the Thendara Golf Course. The rapids can be shot in high water by experienced whitewater paddlers, but you should pull to the left above the rocks of the rapids. A carry of under 0.2 mile leads to a bridge over the rocky stretch of river and takes you to a put-in point on the right bank below the rapids. The banks are once again lined with tall trees and you may see woodchucks peeking out from burrows under the exposed tree roots. You may also see golf balls lying on the sandy river bottom. NY 28 is a mile away and as you near it, the banks open up as before. The Middle Branch, draining the Fulton Chain, enters on the right in a large marsh next to the highway. After crossing under the highway bridge, you can take out on the right where a rough path climbs the bank to the road. If you wish to park in this area, you will have to ask permission at one of the local establishments.

You can easily paddle up the Middle Branch to the dam near the tourist information center, an additional distance of 1.5 miles.

119 Rondaxe Lake

Canoeing, map XII

Most of Rondaxe Lake's shoreline is privately owned and many camps lie along its lower half. The upper reaches of the lake are quite wild, however, and rushes and pickerel-weed rise up from the shallows. Paddling up through a narrow, wooded channel will take you into a large bay where the North Branch of the Moose River enters from the northeast and the outlet of Moss Lake, section 134, enters on the southeast. Slide Off Mountian, section 120, rises steeply to the north, and you may see or hear ravens as they soar to and from their rocky perches scanning the ground for prey.

You can continue up the North Branch a little over 0.5 mile farther before rocky shallows turn you back. Paddling up the Moss Lake Outlet will take you into a large open marsh where you are likely to see great blue herons wading in the grass. You can not go far beyond the marsh since dense alders block the channel.

Access to the lake from state land follows a roundabout route, but unless you can get permission from one of the camp owners to cross their land, it is the only way. Follow Rondaxe Road north from NY 28 for 1.5 miles to the point where North Rondaxe Road comes in from the right. Follow it for 0.6 mile, crossing the bridge over the North Branch, to the intersection where North Shore Road turns off to the right. After 0.5 mile, you will see the yellow-blazed boundary line of state land on the left side of the road that it follows for 0.3 mile. The road then curves right, away from the line and ends at a turnaround near some camps. You should park your vehicle on the side of the road near the blazed boundary in an area where it will not present a hazard to local traffic. Carry your canoe east along the boundary line for 600 feet through the woods and enter the water at a boggy bay on the northwest edge of the lake.

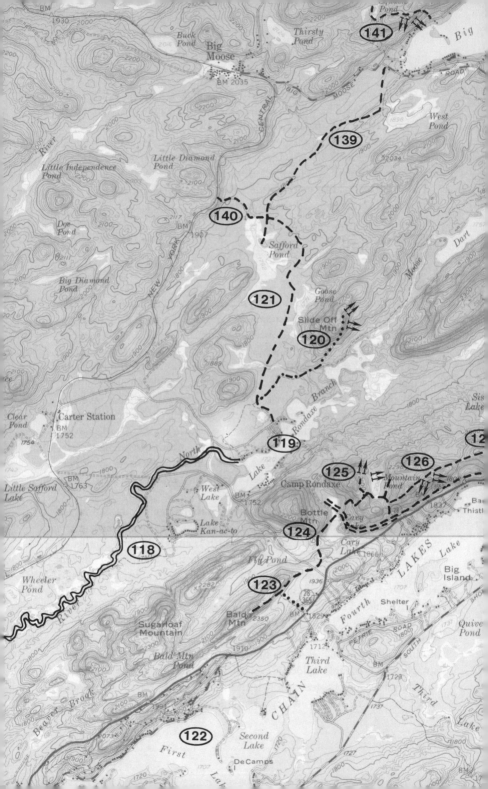

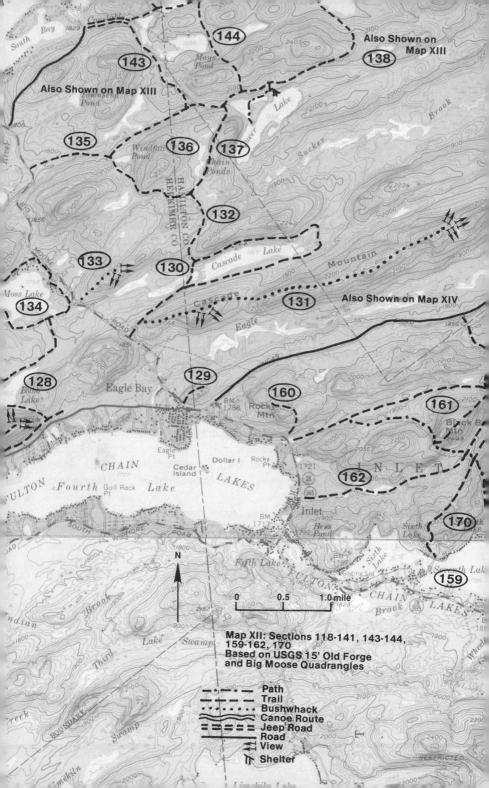

Map XII: Sections 118-141, 143-144, 159-162, 170 Based on USGS 15' Old Forge and Big Moose Quadrangles

·–·–·–	Path
– – –	Trail
········	Bushwhack
≈≈≈≈	Canoe Route
= = =	Jeep Road
———	Road
⤜	View
⌂	Shelter

120   Slide Off Mountain

Bushwhack from snowmobile trail, limited views
1.9 miles, 1½ hours, 280-foot vertical rise, map XII

A snowmobile trail follows an old road from Rondaxe Lake to Dart Lake, paralleling the North Branch of the Moose River on the north. It enters private land near the upper bay of Rondaxe Lake, but the landowners allow snowmobiles to pass through, all the way to Big Moose Road. The area around Dart Lake is owned by the Rochester YMCA, who operate Camp Gorham on its north shore. To climb Slide Off Mountain, you must approach it from the west along this trail.

The trail begins at a sign on the north side of North Shore Road, 0.7 mile from the intersection with North Rondaxe Road, section 119. Park as you would for canoeing Rondaxe Lake. Following orange and red snowmobile trail markers, the trail heads north, coming in under ten minutes to a junction with the trail from Big Moose Road that passes West, Safford, and Goose ponds, sections 121, 139, and 140. Stay on the main trail, now heading east-northeast and in fifteen more minutes, you will come to two bridges at the bottom of a steep drop where the trail crosses the outlet of Goose Pond. In five more minutes, 1.2 miles from the road, the upper bay of Rondaxe Lake appears to your right. The trail enters private land at this point and markers end. To your left, the yellow-blazed state land boundary line angles off to the northeast. A bushwhack along this line will take you to the base of the cliffs of Slide Off Mountain in five minutes.

The woods on the western slopes of the mountain is encumbered with blowdown and tangles, and even though hunters approach the mountain from that direction, you may have difficulty finding or following any paths. You will avoid some difficult navigating if you ascend just to the left of the cliffs even though the way is steep. Reaching the wooded summit after twenty-five minutes, hike around to the eastern side where there is a lookout near the top of the cliffs. A blue-painted can cover marks the end of a path that ascends from private land on the east. Your view is up along the valley of the North Branch of the Moose River where Dart Lake lies off to the east. Hills of the Pigeon Lake Wilderness Area rise up beyond and the summits of Pilgrim and West mountains etch the horizon above Dart Lake. To the southeast, a broad ridge separating Moss Lake from the North Branch blocks more distant views. Below on your right, wetlands of Rondaxe Lake's upper bay spread through the valley. Onondaga Mountain rises to the south, and a tiny portion of Fourth Lake is visible over its eastern shoulder.

121 Goose Pond

Trail, hiking, cross-country skiing
1.5 miles, 1 hour, relatively level, map XII

The shortest approach to Goose Pond is from a snowmobile trail north of Rondaxe Lake. It is the southern end of a trail that heads northeast to Big Moose Road, passing Safford and West ponds along the way, sections 139 and 140. Until recently, snowmobiles used this trail as far north as Safford Pond, but it is now filling in with sapplings and viburnums and appears to be abandoned.

The trail heads northeast from its junction with the snowmobile trail along the North Branch of the Moose River, 0.3 mile from North Shore Road, section 120. It passes through flat terrain crossing a wet vly in fifteen minutes, 0.4 mile from the junction. In another 0.8 mile, you will reach a junction with a side trail that turns right and leads 75 feet to the edge of Goose Pond. Its brushy shoreline is punctuated with dead, standing timber and fallen logs laden with mosses and sundews. Pitcher plants thrive in the quaking sphagnum along its wide, boggy outlet. Traces of corduroy along the eastern edge indicate the route of an old logging road.

The snowmobile trail continues on, joining the blue-marked foot trail, 1.3 miles later near Safford Pond. After paralleling Goose Pond for five minutes, it swings northwest, then turns northeast, crossing a small stream in a vly. A wide swing to the northwest takes you to the junction with the blue-marked trail, thirty-five minutes from Goose Pond.

122 First Lake to Fifth Lake on the Fulton Chain

Canoeing, fishing, camping
11 miles, map XII

In 1811, the New York State Legislature appointed Robert Fulton of steamboat fame, to a commission studying the feasibility of establishing a water route from the Hudson River to the Great Lakes that would pass through the northern part of the state. His reports contained references to the beauty and potential utility of the chain of eight Middle Branch Moose Lakes, as they were then known. Before long, his name came to be associated with these waters and the term Fulton Chain of Lakes spread into common usage. The intended waterway was eventually constructed far to the south of the Adirondacks and though Fulton's name stayed with the lakes, his connection with them passed into obscurity.

Navigation on the Fulton Chain evolved in much the same manner as on other large lakes and chains. Canoes, guideboats, steamers, speedboats, and pleasure craft each experienced their heyday as people and technology changed. As part of a network of canoe routes and carries, however, canoes never lost their appeal on the chain; and, each year, legions of paddlers begin trips here that may end days later on the other side of the park. Time is extremely variable depending on your energy, how much exploration you wish to do and, especially, on how strong the wind is blowing—it can be formidable.

At the tourist information center in Old Forge, a large wooden sign and map show the Fulton Chain canoe route, and you can launch your canoe here. Paddle across the pond created by the dam and proceed up the narrow channel 1.5 miles to First Lake. Heading east along the right, south, edge for 0.8 mile, you soon cross over to the east side and enter Second Lake near DeCamp Island. With not nearly as much development along its shores, Second Lake is a pleasant change of scene. The lake narrows as a long peninsula extends from the right, beyond which, you enter Third Lake. Swinging north, you will come to the slender outlet of Fourth Lake. You paddle 4.5 miles to reach this point.

With a length of 5.5 miles, Fourth Lake is the largest in the chain and this is where poor weather will be noticed the most. On the other hand, you will at least get a little more space between you and shore or other watercraft. The views of the surrounding mountains are exceptional. Most of the high points on the north have trails to lookouts and are descibed later. On days of favorable visibility, distant mountains rising above the expanse of water look farther away than they really are. The large island you see after entering the lake is Alger Island and its fifteen lean-tos are administered by the DEC as a state campground. You can obtain a camping permit from the caretaker for which there is a charge. This is a well-maintained facility with privies, fireplaces, and a lovely picnic area. Public access to the lake is possible from a DEC parking area and boat launch on the shore south of the island, off South Shore Road. There is also a public boat launch off NY 28, 0.5 mile south of Inlet.

The inlet is at the upper end of Fourth Lake, on the southeastern shore. A 0.5 mile paddle up it will take you to Fifth Lake, the smallest of the chain. Once across it, you will only be able to proceed up its inlet about 0.3 mile before reaching a take-out point below unnavigable water. Ahead, you must carry up to NY 28, then along a road to the dam at the foot of Sixth Lake, a distance of 0.7 mile.

123 Bald Mountain Trails
Trail, hiking, views, picnicking
1 mile, 30 minutes, 414-foot vertical rise, map XII

Bald Mountain is the most popular hike in the Fulton Chain region. The hike is short and despite a few steep sections, easy enough that anyone with the inclination can make the trip with little difficulty. A fire tower on its summit is still maintained, but, even without it, you can enjoy good views in all directions from the extensive open rock along the summit ridge.

Originally known as Pond Mountain because of the small pond at the base of its rocky southern face, it was renamed Bald Mountain in reference to its open summit. The trapper, Nat Foster, used to climb the ridge often to survey his surroundings, and one writer of the time penned the term Foster's Observatory in hopes of perpetuating the memory of his woodsman hero.

The open summit played a significant role in Verplanck Colvin's survey work, as it was the only bald summit he found in the western Adirondacks. In October 1876, he described the mountain as he approached it from Fourth Lake.

> Beyond the forest at the foot of Fourth Lake, arose, like a battlement, a mountain crest all devoid of timber; its black front frowning southward upon the valley of the lakes. . . . To avoid the common and indefinite name of 'Bald Mountain,' which is given to so many of the cleared peaks, I now named this Mount St. Louis; a party from that western city having for many seasons annually made their camp on the lake at the foot of the mountain.

The party Colvin referred to was that of Benjamin Stickney, a wealthy businessman. Joseph Grady, historian of the Fulton Chain and Big Moose region, wrote that Stickney christened the peak Mount St. Louis in 1846 when he and his guests conducted the first of twenty-five annual flag-raising ceremonies at its top.

Eventually, Bald Mountain regained its present name, even though the state officially calls it Rondaxe Mountain to avoid confusion with another Bald Mountain fire tower elsewhere in the state.

Rondaxe Road turns left off NY 28, 4.5 miles north of the tourist information center in Old Forge. Follow it just over 0.1 mile to a large parking area on the left. Park here for Bald Mountain and also for the destinations along the blue-marked trail described in sections 124 through 127. As with any popular parking area, it is not wise to leave valuables in plain sight in a locked car.

From the register and wooden map, the trail heads southwest, following red DEC markers through tall hardwoods. In five minutes, you begin to ascend, and the rocky character of the ridge becomes evident. Evergreens are more common as elevation increases and in under fifteen minutes, about 0.4 mile, lookouts appear to your left. Markers are sometimes hard to find, but the trail is well worn. In thirty minutes you should be on the rocky hogback of the summit where the observer's cabin comes into view with the tower just beyond. First through Third lakes lie directly to the south. Huge Fourth Lake stretches away to the east with the broad summit of Wakely Mountain on the horizon over its near end. Blue Mountain's distinct profile is visible over the main body of the lake, and the cone of West Mountain can be seen to the northeast. Between these last two summits, the high peaks of Panther, Santanoni, Colden, and Marcy stand out in the distance.

The original trail to Bald Mountain started inland from the north shore of Third Lake, near the former site of the Bald Mountain House. This trail is now privately maintained, and while it is not quite as long as the newer route, it is steeper and can be very muddy. With the easier and safer DEC trail on nearby Rondaxe Road, this route is not recommended. It meets the red-marked trail just beyond the halfway point and can be very hard to locate on the descent. It begins at a wide turnout on the north side of NY 28, 0.4 mile south of Rondaxe Road. After a steadily ascending for ten minutes, the grade eases up a bit, then climbs steeply to meet the newer trail. The vertical rise on this route is 521 feet.

124 Fly Pond and Cary Lake

Trail, hiking
0.8 mile, 30 minutes, relatively level, map XII

Directly across Rondaxe Road from the Bald Mountain trailhead and parking area, a blue-marked trail begins that gives access to Fly Pond, Cary Lake, the old bed of the Raquette Lake Railway, Scenic Mountain, Mountain Pond, and the Vista Trail. These points are close enough that all can be visited in one day, offering an outing package that has everything from lowland waters to lofty lookouts with a dash of history thrown in.

The first section of trail steadily descends from the road through tall hardwoods and arrives at a junction in less than ten minutes. A red marked side trail leads 200 feet to the brushy edge of Fly Pond. Rondaxe Road is visible across the pond and small Bottle Mountain rises above the north shore.

The blue-marked trail continues on from the junction under tall hemlocks. A herd path forks off to the left only to rejoin the trail in another minute. After walking over an interesting rocky rib, you descend to Cary Lake, commonly known as Carry Lake, less than ten minutes from the junction. Water lilies, pickerel-weed, and coarse grasses line its shore here; an occasional fallen tree breaks the surface. The trail swings to the left, crosses a wet area, then follows along the western edge of the lake. In the next ten minutes, you pass a small campsite then come to the old bed of the Raquette Lake Railway. A wooden sign tells you a bit of this line's history. It was constructed in 1899 and 1900 by the wealthy camp owners to the east who were tired of the inconveniences they encountered with the several transportation links along the lakes. Leaving the Adirondack Division at Carter Station to the northwest, it traveled 18 miles to Raquette Lake and enabled private rail cars to be hauled close to the camps. Service continued until 1933, and the rails were later torn up. Today, sections of the old route serve as seasonal roads and snowmobile trails.

125 Scenic Mountain

Trail, hiking, limited view
1.4 miles, 50 minutes, 470-foot vertical rise, map XII

Scenic Mountain is also known as Cork Mountain to some of the local people since its top rises slightly above that of Bottle Mountain when the two are viewed from the west. At one time, there were more views available from its summit, but all are grown in now except one to the northeast. The view is narrow despite illegal efforts by some to remove vegetation, but it amply rewards your efforts.

The blue-marked trail turns right, 0.8 mile from Rondaxe Road Trailhead, and follows the railroad bed, section 124, as it crosses a wetland along an inlet to Cary Lake. In 0.1 mile, where the railroad bed reenters the woods, the trail turns off to the left. If you were to continue along the bed, you would come to NY 28 in 0.8 mile. (You could approach Scenic Mountain by this route that follows up the Cary Lake outlet, passing some heavily used campsites. It is roughly the same length as the trail described, and it is level.)

Once off the railroad bed, the blue trail becomes quite muddy as it skirts the wetland for a short distance. A steep climb follows that takes you over switchbacks through a mixed woods with interesting rock outcrops. After fifteen minutes, at about 1.3 miles, in the midst of an attractive hemlock grove, you reach a junction in a saddle on the mountain. A red-marked trail turns left and climbs steeply up and over the wooded summit. It then drops a few yards to the lookout on the northeast side. To the north, Slide Off Mountain is barely visible. Behind the marshes of Rondaxe Lake's upper bay, a ridge extends to the east, above Moss Lake Outlet. West Mountain's peak stands out in the distance and to its right, on clear days, you can see the Santanoni Range, Mount Colden, and Mount Marcy. Mountain Pond lies directly below, and the ridge rising behind it blocks any more distant views. The blue-marked trail drops from the junction to the pond, then traverses the ridgeline, sections 126 and 127.

126 Mountain Pond

Trail, hiking, camping
0.5 mile, 30 minutes, 225-foot vertical rise, map XII

The blue-marked trail drops from the junction on Scenic Mountain, section 125, and comes to Mountain Pond 0.4 mile later, a total distance of 1.7 miles from the Rondaxe Road trailhead. A much shorter, direct approach to the pond from the south is along a red-marked trail that intersects the blue-marked trail in a col. It is in a handy location and makes various loop hikes possible.

The Raquette Lake Railroad bed emerges from the woods 1.1 miles north of Rondaxe Road on NY 28. It swings east, paralleling the highway, and a turnoff allows you to drive onto it. The trail to Mountain Pond begins at a widened section of the bed 0.3 mile to the left, west. Except in winter, when the route is a snowmobile trail, you may park here, allowing room for other vehicles to pass.

The trail climbs steeply up a well-worn rocky slope for fifteen minutes before leveling off and ending at the junction. A right turn will take you east along the ridge, section 127. Proceed ahead, following blue markers, to a campsite near the pond. The trail turns left at this point, goes through a short, wet section, then continues on to Scenic Mountain. A path leads right from the campsite to a second, larger campsite in a tall stand of hemlocks. The pond is lined with sheep laurel, sweet gale, and other shrubs. Sundews grow in profusion on the saturated logs that extend into the water surrounded by yellow water lilies.

127 Vista Trail

Trail, hiking, views
3 miles, 1²/₃ hours, 500-foot vertical rise, map XII

A prominent ridge rises steeply above the western half of Fourth Lake, and though it has no official name, it has been called Onondaga Mountain in some texts. The extension of the blue-marked trail that traverses this ridge is referred to as the "Vista Trail" on signs and in DEC literature. There are three very nice lookouts, two out over the Fulton Chain valley to the southeast, and one at the extreme east end, offering views to the northeast. Other lookouts available in the past have mostly grown in, but hints of lost views are possible in seasons of less foliage.

At the junction at the end of the red-marked trail to Mountain Pond, section 124, turn right, east. The ascent resumes through a mixed woods with rocky contours and a section of grasses and ferns. In ten minutes you reach a knob that is followed by a short drop, then another brief climb. After a moderate drop to a wet area, a moderate to steep ascent takes you to the highest point on the trail, twenty-five minutes and 0.6 mile from the Mountain Pond Trail junction. From the bare rock slabs of this first lookout, most of Fourth Lake is visible. Blue Ridge defines the horizon at your extreme left, with Black Bear Mountain in front of it. Wakely Mountain rises above the far end of Fourth Lake, and at a low point way down its right shoulder, Snowy Mountain peeks over. Cellar and Little

Moose mountains lead your eye south to the lower ranges of the Moose River Plains and West Canada Lakes region.

Past the first lookout, the trail dips then rises to a second lookout, passing through a grown-in section where careful attention to the route is necessary. The view here is over the upper portion of Fourth Lake with Black Bear Mountain and Blue Ridge in the distance. A descent takes you past an old fireplace in ten minutes and through another grown-in section. Shortly after passing a steep rocky cut to your right, you ascend to the ridgeline which is quite narrow here. There are limited views through the trees, and it may be possible to see Sis Lake to the north. A steep descent is followed by a short climb, then the ridge begins to rise on the left as you start the final descent.

In ten minutes, before you drop very far below the ridgeline, look for a small cairn on the left of the trail. It marks a junction with a short side trail that is sparsely marked with red DEC markers. This trail climbs steeply for about 100 feet to a lookout to the northeast. A ridge with patches of exposed rock rises to the north, blocking distant views. Bubb Lake lies directly below you with Moss Lake barely visible over its eastern extension. Beyond Moss Lake, hills in the Pigeon Lake Wilderness Area stretch to the horizon. Far to the east, West Mountain stands at the limit of your view.

The trail descends quickly from the junction and ends in ten minutes at the yellow-marked trail to Bubb and Sis lakes, section 128. You may return to your car by turning right and following the trail for five minutes to NY 28 where you will come to the Raquette Lake Railway bed. You can follow the bed west to points mentioned earlier. It is 2.4 miles to the Mountain Pond trailhead.

128 Bubb Lake and Sis Lake

Trail, hiking, camping, swimming, fishing
2.3 miles, 1 hour, 140-foot vertical rise, map XII

The trail to Bubb and Sis lakes follows the route taken by original settlers going between Fourth Lake and Big Moose Lake. Bubb Lake gets its name from a nickname guides gave to Otis Arnold's son, Otis Jr., who frequently fished its waters. Sis Lake may have gotten its name similarly from one of

Bubb Lake from Sis Lake Outlet

the Arnold daughters. The lakes are still favorites for fishing because of frequent stocking and ease of access. Though the trail is not designed for it, carrying a canoe in is not too difficult. The trailhead begins on the north side of NY.28, just north of the Country Lane Gift Shop, 1.5 miles south of Big Moose Road in Eagle Bay or 7.6 miles north of the tourist information center in Old Forge. There is room to park on the widened shoulder on the south side of the highway, although winter snowbanks may not allow this. A sign marks the beginning of the trail, but there is no register.

A steady, moderate ascent brings you to the unmarked junction with the blue-marked Vista Trail, section 127, in five minutes. A height-of-land in a pass lies shortly beyond. Following a stream on your right, you descend from the pass and, after crossing the stream, come to a fork where the trail bears left. The unmarked path straight ahead leads 50 yards to a small opening on the edge of Bubb Lake, less than 0.6 mile and twenty minutes from the highway. It is possible to swim, fish, and picnic here, but the area is too small, too uneven, and too close to the water to allow camping. This is where you would put in a canoe if you chose to carry one.

Resuming on the trail, you recross the stream and contour away from Bubb Lake. In a little over five minutes, a path appears on the left, but it becomes faint as it leads into the woods south of Sis Lake. Stay on the trail and, in a minute, you will come to another path that turns left and leads 200 feet to the brushy shore of Sis Lake. There are tall spruce and hemlocks here, and you can picnic underneath them. This would also be the location for launching a canoe.

The trail continues on under tall hemlocks, passing a large campsite on the right, 25 feet into the woods. The Sis Lake Outlet is just ahead and crossing it on rocks, logs, and mounds of grass can be tricky. This is an attractive place from which you can see both lakes since only about 100 yards separate Sis Lake from Bubb Lake at this point.

The trail rises up slightly from the outlet, swings east and parallels the north shore of Bubb Lake, coming to a campsite at its edge in fifteen minutes. Turning left, you leave the lake and in five minutes, cross its outlet on a good wooden bridge. Downstream, to the left, is a concrete fish barrier dam. Past the bridge, the trail becomes wider as it follows the route of an old road that served the dam. It ends in ten minutes at the Moss Lake circuit trail, section 134.

Along Big Moose Road

BIG MOOSE ROAD branches off NY 28 at Eagle Bay and heads northwest to Stillwater, 18 miles away. It passes through Big Moose Station where the tracks of the Adirondack Division of the New York Central Railroad cross the road. It is maintained year round, but it is subject to rapid snow accumulation, frost heaving, and erosion. The section past Big Moose Station can be rough.

. A part of this road was built in 1892. It began at the station on the just completed railroad and went 2 miles to the west bay of Big Moose Lake. An extension to Eagle Bay was built in 1896 under the direction of William West Durant, the wealthy land and transportation developer of Great Camp fame. These improvements in accessibility led to the rapid development of camps and hotels and also aided the logging industry.

129 Eagle Cliffs

Trail, hiking, picnicking, views
0.3 mile, 15 minutes, 220-foot vertical rise, map XII

A rocky knob rises just north of Eagle Bay and though its height is modest, it offers a surprisingly extensive view over the main body of Fourth Lake. Unfortunately, ease of access has led to its desecration, and the rocks of its crest are covered with spray-painted graffiti. This condition is shameful because the spot is so pretty otherwise. It is an excellent place for a picnic with children or those who cannot hike great distances. Attractive pines, spruces, and hemlocks accent your views of the lake and hills to the south. Off to the west, Onondaga, Bald, and McCauley mountains border the Fulton Chain Valley.

The entire route is on private land, and since there is no designated parking area, you should ask permission to park nearby from one of the local establishments. A driveway turns right, east, from Big Moose Road, 150 feet from NY 28, just past the first camp. The path starts on the left side of the driveway, 100 feet from Big Moose Road. It is marked by a crude plywood sign and though there are no other markers along the way, the privately maintained path is easy to follow. It rises steadily through a mostly hardwood forest with some attractive spruces and hemlocks along the way.

From Eagle Cliffs

130 Cascade Lake

Trail along old road, hiking, cross-country skiing, canoeing, waterfall, camping, swimming, picnicking, fishing, hunting
4.6 miles round trip, 2¼ hours, easy grades, maps XII and XIV

During the first decades of the twentieth century, a girls' camp operated on the north shore of Cascade Lake. Several quality horses were kept at the facility, and the camp became noted for its equestrian exhibitions. The complex of buildings was imposing, and roads encircled the lake. Today, the only signs of the camp are its old foundations and clearings. The old access road provides easy hiking and skiing for most of its length, and it would be easy to carry a canoe along the first 1.2 miles to the lake. It is sparingly marked with yellow ski trail and red DEC markers and is also a designated horse trail. With such easy access, the area is heavily used, especially during hunting season. There are many places to camp in the old clearings and with proper attention to sanitation, campers impact can be kept to a minimum.

The present parking area for Cascade Lake is on the right side of Big Moose Road, 0.9 mile from Eagle Bay. It is on the inside of a curve and, therefore, a hazard to traffic. This may change in the near future as the Pigeon Lake Wilderness Area Unit Management Plan calls for its relocation to a more visible spot away from the curve. The spot is plowed in winter. A short footpath behind the large wooden map and register leads a few feet to the old road. Turning left, you follow the old road as it curves up to the right and comes to a gate in three minutes.

As you walk along a level stretch, you will notice the flank of Cascade Mountain rising to your right. This marks the beginning of the bushwhack of section 131. The road soon makes a steady, gradual descent and after fifteen minutes passes an iron post on the right that marks the Herkimer-Hamilton county line. Just beyond, you come to a junction where the loop trail around the lake comes in on the right. The main road curves down to the left, passing a spring on the right whose overflow drains down the road's gravel. Spruce and balsam become more common and after passing two clearings on the right, you come to the lake's outlet, which you cross on a bridge made of boards and iron rails. Upstream, on your right are the remains of a wooden fish barrier dam.

At a junction just past the outlet, a red-marked trail comes in on the left. It is a link trail giving access to the trail system to the north, section 132. Within five minutes, the lake appears to the right and a path leads 30 feet to its brushy edge where you can launch a canoe. In three more minutes, another path leads 30 feet to a campsite where you can swim and picnic. Just ahead, 1.6 miles and thirty-five minutes from the trailhead, a path to the left leads past an outhouse to the brick rubble of an old foundation. The road curves down to the right to a very large, grassy camping area under tall pines and hemlocks. This area has seen a lot of use, but remains attractive. To the right there is a sandy beach.

The trail narrows beyond this point and continues through an open area where the remains of an old wall stand off to the left. Stonework occasionally lines the old roadway or appears in the nearby woods. In five minutes, you come to a large clearing where a path drops to a campsite at the edge of the lake, 100 feet away. This spot is more exposed than the others, but on fair days it is a good place to sunbathe after a swim. A path on the right leads to the previous camping area, while a path to the left goes to a little-used campsite.

More remains of the girls' camp await your discovery as you come to a small briar-filled area where the old tennis courts lie off to the right. From here, you pass through another large clearing, then a smaller one with more stonework on the left. A short bushwhack north, into the woods will take you to the base of a sheer cliff, rising over one hundred feet. The woods along the top are extremely dense, and there are no safe views from it. However, interesting rock formations and crevices can be found along the bottom.

The trail narrows considerably as it descends from the clearing and passes through a muddy stretch before coming to a swampy area at the head of the lake. It is extremely wet and the trail is difficult to discern, but that situation does not last long and, after crossing an inlet, you reenter drier woods. The trail now follows an old roadway through fragrant balsams, passing a path on the left that goes back to the inlet. In less than five minutes, you reach an open area where you must hop across another inlet. This area can be a bit wet at times, but just out of sight, up the inlet is a pretty twenty-five-foot waterfall from which the lake gets its name.

The trail continues west from the open area and though markers are scarce, the route is obvious as it follows the old roadway. This section is uneventful; there are occasional mud puddles, and the lake remains out of sight for the rest of the way. The junction with the main trail is thirty-five minutes away, making this stretch the shortest route to the cascade.

131 Cascade Mountain
Moderate bushwhack, views, maps XII and XIV

Long and narrow, Cascade Mountain extends for 6 miles from Big Moose Road, east to the Brown's Tract Ponds. Though it has some rocky cliffs and outcrops, they are for the most part, too steep or dense to stand above, or too difficult and tiring to reach. However, for those who enjoy exploring ridges and consider views incidental, a hike along the spine of this mountain offers a rewarding day. Three locations providing the best views are described here.

The best way to approach the mountain is to park at the Cascade Lake trailhead and hike up the trail, past the gate to where it levels out, section 130. You will notice the ridge rising up to your right so you should leave the trail here and climb straight up onto it. Turn left and follow along the ridgeline to the east through mixed forest. Blowdown may give you a little trouble, but herd paths make some of the route interesting.

First Lookout on Cascade Lake Mountain

In under forty-five minutes, you will come to an extensive bald crest on the ridge with two large balancing rocks. This is a peaceful, scenic place, and you have a view that extends from Blue Ridge on the east to Fourth Lake on the southwest. A small wetland along Eagle Creek lies below you to the right.

If you choose to continue on the mountain, there will be no more views for the next two hours. Descending from the first lookout, you will drop into a col with many saplings and where the going is rough. Climbing up to the next high spot, you pass many interesting rock outcroppings. A slight descent leads to an unexpected wet, grassy area. The next ascent is rockier than the previous one, and the woods are a bit thicker. After another significant descent, you will begin a climb to the highest point of the mountain. This summit offers the best views on the mountain, but finding the lookouts is very difficult.

Staying to the south side of the ridgeline, you reach the first lookout just before the true summit. Dense evergreens hide a narrow ledge at the top of a steep cliff. Be very careful pushing through the trees; there is little to stand on once you are through! The field of view is about 100°, extending from Wakely Mountain on the east to the hills of the Moose River Plains. On a clear day, you can see exposed rock on the flanks of Cellar and Blue Ridge mountains as well as the tower on Pillsbury Mountain near Speculator.

The next lookout is about fifteen minutes farther east and also on the south side of the ridge. As you emerge from the trees onto the bare rock, you will notice that it is more open and, therefore, much safer. The view is slightly shifted to the east, and Blue Mountain is now visible. Ferd's Bog is directly below you, its extensive sphagnum mat surrounded by dense spruce stands, section 171. Your best views are not from here, however, because a few feet down and to your left is another lookout. Go back into the trees, drop down to the level of the lookout and push out onto the rock. From this vantage point, your field of view has extended as far northeast as the Seward Range. The Santanoni Range with its recent rock slide scar is next on the horizon, followed by mounts Colden and Marcy. Closer in are Kempshall Mountain and the Fishing Brook Range.

One more lookout awaits you. It is back through the trees to the rear. From a small bald hump on the north side, you can get a unique view of West Mountain with Shallow Lake at its base. Pilgrim Mountain rises behind to the right and the Seward Range defines the far horizon. You have come about four miles from Big Moose Road, but it seems much longer. A shorter approach to these last lookouts would be from Uncas Road on the other side of Ferd's Bog, a distance of just over 1 mile. This would involve crossing Eagle Creek and going through its dense spruce thickets. If you choose to try this route, plan it carefully so that you do not disturb the fragile bog environment of the creek valley.

132 Cascade Lake Link Trail

Trail, hiking
1 mile, 30 minutes, 270-foot vertical rise, map XII

This red-marked trail heads north from the Cascade Lake Trail, 1.1 miles from the parking area and climbs to a junction with the blue-marked trail from Windfall Pond to Chain Ponds, section 136. There may be some minor blowdown and a few wet spots along the way, but you will also see evidence of old logging roads that the trail occasionally follows. Starting out on the level, you soon begin an easy ascent through a tall hardwood dominated forest with a dense understory composed of saplings and tiny spruces. A long level stretch is followed by a series of short pitches that take you up to the junction, located on a small ridge. A left turn will take you to Windfall Pond; Chain Ponds are down the trail ahead.

133 Cliffs above Cascade Lake Outlet

Bushwhack, views
0.6 mile, 30 minutes, 280-foot vertical rise, map XII

The bushwhack to these cliffs is a little rough, but they provide a unique view of Cascade Lake and its outlet. If you don't have time for a longer hike or are looking for something a little different to round out a full day, the trip is worth your effort.

After crossing Cascade Lake Outlet, Big Moose Road rises and curves to the right. A wide turnoff located on the outside of this curve, 1.6 miles from Eagle Bay, is primarily used for access to the Moss Lake area, section 132, and this is the best place to park for your bushwhack. Cross the road and enter the woods about halfway between the parking area and the outlet. Head east-northeast, staying above the dense conifers along the outlet. Gradually work your way toward the left, ascending the ridgeline as you go. The forest floor is tangled with viburnums and light blowdown so progress may be slower than you like. Within half an hour you will be at a high point on the ridge and by pushing through the trees to the right, you will come out at the top of an area of exposed rock. To the left, Cascade Lake stretches out in the distance. The long range of Cascade Mountain rises beyond, and the unmistakable profile of Blue Mountain is visible at the range's far end. Below to the left, the outlet snakes its way through spruce-lined wetlands. The near hills to the south part enough to allow a partial view of Fourth Lake and the mountains beyond. At your extreme right, Onondaga Mountain stands in the distance with a tiny portion of Bubb Lake visible below it.

134 Moss Lake

Trail along old road, hiking, cross-country skiing, canoeing,
camping, swimming, picnicking, fishing, hunting
2.5-mile loop, 1 hour, relatively level, map XII

Moss Lake was originally known as Whipple's Lake, and later became Morse Lake, both names in reference to prominent visitors of its shores. As time passed, Morse was corrupted into Moss, the name that remains in use today. The original trail north from the Fulton Chain passed along the lake's eastern shore on its way to Dart Lake and the North Branch of the Moose River.

In 1923, an exclusive girls' camp was opened at the lake with a complex of buildings spread along the north and east shores. The recreation hall was said to be one of the largest in the world at the time, and famous sports personalities were among the instructors for the programs of archery, swimming, tennis, and horsemanship. The camp eventually closed; and in 1973 the property was sold to the state for inclusion in the Forest Preserve.

In May of 1974, however, before the buildings were removed, Indians from several reservations in New York and Canada, converged on the 612 acre site to set up what they hoped would be a self-sufficient and sovereign community. Stating that they were only trying to reclaim land swindled from their ancestors, thirty-five families moved onto the site they called *Ganienkeh*, meaning "land of the flint." Many local residents opposed the takeover saying that they were being harassed and that the economy would be disrupted by fear of the Indians' potential for violence and their occupation of taxpayers' public land. This was a strange irony in an area of Indian names where shops sell Indian pottery, jewelry, and rugs. Both sides reported shooting incidents and as feelings ran high, the situation gained national attention. Eventually, after three years of negotiations with the state, the Indians agreed to move to a leased site near Altona, north of Plattsburg. They took with them materials from the demolished dormitories after which the state removed the rest of complex.

Little is left to suggest the prominence of the camp, and as you walk through the clearings and along the old driveways, you can only imagine the activities of the Indian families. The encircling road is now an excellent novice ski trail, and with the placement of nearby fireplaces and outhouses, the clearings can support several groups of campers and hunters. A path from the parking area leads 400 feet to a sandy beach where you can launch a canoe to visit the island or the scenic bays. It is possible to paddle a short way down the outlet to the site of an old dam used during logging days. From a wetland beyond, there is a lovely view of the ridge to the north with its patches of exposed rock.

The parking area and trailhead are located on the left side of Big Moose Road, 2.1 miles from Eagle Bay. It is kept open in winter for the benefit of cross-country skiers. The trail around the lake has yellow DEC markers and occasional ski trail markers. It is also a designated horse trail. While you can cover the whole circuit in an hour, you will likely take much longer as you explore the clearings. Sandy beaches are the rule, offering excellent opportunities for swimming and picnicking. Camping permits must be obtained from the ranger in Old Forge.

Starting from the left corner of the parking area, the trail comes to several large clearings in three minutes. There is a privy here and some campsites can be found toward the lake. Different paths lead down through tall pines to the water's edge. One comes out on a rocky shelf while another leads down to some old stone steps. Beyond the clearings, the trail swings away from the lake, drops to cross an inlet, then rises up and meets a road coming in on the left. This road leads 100 yards to a wide turnout on a curve on Big Moose Road where you can also park.

After dropping to cross the bridge over the outlet of Cascade Lake, the trail soon comes to a junction where a yellow-marked trail heads south to Bubb and Sis lakes, section 128. This is 0.7 mile and fifteen minutes from the parking area. Past the junction, look for an old iron wheel on an axle. A path turns right here and leads 0.1 mile to the edge of a bay where you can swim. For the next ten minutes, the trail remains out of sight of the lake until it nears the outlet, which it crosses on a wooden bridge at 1.3 miles.

Curving up from the outlet, the trail comes much closer to the lake as it swings around the west bay and heads to the camp clearings along the north shore. Many campsites can be found here and two privies have been placed nearby. Paths lead to the long sandy beach and, as at the other location, there is a set of large stone steps. The trail leaves the clearings along a driveway that heads out to the road where there is a barrier. It turns right before the barrier onto another driveway and follows it to the parking area.

Trail crossing, Inlet to Chub Lake northeast of Queer Lake

135 Windfall Pond

Trail, hiking, camping
1 mile, 30 minutes, easy grades, maps XII and XIII

A system of trails in the lower Pigeon Lake Wilderness Area visits the major ponds and lakes between Cascade Lake and Big Moose Lake. Many possibilities exist for loop hikes that can last an afternoon or be expanded into multi-day outings. The only lean-to in the area is at Queer Lake, but there are campsites in several other locations. The central access to this area is from a parking area on the right side of Big Moose Road, 3.3 miles from Eagle Bay. It is now kept open in winter, however. A well-used trail with yellow DEC markers heads east from the trailhead register and map, stopping first at Windfall Pond.

In five minutes, a path turns right off the trail at a campsite and heads up along a stream. The trail turns left and crosses the stream to parallel its rocky course on the opposite bank. There are a few muddy spots, but the trail is otherwise delightful. Easy ups and downs take you through the lush forest you would expect to find in the wilderness. After fifteen minutes, you recross the stream on a bridge above a rocky chute. The path from the campsite rejoins on the right and a small vly is passed on the left. After crossing a small stream on rotting planks, another vly is seen to the left and more muddy spots appear.

You are now following the outlet of Windfall Pond, and at a bend, where an old sign points the way, you begin a slight ascent. After crossing and recrossing the outlet on rocks, you reach a junction near the end of the pond. The blue-marked trail to the right goes to the Cascade Lake Link Trail and Chain Ponds, section 136. The yellow-marked trail turns left, crosses the beaver-dammed outlet and heads east to Queer Lake, section 137. In two minutes, a path leads right, to a small campsite between the trail and the pond. There are slabs of rock at the water's edge where you can picnic, but it is a poor place to swim. Otherwise, the pond's shoreline is mostly swampy with dead timber.

136 Chain Ponds

Trail, hiking
2.7 miles, 1¹/₃ hours, moderate grades, maps XII and XIII

A trail with blue DEC markers leaves the yellow-marked trail at 1 mile, near Windfall Pond and heads southeast to meet the red-marked Cascade Lake Link Trail. It then swings northeast, passing the lower end of Chain Ponds to rejoin the yellow-marked trail west of Queer Lake. This loop passes through some very wild terrain where the feeling of wilderness is great. The mixed forest is tall and rich, and there are many rock outcroppings along the way. However, the trail can be very wet in places and markers are scarce in a few sections.

From the junction, the trail climbs high and away from Windfall Pond through tall hardwoods. Leveling off, you pass interesting rock outcrops on the left, then come to a wet area where a swamp is visible through the trees to the right. After a short ascent, you pass another outcrop covered with rock tripe lichen on the left. After twenty minutes, the trail begins a rough descent where you must pay careful attention to stay on the correct route since it is very wet and poorly marked. After crossing two streams, the way is easier and more rock appears. The trail rises along the right-hand edge of a ravine and comes to the junction where the Cascade Lake Link Trail, section 132, comes in on the right. This is about forty minutes from Windfall Pond.

The blue-marked trail turns left and descends to the Chain Ponds outlet, which it crosses on stones, in just over ten minutes. The ponds can really be considered one body of water divided into three ponds where opposite banks close in. A small area off to the left is not suitable for camping, but it makes a good spot to rest and eat lunch. From it you can look across the first pond with its brushy shores and stump-filled waters.

After following along the pond for a few minutes, the trail becomes wet and ascends through a narrow draw with imposing rock outcroppings on the right. Once past the height-of-land, wet sections continue where water frequently runs down the trail. Gradual descents lead to drier land and, thirty minutes from the ponds, the junction with the yellow-marked trail. Windfall Pond is 1.6 miles and thirty-five minutes to the left; the northwest bay of Queer Lake is 350 feet to the right.

137 Queer Lake

Trail, hiking, lean-to, camping, swimming
3.4 miles, 1½ hours, easy grades, maps XII and XIII

The yellow-marked trail continues on from Windfall Pond, 1 mile from Big Moose Road, section 133, and at 1 mile enters the hub of the trail system near Queer Lake, so named for its odd shape. The wild beauty of the lake, and the fact that it has the only lean-to on the whole trail system, make it the most popular destination in the area. With several well-used campsites nearby to accommodate the overflow, there is a potential for high impact on the resource resulting in a less than wilderness experience. Visitors should therefore make every possible effort to lessen their impact on both the land and the atmoshpere.

After crossing the outlet of Windfall Pond, continue east on the yellow-marked trail. The pond is visible through the trees to your right. The trail contours along the north side of a hill, then drops to cross a small stream. Just over thirty minutes from the last junction, at 2.1 miles from Big Moose Road, you reach a second junction where the red-marked Hermitage Trail, section 143, comes in from the north. A path straight ahead goes to camps on a parcel of private land that extends into the wilderness area from the north. The yellow-marked trail turns right and ascends as it swings south, rounding the tip of the private land. During a moderately steep descent, the camps may be seen to the left through the trees. After crossing a stream, the trail turns right and a path to the camps turns left. Be careful not to miss this turn on the way out; the camp owners' privacy relies on hikers' respect.

Western bay of Queer Lake near the trail

The trail parallels the stream, which is erroneously shown as the outlet of Queer Lake on the 1954 USGS topographic map of Big Moose. The real outlet drains from the lake's south bay into Sucker Brook. The trail crosses to the south side of the stream in a very wet area where several paths can cause temporary confusion. At 2.6 miles, the blue-marked trail from Chain Ponds soon enters on the right and, less than 50 feet beyond, the yellow-marked trail turns left. The northwest bay of Queer Lake can be seen from this bend and a path leads straight ahead past a campsite to follow along the bank for a short distance. The bay's brushy edges are lined with fallen timber and patches of sphagnum where many pitcher plants abound.

The yellow-marked trail climbs high above the lake and in ten minutes, at 2.9 miles, comes to a junction where the yellow-marked trail from Mays Pond, section 144, comes in from the north. Continuing east, you cross a small stream and come to another junction in under ten minutes, at 3.2 miles. The trail swings to the left and heads toward Chub Lake, section 138. To get to the Queer Lake lean-to, you should turn right onto a red-marked trail that descends to the narrow land bridge connecting the lake's large peninsula to the mainland. The area is boggy and fallen timbers line the waters' edge. The trail enters the tall evergreen woods that dominates the peninsula, passes several campsites on the left and reaches the lean-to, 0.2 mile from the junction. The lean-to sits in a small south-facing clearing with large rocks along the shore. One large squared-off rock under a tall white pine provides an attractive spot for eating, sunbathing, or just taking in the view down the lake.

Of several paths found around the lean-to, one pushes through the brush to the west and goes to the end of the peninsula. It is fairly easy to follow and stays within sight of the northwest bay, passing first through one campsite then rising above another on the right in a low area. The path becomes quite narrow and climbs through a dense section before coming to the beautiful tip of the peninsula. Tall pines stand near the deep, narrow channel connecting the bay and large rocks extend into the water. There are two campsites here, both so close to shore that use is questionable unless they become designated sites. You can push a little farther along the edge to a steep, rocky hogback that rises thirty feet above the lake. It should take about twenty minutes to reach this point from the lean-to.

138 Chub Lake

Trail, hiking, camping, swimming
5.5 miles, 2¹/₂ hours, easy grades, maps XII and XIII

From Queer Lake, the yellow-marked trail heads deeper into the wilderness area on its way to Chub Lake. Since the main approach is from Higby Road, section 145, the lake is described in detail in that section. This trail however, provides yet another useful loop for your trip planning. Though it is the longer way to the lake, it is in good shape and gives you a strong sense of remoteness. Allow one hour for the 2.1 miles between the lakes.

The yellow-marked trail turns left at the junction with the red-marked Queer Lake lean-to trail, section 137, then swings east and begins a long, easy ascent through tall hardwoods. After thirty-five minutes, at 4.5 miles, you arrive at a height-of-land where the trail makes a sharp right turn as it begins to descend. The trail skirts to the left of a small flooded area and in ten more minutes you cross an inlet of Chub Lake on a raised plank bridge that is in poor shape. The wetland upstream is particularly scenic as is a bay of the lake which lies to your right. The trail reenters the woods and comes to a junction in five minutes. A yellow-marked side trail goes straight ahead, then swings right and drops to campsites at the edge of the lake.

The main trail continues on another 0.3 mile to the blue-marked trail from Higby Road.

139 West Pond

Trail, hiking, cross-country skiing
0.7 mile, 30 minutes, easy grades, maps XII and XIII

The trail to West Pond is the first section of a combination foot and snowmobile trail that heads southwest, passing Safford Pond and Goose Pond. It continues on as a snowmobile trail to connect with another snowmobile trail that parallels the North Branch of the Moose River between Rondaxe Road and Big Moose Road. The trail has received little, if any maintenance in recent years from the trailhead to Safford Pond. Blowdown, grown-in areas, and a scarcity of markers mean that this is not a trail for beginning hikers or skiers. Junctions are usually marked, but the signs are old and deteriorating. However, if you are up to a little route-finding challenge and don't mind a few inconveniences, you can make a delightful trip to these ponds, enjoying the solitude that comes from such little use. Snowmobile trail markers are used along the entire stretch. Blue DEC markers are found on the main trail as far as Safford Pond.

The trailhead is a parking area on the left, west, side of Big Moose Road, just before the road turns sharply left at an intersection, 5.8 miles north of Eagle Bay. It is called the Orvis Trailhead and is not plowed out in the winter, in which case, you will have to ask permission to park nearby. A large wooden map of the area next to the register is oriented according to your direction of travel and not with the top being north as is usual. The original trailhead was located about 300 yards to the south on private land.

The trail heads into the woods along an obvious route and gradually curves left. In ten minutes, at a small opening in the woods, the trail from the old trailhead comes in on the left. A shortage of markers creates confusion here. The land rises ahead and the tendency is to swing to the left staying on the level. That is the old route and it will take you directly to the outlet of West Pond where it becomes virtually impossible to trace. The correct route leads along the right edge of the opening and climbs the hill. You should be able to locate the trail at the top and it will take you past a wetland at the end of West Pond from which the outlet tumbles away into the woods. You soon come to a not-so-obvious junction where an old sign points ahead to Safford Pond. A faint trail with a few red DEC markers turns left here. It leads past a fine grove of hemlocks on the left and comes to the rocky shore of West Pond in five minutes. There are no good places to camp but it is a good place to have a snack. Most of the shoreline is brushy and the best way to explore the pond is on skis or snowshoes.

140   Safford Pond

Trail, hiking, cross-country skiing, camping, fishing, hunting
2.7 miles, 1½ hours, easy grades, map XII

The 1954 USGS topographic map of Big Moose refers to it as Safford Pond, but DEC signs in the area sometimes call it Big Safford Pond. Perhaps this is done to avoid confusion with Little Safford Lake to the southwest.

From the junction with the side trail to West Pond, 0.5 mile from Big Moose Road, section 139, the blue-marked trail continues southwest. There are few markers at first, but it is not difficult to see the correct route and in ten minutes, their frequency improves. You steadily descend along small hogbacks through a dense hardwood forest and in ten more minutes, you drop into a small, wet hollow. The trail climbs the opposite bank and turns sharply left at its top where a small wetland is visible through the trees to the right.

A valley forms to your right, but you stay above it in the open woods for the next fifteen minutes. At one point, the trail splits, only to come together a few yards ahead. As you near a dense spruce and balsam section, the trail seems to disappear, but it really turns right, and you must push through under the trees to continue. You arrive at a junction in another fifteen minutes. Here, at 2.4 miles, a blue-marked trail turns right and takes you to a major inlet of Safford Pond, less than 0.1 mile away. This trail is especially hard to follow because there are few markers and no definite treadway, but if you stay to the right as you dip to the inlet, you will not be far off.

From a campsite near the inlet, signs point the way back to the main trail, but the side trail does not end here. If you can manage to follow it farther, you will come to a sign pointing the way to the tracks of the Adirondack Division Railroad, less than 1 mile away. It is a challenge to find the trail as it follows an old path, which is shown on the 1954

Safford Pond

topographic map. Markers are hard to spot as the trail winds through dense woods with wet areas and stream crossings before climbing to the railroad grade where there is still an old trail sign. This point is about 2.5 miles south of Big Moose Station.

The main trail continues south and comes to a second junction five minutes later, at 2.5 miles. The snowmobile trail forks left and heads to Goose Pond and the North Branch. The trail straight ahead goes on for another 0.3 mile, emerging from the woods briefly to cross a boggy section at the pond's edge. It reenters the woods, goes over a small rise and comes to an open spot near a small beach where you can swim, rest, or have lunch. The pond's shoreline is mostly brushy with scattered tamaracks and some dead standing timber. This is a favorite haunt of sportsmen, and back in the woods, you may find an old row boat used by anglers and hunters.

141 Billy's Bald Spot and Squash Pond

Trail, hiking, lean-to, picnicking, views
1 mile, 40 minutes, 400-foot vertical rise, maps XII and XIII

Big Moose Road makes a sharp left turn at an intersection, 5.8 miles from Eagle Bay. The road turning right at this intersection is Martin Road, and if you follow it 0.6 mile, you will notice a small sign on the left that says "Billy's Squash." It is just before the pavement ends and marks the start of a trail that climbs 350 feet in 0.4 mile to a rocky bluff known as Billy's Bald Spot, from which most of Big Moose Lake can be seen. The trail then continues to the northwest to Squash Pond. Most of this hike is on private land, but it is a traditional route and the landowner has kept it open to the public. The trail is privately maintained, but is badly eroded since water frequently runs down it. Dense growth and blowdown are frequent on the Squash Pond section. Use care in parking on the shoulder of the road so you do not interfere with local traffic.

The trail begins its steep climb immediately, winding up a rocky hardwood slope. It follows a variety of markings including red and orange paint blazes, yellow metal disks, and occasional blue DEC markers. After fifteen minutes, you come to an opening where a privately constructed, but deteriorating lean-to sits in a small clearing.

The lake lies in its basin below you, cradled by a series of ridges and hills. A few distant mountains rise up in the distance to the east and south. Far to the left of your field of view, West Mountain dominates the horizon over East Bay. The range with Metcalf and Wakely mountains is beyond South Bay and hills beyond the Fulton Chain lie far to the south. Directly below you is an island where, in 1880, William Dutton of Philadelphia had a camp built. An intense lover of the wilds, he spent lazy hours on this rocky lookout, leading guides to refer to it as "Billy's Bald Spot." While it may have been naturally bald in his time, trees have been cut in recent years to maintain the view.

The trail to Squash Pond begins directly behind the lean-to and is similarly marked. It heads generally west over the crest of the ridge, dropping to cross the outlet of the pond in just over 10 minutes. A path heads left and drops back down to the road, but it is not maintained for the public, and you are advised not to use it. The trail to the pond enters state land in this area and is hard to follow, but if you turn right and head upstream over a small rise, you will not be far off. A wetland is passed on the right, and after pushing through a dense evergreen section you will emerge on a rocky rib at the edge of the pond. Most of the shoreline is brushy so this a good place to take a break and enjoy the peaceful character of the area.

Higby Road and Big Moose Lake

INACCESSIBILITY KEPT BIG Moose Lake the wild haunt of a few hardy mountain men for most of the nineteenth century. As development increased on the Fulton Chain to the south, sportsmen occasionally made their way over the rough trails to the lakes of the North Branch of the Moose River, and soon primitive camps appeared on its shores. With the constuction of the Adirondack Division Railroad and associated service roads in the 1890s, permanent camps and inns flourished. One of the early settlers on the lake was James Higby who became noted for his diverse talents in guiding, camp building, and pancake flipping. Higby Road is so named since it was the route to Jim's hotel on the south shore of East Bay.

In July of 1906, Big Moose Lake received national attention when Chester Gillette, a young businessman from Cortland, murdered Grace Brown who was carrying his illegitimate child. When her bruised body was found in the South Bay, it appeared she had struck her head and drowned when their small boat overturned. Suspicion arose when Gillette was found days later in an Inlet hotel. Despite his claim that she killed herself in shame and he fled in fright, he was charged with her murder and electrocuted at Auburn State Prison in 1908. An erie fascination with the incident arose as people came to see the lake and the Glenmore Hotel where the couple had registered. Theodore Dreiser based his famous novel *An American Tragedy* on the story and a broadway production followed. It also inspired a popular movie called *A Place in the Sun.*

Most of Big Moose Lake's shoreline is privately owned and many prominent camps stand along its edge. A second Glenmore Hotel has replaced the first, and other hotels operate nearby. State land touches the north shore of East Bay and surrounds both the eastern extension of North Bay and the Inlet, a marshy bay to the northeast. Several trails described in this section originate in these areas and are only accessible by canoe or boat.

Public access to the lake can be found by turning right from Big Moose Road at 3.9 miles onto Higby Road and following it 1.5 miles to a fork where a right turn will take you to a dock maintained by the Big Moose

Lake Property Owners' Association. There is room to park off to the right. This access is the closest one for the trails, and mileages and times are given for it.

When William Seward Webb sold off all the lakeshore lands he owned in the area, he specified that trails along the shores should remain public footpaths forever. Some property owners not only respect this covenant, they maintain parts of the trails along the shore of Big Moose Lake, permitting people to walk to such destinations as Russian Lake and Merriam Pond.

142   Constable Pond, Pigeon Lake, Otter Pond, and West Mountain

Trail, hiking, fishing, views
8.2 miles, 3½ hours, 1073-foot vertical rise, maps XIII and XV

This long trail is the western approach to West Mountain, the highest mountain in the area and the former site of a fire tower. Trails to Queer Lake, Mays Pond, and Chub Lake branch south in its first 2.5 miles, so parts of it can be used for various loop hikes. Passing Constable Pond, it ascends into the remote foothills around Pigeon Lake and Otter Pond. The edges of these bodies of water are generally boggy, limiting access to them. The woods around them are frequently dense making selection of a place to camp difficult, although a campsite does exist near the upper end of Constable Pond. If you plan to camp farther up the trail, your best bet is to locate a stream for a water source and search nearby hardwood stands for areas open enough for your needs. There is a clearing on the southeast side of West Mountain, just below the summit. Using it means a long, tiring backpack to an area of weather extremes. Your other alternative, if your stamina allows, is to do the trail as a day hike, meaning a round trip distance of 16.4 miles. This can be shortened to 13.1 miles if you leave a second car parked at the end of the trail to West Mountain from Brown's Tract Road near Raquette Lake, section 176, and descend by that route. Day hiking may limit the amount of time you have to explore, and since there is much to see along the way, careful planning is a must. Markers are adequate, but some sections are encumbered with blowdown, and there are many stream crossings without bridges where you may have difficulty in wet seasons.

To reach the beginning of the trail, drive 1.4 miles over Higby Road to Judson Road, a private road that comes in on the right at the bottom of a hill. There is no formal trailhead and until adjacent land can be aquired, you must park on the right shoulder, being careful not to interfere with local traffic on either road. The blue-marked trail follows along Judson Road for 0.2 mile before turning off to the right onto an old woods road. After passing a gate marking the beginning of state land, you will come to a register and wooden map of the area. In three minutes, the red-marked Hermitage Trail, section 143, ascends to the right from a junction marked only by an arrow on your left. Just ahead, the trail turns left, leaving the road to cross Constable Creek on a strong wooden bridge with a rail. The road continues southeast to a private camp on Mays Pond.

The blue-marked trail passes through private land as it parallels a wetland along the creek. In ten minutes, a woods road enters from the left and you follow it, crossing the creek again on a bridge suitable for light vehicles. The remains of a fish barrier dam can be seen to your right and upstream to the left, the extensive wetlands along Constable Creek begin here. At the other end of the bridge, the trail forks left while the road goes southwest to join the Mays Pond road.

You now follow a long even stretch of trail with the conifer-lined wetlands to your left and a higher mixed woods on the right. The trail reenters state land after thirty-five minutes at 1.3 miles, and you come to a junction where the yellow-marked trail to Mays Pond heads south, section 144. The wetland along the creek to the north is especially scenic here and a bushwhack to its edge will allow you to see its sweet gale, bottled gentians, and flowering sedges. In the next fifteen minutes, the wetland will give way to Constable Pond and a path leads 75 feet to its edge. Not long after passing an old sign with the pond's name on the left, you will come to the junction with the yellow-marked trail to Chub Lake, section 145. This is 2.6 miles and an hour and a quarter from Higby Road, and just beyond, on the right, is a small campsite.

From this point on, the trail is wilder and rougher. You will spend the next ten minutes getting through a very difficult section with heavy blowdown and two stream crossings. The second stream is the sizeable outlet of Chub Lake, and since there is no bridge, crossing may pose problems, depending on water levels. Several huge white pines tower from the dense mixed woods around the outlet. The trail greatly improves, and as you slowly gain elevation, the woods become more hardwood dominant. After twenty-five minutes, at 3.5 miles, you cross another stream, and the Pigeon Lake Outlet appears to your left. Shortly, you cross that outlet in a

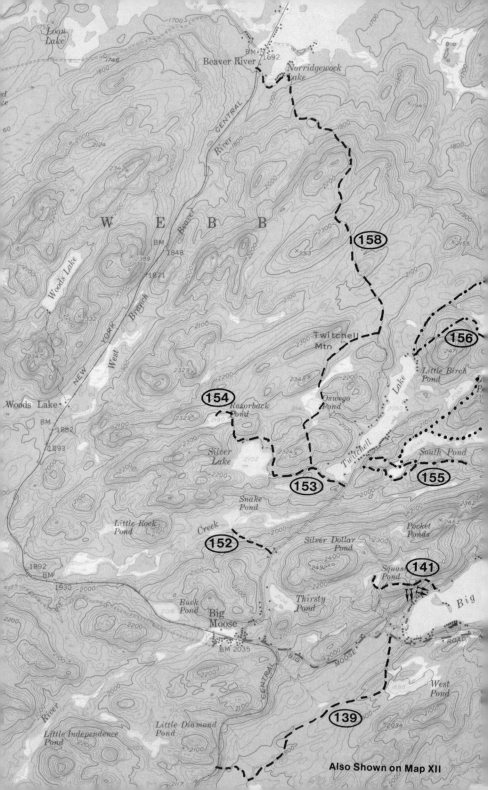

Also Shown on Map XII

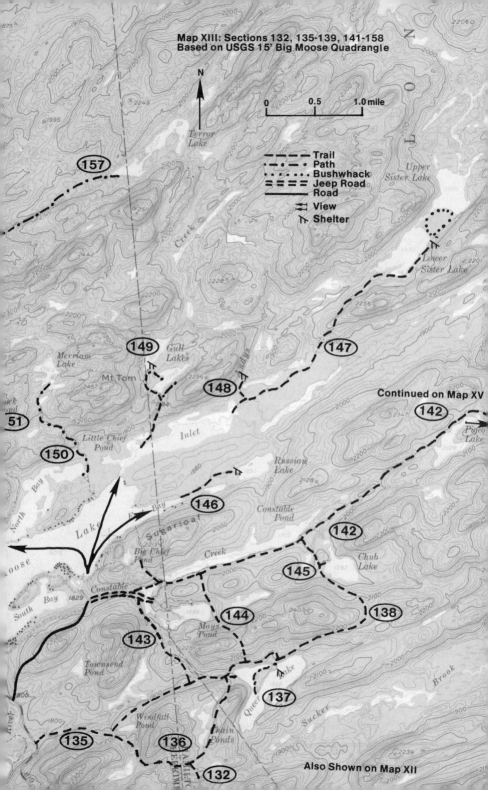

Map XIII: Sections 132, 135-139, 141-158
Based on USGS 15' Big Moose Quadrangle

N

0   0.5   1.0 mile

— — — Trail
—·—·— Path
·········· Bushwhack
═══ Jeep Road
——— Road
⇄ View
⋎ Shelter

Terror Lake

Upper Sister Lake

Lower Sister Lake

(157)

(149)   Gull Lakes
Merriam Lake
Mt Tom
(148)
(147)

Continued on Map XV

(51)
Little Chief Pond
(150)
Inlet
Russian Lake
(142)
Pigeon Lake

North Bay
East Bay
Sugarloaf
(146)
Constable Pond
(142)
Chub Lake

Moose
Lake
Big Chief Pond
Creek
(145)
(138)

Constable Bay
1829
(144)
Mays Pond
(143)
Townsend Pond
(137)

South Bay
Queer Lake
Sucker Brook

Windfall Pond
Chain Ponds

(135)   (136)
(132)

Also Shown on Map XII

Russian Lake

dense area, and a little farther on pass on the right a small wetland that lies along the outlet. An old sign, seen ten minutes later, tells you that you have finally reached Pigeon Lake. Because of dense spruce and balsam, it is difficult to bushwhack to its brushy shore. In this area, you will start to see red trail markers mixed in with the blue, and this condition lasts for the rest of the way.

In the next thirty minutes, the trail crosses two more streams, the second on a sturdy log high above the water. The trail beyond is quite enjoyable as it eases across the north side of a hill through mixed trees. Ferns and low plants carpet the ground, and there is surprisingly little blowdown. Another thirty minutes pass before you cross the outlet of Otter Pond in a small wet area. It is hard to see the pond itself through the dense trees when you pass it ten minutes later. You need two and a half hours to cover the 6.8 miles to this point.

After Otter Pond, the trail becomes noticeably steeper, and the forest is mostly tall maple, yellow birch, and ash. An easy stream crossing signals the last water on the trail, and the final steep climb to the summit begins. The trail is vague in a few places, but careful scouting will reveal the correct route, and fifty minutes past Otter Pond, you should be in a level draw on the summit ridge. Markers are scarce, but by swinging to the right, you will come to a junction where the trail from Brown's Tract Road, section 176, comes in from the southeast. A 200-foot spur trail pitches up to the right through dense growth. The summit is just beyond, and you come out in the rocky opening where the tower stood.

Your view is from the east-northeast to the south and to your left, the Fishing Brook Range and Blue Mountain are seen. Blue Ridge and Wakely Mountain define the horizon to the southeast and Raquette Lake dominates the foreground. The tower was removed in the 1970s because fire patrol planes were considered adequate and because the State Land Master Plan states that fire towers are nonconforming structures in Wilderness Areas. The unique views of the lakes and ridges to the north and west are now gone, and it is evident that some illegal tree cutting has been done to maintain the existing view.

143　Queer Lake via Hermitage Trail

Trail, hiking, lean-to, camping, swimming, fishing
3.1 miles (Judson Road to Queer Lake), 1½ hours, easy grades,
maps XII and XIII

The 1.3-mile-long Hermitage Trail connects the blue-marked trail from Judson Road, section 142, with the yellow-marked trail from Big Moose Road, section 133. It gets its name from the rustic camp at the tip of a private parcel of land near the west end of Queer Lake. Built in the 1920s, the main building has a stone foundation and large porch. The trail parallels the western boundary of the parcel and is the shortest approach to Queer Lake. It is a delightful trail, and its deep-woods character quickly gives you a wilderness feeling.

The turn-off for this red-marked trail is 0.5 mile from Higby Road along the blue-marked trail. It can be easily missed since the only sign at the junction is an arrow on the north side. The trail turns right and ascends into tall hardwoods. At the top of the rise, an old path joins the trail on the left. It comes up from the blue-marked trail from a point just beyond the junction. It splits off to the left again, then rejoins the trail a few yards later. You may take this path by mistake on the way back so stay alert.

The trail enters a mixed woods and in twenty-five minutes, at 1.5 miles, comes to a junction with a private trail on your left. Yellow state land boundary paint blazes are just off the trail to the left. An easy descent takes you to a wet area after which you ascend to the junction with the yellow-marked trail from Big Moose Road. It should take you about forty-five minutes to reach this point, 1.8 miles from Higby Road, and you can now proceed as described in section 135.

144 Mays Pond

Trail, hiking
1.7 miles, 45 minutes to Mays Pond; 2.6 miles, 1½ hours to
yellow-marked trail, 300-foot vertical rise, maps XII and XIII

A yellow-marked trail parallels the Hermitage Trail to the east, passing along the east shore of Mays Pond. It connects the same trails as the Hermitage Trail does, making it yet another valuable link for planning loop hikes. As of 1987, however, the section south of Mays Pond is almost impassable due to severe blowdown and overgrown areas. Jim Higby claimed to have discovered the pond on May 1 and so named it.

Turning south from the junction on the blue-marked trail, 1.3 miles from Higby Road, section 142, the trail climbs steadily for five minutes, levels briefly, then begins to descend. Markers are few and hard to spot so careful scouting is necessary to stay on course. You soon see Mays Pond through the trees to the right and a side path leads 50 feet to a small, rocky opening on its edge. Tall pines rise above the dense woods along the pond's edge, and this is a good place to rest and refresh. A rough path goes right, through brush along the rocky shore for a short distance. Far down the shore to the right, you can see a point with a dock and a cabin under tall pines. This is the private parcel reached by the woods roads to the north.

The trail curves around the east end of the pond, passing some huge white pines. A sign on the left tells you that you're at Mays Pond, and a path descends 25 feet to its edge. Another path just ahead drops to the shore and signs point the correct direction of the trail. After five more minutes, you hop rocks to cross a stream that drains a swampy, unnamed pond to the east. If you have time, a short bushwhack up the stream is a nice diversion. In two places, the water shoots through straight-sided flumes that resemble canal locks.

A moderate ascent follows and it is complicated by a lack of markers. As you climb higher, blowdown and dense undergrowth confuse you and make the ascent tiring. It will take you almost twenty minutes to go 0.3 mile. After reaching the height-of-land, the blowdown lessens somewhat, and your pace increases. The descent is much easier, and you quickly reach the junction with the yellow-marked trail to the north of Queer Lake.

145 Chub Lake

Trail, hiking, camping, swimming, fishing
3 miles, 1½ hours, easy grades, map XIII

This approach to Chub Lake is much shorter than the one from Big Moose Road described in section 138. From the junction on the blue-marked trail of section 142, 2.5 miles from Higby Road, turn right onto the yellow-marked trail and follow it 0.3 mile to the side trail to Chub Lake.

The side trail, also with yellow markers, swings right and descends in less than five minutes to a large informal campsite on the edge of the lake. A large rock slab leads into the water, making this spot good for swimming. There is a second campsite to the left.

146 Russian Lake

Trail accessible by canoe, hiking, lean-to, camping, swimming,
picnicking
1.3 miles canoeing, 0.8 miles on foot, 1 hour, relatively level,
map XIII

From the property Owners' dock off Higby Road, paddle out to the right and parallel the right, south shore, entering the narrow East Bay. Near the end of the bay, on the north shore, a newly rebuilt dock marks the beginning of the trail, which follows blue DEC markers east along the edge of the bay before heading north to high ground.

The trail passes through one of the most spectacular forest stands in the Adirondacks, huge spruce and hemlock border the trail, tremendous pines appear nearer the lake. Wetlands along Russian Lake Outlet appear occasionally through the trees to the right. After only twenty minutes on the short, easy trail, you reach a lean-to in an open area at the west end of Russian Lake. It is in good shape, as is the privy, but there are signs of inconsiderate tree cutting in the area. A path leads from the lean-to out onto the slabs of rock along the shore where you can easily get into the water for a good swim, sunbathe, or just relax and enjoy the view. Rocks occasionally break the brushy shoreline and white pines randomly rise above the surrounding woods. A small pine-covered island sits next to the north shore.

147 Andys Creek

Trail accessible by canoe, hiking, lean-to, camping, swimming, fishing, hunting
2.6 miles canoeing, 0.5 mile on foot, 1¹/₄ hours, easy grades, map XIII

If you paddle northeast from the Property Owners' dock and cross the broad eastern end of Big Moose Lake, you will come to the grassy entrance of the Inlet. This marshy bay extends northeast from the lake and is completely surrounded by Forest Preserve lands. It is not part of the Pigeon Lake Wilderness Area Unit Management Plan and its monitoring is left up to the lake's residents and visitors. Power boats are discouraged from entering the Inlet because of possible damage to the marsh environment as well as the navigational hazards of submerged obstacles and tangles of vegetation. They do enter though and operators are advised to maintain low speeds. This is a good area for observing wildlife. Its diversity supports a variety of birds such as ducks, great blue herons, cedar waxwings, and belted kingfishers. A large abandoned nest at the far end was once the breeding place for ospreys. Animals such as deer, otters, muskrats, beavers, fishers, and foxes depend on this area for food and cover.

To find the trails to Andys Creek and Sister Lakes, you must locate a channel in the vegetation at the east end of the Inlet. Open water extends for a short distance to the right, but you should paddle toward the center of the pickerel-weed and grasses where the channel emerges. A 0.3-mile paddle up the channel will take you to the trailhead, a wet little indent on the right side. By paddling a few yards past the trailhead, you will swing right around a point and come to a campsite on the right bank.

The trail follows blue markers through a muddy section, passing the campsite on the left. After five minutes, 0.2 mile, you will come to a junction where the yellow-marked trail to Sister Lakes goes right. Rising slightly from the junction, your trail to the left soon crosses Andys Creek on a sturdy bridge with a railing. As you climb away from the bridge, notice a small sign on the left at a small stream crossing. It indicates a spring. The lean-to and privy are just ahead and both are in good condition. They are situated in a spruce grove at the edge of the creek where it tumbles over large slabs of rock. This scenic area is popular with sportsmen and during hunting seasons, the lean-to and campsites will likely be full.

148 Sister Lakes

Trail accessible by canoe, hiking, lean-to, camping, swimming, fishing, hunting
2.6 miles canoeing, 3.3 miles on foot to Lower Sister Lake, 3 to 3½ hours one way, 200-foot vertical rise, map XIII

This yellow-marked trail heads east-northeast from the junction on the Andys Creek trail, section 147. Its first part is flat and dry as it passes through a pretty lowland forest of mixed trees. This section ends in thirty-five minutes as you drop to cross wet ground on planks at 1.1 miles. The trail then passes between two large white pines and begins to climb steadily for twenty minutes. An intermittent stream appears on your left and an old fading sign indicates a spring on it. Height-of-land is reached at 1.8 miles, and a 0.5-mile descent follows, taking you almost down to the level of the swamps surrounding the outlet of Lower Sister Lake. A trail used to lead to the swampy outlet end of the lake, but almost all sign of it is gone. The trail continues along but way back from the shore of the lake heading to the lean-to at the far eastern end. Here, the trail traces an uneven course up small rises and down again. There are some wet areas and small streams to ford. You glimpse the lake through the trees and you may want to leave the trail to photograph the outlet end which is studded with bleached boulders.

After passing through a large blowdown area, you soon arrive at a second area of devastation directly behind the lean-to. It is amazing that a lean-to survived winds that toppled so many trees, but it and the privy, both in good shape, are still standing. A path in front drops down to slabs of rock along the shore. The rock extends around to the left providing many places from which to swim or relax and sunbathe.

A leaky canoe can be found near the lean-to. It is probably not seaworthy enough to take you to the 0.5 mile to Upper Sister Lake. Following land features, such as the outlet of Upper Sister Lake, will take you on a much longer and very difficult bushwhack to the Upper Lake. The woods between the lakes are dense, wet and tangled with blowdown. Land features such as the outlet to the northwest or the ridge to the southeast will guide you to the lake, but it will be a time-consuming, tiring effort and the brushy shoreline renders the lake virtually inaccessible. Just to see it you must travel a very long way, crossing through the center of the Pigeon Lake Wilderness.

149 Gull Lakes

Trail accessible by canoe, hiking, lean-to, swimming, fishing
1.8 miles canoeing, 1.2 miles on foot, 1⅓ hours, 150-foot
vertical rise, map XIII

The landing for the trail to the two Gull Lakes is on the north edge of Big Moose Lake Inlet, where it widens out from the entrance channel. A wilderness area sign hangs on a nearby tree. The trail is initially wet, but soon improves as it climbs through tall hardwoods away from the water. The outlet to the lower lake appears to the left, and after leveling off at twenty minutes, about 0.6 miles, an unmarked path forks right from the trail, leading 150 feet to the edge of the lake. This appears to be a point where people frequently launch canoes. It is entirely practical since it is just a short climb from the inlet and is the best way to explore the lake.

The trail turns left and drops to cross the outlet where another path branches off to the right and leads to a rock overlooking a beaver dam with the lake beyond. After following along the southwest edge of the lake for a few minutes, you climb over a small rise, then drop to cross a stream. The southwest end of the upper Gull Lake is just ahead, and its lean-to is nestled in a small opening where you have a scenic view down the peaceful waters. Tall evergreens rise from the edges of the opening and a path behind the lean-to leads to the privy. Both structures are in good condition. The privy path swings left and drops to a narrow bay on the lower lake less than 0.1 mile away. This is the best way to get your canoe to the upper lake.

150 Pine Point

Canoeing, camping, swimming, picnicking, fishing
2.1 miles, 1 hour, map XIII

A popular picnic site is ensconced on the far north shore of the eastern extension of North Bay. Known locally as Pine Point after the tall, double-trunked white pine found at its edge, many people enjoy the peace and scenery found at this small opening. It is also the jumping-off point for the old trail to Merriam Lake, section 151. In recent years, there has been concern over adverse impact from campers. A private group has agreed to fund a DEC constructed lean-to somewhere on Big Moose Lake, and this is one of the areas under consideration. This would localize camping and reduce impact.

To find Pine Point, paddle out to the left from the Property Owners' dock and cross the lake at its narrowest section. Head west along the north shore to the tip of a long, narrow extension of land. Turn right, entering the North Bay and paddle straight up the length of it on a northeast heading. Even paddling through North Bay is a delightful adventure. Colvin described it as "a bay of singular shape, almost separated from the main body of water, and extremely picturesque in its own islands, bays and points." He thought it "worthy of name as a separate lake."

You will pass an island on the right and beyond it, a brushy point of land signals you to turn right into the eastern extension. After passing a wooded peninsula on the left, swing left and follow along the north shore to the tall pine of Pine Point.

151 Merriam Lake

Path accessible by canoe, hiking, fishing, hunting
2.1 miles canoeing, 1.4 miles on foot, 1²/₃ hours, 320-foot
vertical rise, map XIII

An old trail heads north from private camps on the far north shore of Big Moose Lake to Merriam Lake. There are a very few old axe blazes to mark the route, but it is kept clear by hunters and north shore campowners and is easy to follow. You can reach it from a short path heading east from Pine Point, section 150. At the junction, a right turn goes directly to private land, passing a path branching right to the east edge of North Bay. You should turn left, following the path as it ascends by degrees to the outlet of Merriam Lake. The path eventually crosses the tumbling outlet, and in times of high water this crossing will be very difficult. Above the crossing point, the outlet slackens into a grassy wetland and you will probably have to skirt the area on the left. The path ends shortly afterward at the edge of the lake where its outlet slides over various levels of rock slabs. With its brushy shoreline and aquatic plants, it is typical of small Adirondack lakes, but because you reached it along a less-traveled route, it will seem especially wild.

Silver Lake

Twitchell Lake Area

REMOVED FROM THE tides of development and exploitation, Twitchell Lake has had a relatively quiet place in Adirondack history. Its remoteness caused it to be one of the last wilderness holdouts of a few hardy mountain men and "sports." Slowly, hunters and anglers from the Moose and Beaver River regions descended upon its pristine shores and, like other lakes before it, camps and hotels sprang up. One of the earliest sportsmen to frequent its waters was Charles Twitchell, whose name became affixed to the lake. Small camps and shanties sprung up in the latter half of the nineteenth century, but it wasn't until 1897 that the first public camp, the Twitchell Lake Inn on the southeastern shore, opened its doors. This magnificent rustic inn and several of its secondary buildings still stand, although it is not now open to the public.

Most of the land around the lake remains in private ownership, and many fine camps lie along its shores. Telephone and electric services are now available and in the summer, power boats and float planes are in common use. However, the area still retains a quiet backwoods quality valued by Twitchell Lake residents. Access to the lake is along Twitchell Road, which turns right off Big Moose Road, 7.6 miles from Eagle Bay. The road goes 2.1 miles to a public parking area at the state-owned southern end of the lake. Boats and canoes can be put in at this point.

To your right, a small dam across the outlet raises the level of the lake. The outlet, known as Twitchell Creek, tumbles over a series of rocky falls and chutes, dropping over one hundred feet in its first third mile.

152 Snake Pond

Trail, hiking, snowshoeing
0.5 mile, 15 minutes, 200-foot vertical drop, map XIII

This trail begins on the right side of Twitchell Road, 1 mile from Big Moose Road. It is marked by a sign, but it is easy to miss since there is no parking area, and you must therefore park carefully on the shoulder of the road. The trail starts on the level, but soon begins a steady descent, becoming wet and eroded in places. It then tunnels through a dense spruce and balsam stand, emerging on the brushy edge of Twitchell Creek. Snake Pond is actually a bulge on the north side of the creek, and from the trail's end, it is hidden from view by a point of land that separates it from the creek. The water is quite deep for wading in this area, so the best time to explore the lake is during the winter freeze.

153 Silver Lake

Trail, hiking, picnicking
0.9 mile, 30 minutes, relatively level, map XIII

Silver Lake lies off to the left of the trail to Razorback Pond, section 154, on private land west of Twitchell Lake. Though the property is posted, the owners will allow picnicking at a point near the outlet.

The yellow-marked trail begins at the Twitchell Lake parking area and follows an old woods road that has some very muddy sections. The road gently rises up, then levels at 0.4 mile. Just ahead is the junction where the new trail to Beaver River begins, section 158. The private land boundary is reached in fifteen minutes and a sign tells you that a campsite is available on state land at Razorback Pond. In ten minutes, an unmarked side trail leads to the edge of the lake where there is a rough fireplace. A No Camping sign is supplemented by another sign that says, "Fires prohibited on this property except in this fireplace."

You have a narrow view up the southern edge of the lake toward a small island. The bulk of the lake where two camps are located is out of sight to the right. The rocky outlet to your left contains the remains of an old beaver dam.

154 Razorback Pond

Trail, hiking, camping, fishing
2 miles, 1¼ hours, 170-foot vertical rise, map XIII

Anglers know Razorback Pond as a traditional trophy fishing area where stocked brook trout must be caught with an artificial lure. The walk to this quiet little pond will appeal to all hikers. From the junction with the side trail to Silver Lake, section 153, the trail swings right following yellow markers along the route of an old road. Hardwoods dominate the forest, and you may encounter some blowdown, but the trail is well defined. In ten minutes, you go over a shoulder to a stream crossing where the old road fades. The trail rises higher on the hillside and begins a moderate climb, easing off as an old road enters on the left. A height-of-land is at 0.8 mile, about thirty minutes, past Silver Lake, and as you begin to descend, the old road turns off to the right. A DEC sign nearby tells you about the special trout waters. The trail drops quickly to the edge of the pond, and at a wet spot with a stump on the right, the state land boundary line enters from the northeast. A good path continues on from this point. Moving back into the woods, it swings around to a campsite on the north shore. The campsite is, unfortunately, littered with pieces of plastic, cans, and bottles. There are slabs of rock along the shore here, offering you a good place to rest or try your skill with rod and reel.

155 South Pond, Lilypad Ponds, and Jock Pond

Paths, bushwhacks, hiking, hunting
0.4 mile, 15 minutes to South Pond, easy grades, map XIII

South Pond is one of several small bodies of water lying between Twitchell Lake and Big Moose Lake. Their shorelines are mostly brushy, like so many other Adirondack ponds, but they are interesting to explore. Seldom visited, except during hunting season, they will quickly give you a sense of solitude and an opportunity to observe wildlife undisturbed.

Park at the public parking area at the southern end of Twitchell Lake and walk over to the road that crosses the outlet. Follow the road for about 0.5 mile until you see the rustic log structure that was the Twitchell Lake Inn. To your right, a wooden water tower stands off in the woods. A path to South Pond begins behind it and leads 0.4 mile over a small ridge to the edge of the pond. It follows infrequent red and orange rings painted around trees, intersecting the yellow-blazed state land boundary line at the half-way point. You may have difficulty following it, but if you stray, a compass bearing east-southeast should get you to the pond. The path swings south and crosses the pond's outlet, becoming extremely hard to find.

Other paths lie to the south, one of which was once a snowmobile trail that ran along the boundary between the wilderness and wild forest areas.

There is currently a private effort to clear and mark this old trail, but since completion of this project is questionable and both of its ends are on private lands, it is not described in detail here. It is interesting to note that when William Seward Webb sold parcels of his extensive holdings along Twitchell and Big Moose lakes, he stipulated in the deeds that the trails and waterways should remain open for the public forever. Known as the "Webb Covenant," this declaration has met with considerable controversy over the years, and its validity is still questioned. While this would be of great help to the woods explorer, you may correctly assume that it will not be honored by every resident unless they have so indicated.

To reach Lilypad Ponds, bushwhack along the western edge of South Pond on a northeast heading. In 0.5 mile, the shoreline curves to the southeast. Continue on your northeast bearing, which will take you up through a draw to the first of the two ponds, 0.4 mile away. To avoid private land on the west, bushwhack along the eastern edge to the second pond, 0.5 mile away.

Jock Pond's outlet drains into the far end of the eastern extension of South Pond. A bushwhack along this extension on either side is not easy because of dense growth and uneven contours, but the distance to Jock Pond is shorter if you approach along the north edge. It is 1 mile to the outlet, and it will take you the better part of an hour to reach it. The pond lies up in a narrow draw 0.3 mile away to the northeast.

156 East Pond

Path accessible by canoe, hiking, hunting
1.1 mile, 45 minutes, easy grades, map XIII

The path to East Pond, as well as the path to Terror Lake, section 157, begins at the Lone Pine Camp at the far end of Twitchell Lake. Both are maintained by camp owners and hunters and have been traditionally open to the public. If you decide to use these paths, leave your canoe next to the woods, out of the way of camp users and respect the cleanliness and peace of the property as you pass through.

A well-worn path leads back from the shore of Twitchell Lake, passing a private lean-to on the right. A large green camp appears ahead to your left, and the path to East Pond forks off to the right. ATV tracks score the path climbs and swing to the left. It soon narrows to a foot path as it enters an open hardwood section and is marked by red tape, occasional unpainted

Terror Lake

disks, and a few paint and axe blazes. In less than ten minutes, you will arrive at the state land boundary, marked by yellow blazes and a wilderness-area sign. The path continues its slight ascent as it curves around on the north shoulder of a hill. In twenty minutes, the path drops quickly to a wet area where an arrow-shaped board points the way back to the lake. The outlet of East Pond is just beyond, and the path turns right, taking you to the pond itself where there is a large beaver lodge.

A broad, swampy inlet enters the pond at its extreme eastern end, and there are abundant signs of past and present beaver activity along its length.

157 Terror Lake

Path, hiking, hunting
3.6 miles, 2 hours, moderate grades, map XIII

In the fall of 1844, George and Charles Fenton were trapping in the area between Twitchell Lake and the Beaver River. The fair weather they started out in had deteriorated into a freezing rainstorm and as it continued through the second day, they decided to build a brush shanty. Realizing that they could not start a fire with their wet matches, and their lives were in jeopardy, they continued east, hoping to make it to the

Carthage Road, then under construction. This was one of the so-called "military roads" that was to have led from Crown Point to Carthage, a distance of 150 miles. Such a road would not only allow the rapid movement of the militia across the state, but it would also benefit industry, tourists, and settlers. The cold, wet, and weary Fenton brothers hoped they could find relief in the camp of a construction crew, but when darkness fell, they found themselves on a lonely mountain. All through the night, they moved around and wrung water from their clothing until, in the first light of day, they descended to the shores of an obscure lake that they named Terror Lake in light of their desperate situation. Later that day, they did make it to the road and safety, but the name they had given the lake remained.

The wildness and solitude of Terror Lake drew generations of sportsmen to its shores and trails were cut in to it from several directions. Many remote hunting camps were built in the vicinity, and during the first half of the twentieth century, the area reached its peak popularity. After the 1950s, however, fishing and hunting began to decline and fewer people visited the area. The reasons for this are unclear, but changing habits and attitudes of hunters, as well as forest decline due to acid precipitation were contributing factors. Today the lake is as quiet as it was when the Fentons found it; but, sadly, it is less productive.

The main access to Terror Lake is along a path from Lone Pine Camp, described in section 156, It is marked in a variety of ways, red and blue tape, paint, and disks. The first third is quite easy to follow, but as you approach wet areas near the South Branch of the Beaver River, the route is less well defined. The closer you get to the lake, the harder the path is to find, and between markings, you must resort to looking for signs of past maintenance and a foot tread on the forest floor. The land you pass through is truly wild with mature hardwoods dominating. The feeling of wilderness is intense.

Following the path back from the shore of Twitchell Lake, you pass the private lean-to on the right and continue on in front of the large green camp on the left. The path enters the woods and skirts a wet area on the left. In ten minutes, you cross a wet spot on a rotting wooden bridge just before entering state land. After thirty minutes, you enter a section where many streams and swamps form the headwaters of the South Branch of the Beaver River. The path crosses one that is the outlet of East Pond and follows along its right bank as it tumbles down a moderate slope. Using an old beaver dam, you recross the outlet just above a wetland. You cross another stream; then, for the last time, cross the outlet in a picturesque little spot near the site of a former hunting camp. Just downstream from this crossing is a pretty little waterfall; those old hunters knew how to pick campsites. It will take you an hour to reach this spot.

The path climbs up away from the South Branch and generally follows a northeast course through a dense, unchanging forest that will test your route-finding abilities. It will be another hour before you drop to the multi-dammed inlet that feeds the southwestern end of Terror Lake. The path ends in a dense stand of conifers on the lake's edge where a fiberglass boat and some paddles are located. Much of the shoreline is either densely wooded or swampy or both, so the best way to explore this odd-shaped lake is in the boat or with snowshoes in the winter. Evidence of former camps is rapidly vanishing as the forest reclaims the sites.

158 Norridge Trail from Twitchell Lake to Beaver River

Hiking, hunting
7.5 miles, 3¾ hours, map XIII.

Until 1988, the trail to Beaver River was accessible only by canoeing three-quarters of the way up Twitchell Lake to a point on private land where it began. After hiking 0.7 mile, you reached Forest Preserve and continued on to Beaver River. A new section of trail, completed in 1993, now bypasses the lake and private land.

The trail begins on the yellow-marked trail to Silver Lake, section 153. At the junction 0.5 mile from the parking area, the new blue-marked trail pitches up to the right and climbs steeply for 0.4 mile to the top of a hill. Swinging right, you begin a moderate descent that takes you to the outlet of Oswego Pond in fifteen minutes. Cross the outlet on rocks and follow markers through a dense stand of spruce and balsam.

The trail continues around the east side of the pond and leads you to an inlet in fifteen minutes where you must cross on logs and rocks. Once on the other side, the markers direct you along the edge of the grassy wetland along the inlet. Passing an old beaver lodge on the right, you come to a point where the wetland begins to widen out and it is here that the trail turns left and enters the woods again. You begin a series of ups and downs, following the contours of the land north of the wetland. This is an especially wild area, beautiful yet mysterious in its dense cover. After crossing a stream where a small open area is visible through the trees to the right, you begin a steady ascent that ends at an intersection with the original yellow-marked trail. This point is 0.7 miles from Twitchell Lake, 2.6 miles and two hours from parking area.

Turn left, north and follow the trail as it begins a descent to a dense spruce and balsam wetland. The trail crosses the swamp on a long plank walkway that is in fair condition, but very slippery. After rising away from the swamp, the trail levels off, and you encounter some wet areas in a dense evergreen section.

The trail becomes drier as you begin an ascent that will take you over its highest point. Tall maples, yellow birch and beech dominate the hardwood forest and the route becomes quite enjoyable. Almost three hours have passed now and at 4.9 miles, you begin to descend, crossing two pretty streams, two minutes apart. Blue markers appear at this point, and their numbers increase as you get closer to Beaver River. The trail gradually contours around to the west, and when leaves are off the trees, you can see Stillwater Reservoir ahead in the distance. A steep descent follows and the trail can be wet and slipper in places. The grade eases up after ten minutes and the trail crosses a stream. An old road comes in on the left and you descend along it to the state land boundary behind a camp. A road is just ahead and signs pointing the way to Twitchell Lake can be found at both the road and the boundary.

You are now at Norridgewock Lake, a tiny bay separated from Stillwater Reservoir by an earthen causeway and dam. You can get to Beaver River station by turning right and walking along the road around the lake. The original trail, however, forked left about 1000 feet from the road and struck the boundary about 100 yards west of the present terminus. It then turned west and followed the boundary toward a stream that it crossed. Beyond the stream, it swung northwest and came out on the tracks of the Adirondack Division Railroad, about 500 feet south of the present Norridgewock III hotel. If you try to follow it, you will find several old signs in the woods, DEC markers of all three colors, a rerouted stream crossing, and rough going most of the way.

Beaver River is an interesting community. The only road to it was cut off when Stillwater Reservoir was created. Access today is by boat, floatplane, trail, or snowmobile.

Near Inlet and the Upper Fulton Chain Lakes

EARLY SETTLERS WERE so impressed with the beauty of the half-mile-long inlet to Fourth Lake from Fifth Lake, that the name was given to the community that rose up around it. Fred Hess, a famous woodsman of the latter half of the 1800s, was responsible for the construction of many of the settlement's camps and hotels. He also tried to operate some of the establishments he built, but found out the hard way that business and finance were less easy to manage than tools and materials. He left the Fulton Chain region in 1899, but returned in 1923 at the age of eighty-three. Still in fine physical shape, he continued to travel miles into the wilderness to trap in the Moose River Plains area.

The upper lakes of the Fulton Chain saw some development, but not to the extent of the other lakes. The hermit, Alvah Dunning, deeply resented the intrusion of "fools" in "his" woods, and was able to find some relief in his lonely hermitage on Eighth Lake. Today Eighth Lake and the upper half of Seventh Lake remain free of development except for the Eighth Lake DEC campground facility.

159 Sixth Lake to Eighth Lake on the Fulton Chain

Canoeing, lean-tos, camping, swimming, fishing
Approximately 5.3 miles canoeing, 1 mile maximum carry, maps XII and XIV

The popular canoe route up through the Fulton Chain, begun in section 120, continues on from the dam at Sixth Lake. Many homes, camps, and businesses are found along the shores of this mile-long lake and it is busy with floatplane and motorboat traffic. By following along the southern shore, you round a point at its far end and, turning right, come to a road bridge over the entrance to Seventh Lake.

The second largest lake in the chain, Seventh Lake was a favorite of some of the earliest woodsmen. Nat Foster, who took up residence in the abandoned Herreshoff Manor near present-day Thendara, called it "the noble Seventh." The large island near its south shore was once called White's Island since the trapper Green White had a shanty located there. Today, the upper half of the lake is surrounded by Forest Preserve land with the boundary going through the center of the island, now known as Goff Island. A public launching site is located just off NY 28 near the Buck Creek Inlet on the lake's southeast shore. Three lean-tos are situated on the north shore, and a path connects the two westernmost ones and several other campsites with Seventh Lake Road, section 164. Another large island lies east of the middle lean-to, about 2 miles from Sixth Lake. It has an extensive sandy beach and a privy located back in on a path. No camping is permitted here however. The third lean-to is found on a spade-shaped peninsula protruding from the north shore, 0.5 mile past the island.

The normal take-out point is across the channel from the last lean-to, to the northeast. It is a landing that is part of the DEC's Eighth Lake Campground facility. Following signs, a carry of 1 mile takes you through the center of the campgrounds along a paved road to the south shore of Eighth Lake. In times of higher water, it is possible to canoe past the take-out landing and continue up the stump-filled upper channel of Seventh Lake. This will bring you in 0.5 mile to the bridge on the Uncas Trail, section 166. The carry from the bridge to Eighth Lake is about 0.6 mile.

Pretty Eighth Lake is the only lake in the Fulton Chain completely surrounded by state land. It is 1.5 miles in length and also has three lean-tos. One is on an island half way up the lake; another large one sits across from the island on the nearby northwest shore. The third lean-to is on the northernmost tip of the lake near an extensive sandy beach. It is referred to as the Dunning lean-to since the hermit, Alvah Dunning, had a shanty located in its vicinity. This is the farthest point of canoeing on the Fulton Chain, and you can follow a carry north-northeast for 0.5 mile to a register near NY 28 where there is a wide turnoff on the west side of the highway. This area is 2.3 miles north of the Eighth Lake Campground entrance and 2.3 miles south of the intersection for Raquette Lake Village. The carry continues on another 0.7 mile to the Browns Tract Inlet, a winding channel that goes for 2.5 miles through a magnificent wetland before entering Raquette Lake. This carry, which is also part of a snowmobile trail, is described in section 168.

160 Rocky Mountain

Trail, hiking, views
0.5 mile, 30 minutes, 450-foot vertical rise, maps XII and XIV

The popular climb up Rocky Mountain begins in the middle of an extensive turnoff on the northeast side of NY 28, 1.2 miles north of Eagle Bay or 0.9 mile south of Inlet. There is no trail sign, but the wide, eroded beginning is obvious.

The trail is randomly marked with yellow DEC markers and orange paint blazes, and, while there is usually no blowdown, rocks and roots present their own hazards. The first few feet are very muddy, but you soon rise above the wetness as the climbing begins. A few steep sections can be tiring, but the surrounding forest is mixed and the understory varied, so you have a good reason to stop for a rest while you study the landscape. As you reach the summit, the bedrock trail leads you out onto open rock where views over Fourth Lake from the southeast to the west await you. Nearby to the southeast, Seventh Lake Mountain dominates the view. Low hills beyond the south shore of Fourth Lake stretch away to McCauley Mountain in the west. Bald Mountain and Onondaga Mountain stand above the north shore and the village of Eagle Bay can be seen along a section of the highway below to the west.

The summit rocks provide a sunny location for a picnic and ledges just below offer shelter from cold winds. Unfortunately, graffiti has marred much of this frequently visited lookout, and it is hard to find a spot free of its intrusion.

161 Black Bear Mountain from NY 28

Loop with trail and path, hiking, views
3 miles, 1½ hours, by trail; 2 miles, 1 hour, by path; 700-foot vertical rise; maps XII and XIV

The summit of Black Bear Mountain was once burned over by a severe forest fire, and the charred dome reminded local people of a big black bear. Colvin called it Mt. Devastation. Many years have passed since the fire, but the summit has been slow to recover. It is a perfect area in which to study the impact of fires and the pioneering vegetation that follows. Though large amounts of rock are still exposed, stands of white birch,

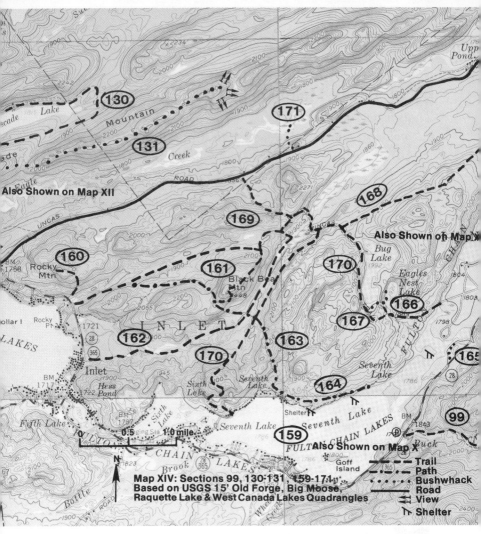

Map XIV: Sections 99, 130-131, 159-171
Based on USGS 15' Old Forge, Big Moose,
Raquette Lake & West Canada Lakes Quadrangles

Trail
Path
Bushwhack
Road
View
Shelter

mountain ash, spruce, and balsam have taken hold where enough soil is present. Mosses, lichens, and small hardy plants such as the three-toothed cinquefoil reach out along cracks and between layers of rock. As you study the summit plant life, rock-hop where you can to avoid damaging it by unnecessary trampling. Much time can be spent studying such a varied landscape, and when you combine it with the superb views to be found, it adds up to a rewarding adventure. Though the mountain can be approached from several directions, its modest distance is just enough to keep it from being overwhelmed by the number of visitors that flock to other peaks and lookouts to the west.

In the early 1920s, Black Bear was one of the Adirondack Mountain Club's first trail projects.

A trail begins at the extreme south end of the same turnoff used for Rocky Mountain, section 160, and heads east toward Black Bear Mountain. There are very few yellow DEC trail markers and no trail register, though yellow ski trail markers appear occasionally as this route is part of the cross-country ski trail described in section 162.

In 1950, high winds caused "The Big Blow," which leveled over one-quarter million acres of trees on Forest Preserve lands. Though the destruction was mostly in the High Peak region, other locations were affected, including this area. The first part of this trail follows one of several old roads that were constructed to remove fallen timber that presented a fire hazard. It is now a grassy lane that tends to be wet in rainy seasons. As you walk along, you will see many other roads intersecting the trail, so care is needed to stay on the correct route. In fifteen minutes, at 0.7 mile, you reach a junction where an alternate route forks right, following blue painted blazes on a more direct approach to the summit. It is described later in this section.

The yellow-marked trail bears left, passing roads on the left and right and emerges in a large clearing less than ten minutes from the junction. Just beyond the clearing, there is a wooden bridge over a stream. You have been ascending since the beginning, but now the grade becomes more noticeable and the trail narrows, leaving the major road work behind. The hardwood-dominant forest is now tall and full, and the understory is rich with ferns, club mosses, and several varieties of wildflowers. In twenty-five minutes, after crossing and recrossing the stream, you come to a junction at 2.2 miles with the yellow-marked trail that comes in from the Uncas Road, section 169. The ski trail turns left at this junction and is described in section 162.

Turning right, you encounter a few eroded sections as the trail steepens on its way to the summit. In some places, the soil has worn away, exposing the bedrock. The forest slowly changes as you gain elevation and the number of conifers increases. In an area of short balsams, ten minutes from the last junction, a path turns left and climbs to an extensive open ledge, 100 feet away. There is an excellent view to the northeast overlooking No Luck Brook. You can walk along the rock escarpment to the right, southwest and slightly uphill, for about 150 yards to a path that will take you back to the trail. While you can see the summit to the southwest, you cannot get to it by continuing along the ledge.

Return to the trail, which leaves the area of the ledge and winds through dense, fragrant spruces and balsams before coming out in the open at 2.8 miles. Cairns and paint blazes guide you between the small stands of trees

View from Rocky Mountain

to the edge of the summit rocks. The way is not always readily visible, and if you return this way, you will need to take time to search for the proper route. This will not only keep you on the right track, but it will also limit the impact off-trail hiking has on the summit vegetation.

Views are possible in all directions, though not at the same time. That is part of the summit's charm; as you explore the landscape, new views continually reveal themselves. Cascade Mountain dominates the view to the north with West and Pilgrim mountains rising over its right shoulder. No Luck Brook, a major inlet to the Brown's Tract Ponds, lies below to the northeast. Raquette Lake is beyond with the Seward and Santanoni ranges looming on the horizon above the lake's basin. Blue Mountain, Blue Ridge, and Wakely Mountain stand off to the east and closer in to the south; Seventh Lake with Goff Island lies at the base of Seventh Lake Mountain. Fourth Lake stretches out to the west, with Bald Mountain and Onondaga Mountain to its north.

The blue-blazed path that forks right from the yellow-marked trail, 0.7 mile from NY 28, is the old trail to Black Bear Mountain. It is much steeper and wetter, but it is 1 mile shorter and passes through a nice mature hardwood-dominated forest near the base of the mountain. It is regularly maintained and can be used with the yellow-marked trail to make a pleasant loop hike over the summit possible.

From the junction on the yellow trail, fifteen minutes and 0.7 mile from the trailhead on NY 28, the path begins a slight but steady ascent along the route of an old road, coming to a clearing in five minutes. Swinging left, the road continues through disturbed lands that gradually give way to beautiful mature hardwoods. After 1.5 miles, as you near the base of the mountain, the grade becomes more evident and the path is eroded in several places. The number of hemlocks, spruces, and balsams increases, and soon the path becomes very steep and rocky. You will come to a junction on this steep section in under ten minutes. The privately maintained path to Seventh Lake, section 163, drops away to the right. Signs at this junction point correctly to Seventh Lake and Fourth Lake, but misplaced yellow DEC markers might lead someone descending from the mountain to believe that the paths are so marked.

Turning left, a final rocky ascent follows blue blazes and random yellow DEC markers past lookouts to the southwest before reaching the summit, 2 miles from NY 28. Obviously, the two routes to the summit can be combined into a loop walk from either direction, though you are cautioned to watch your footing if you walk in a clockwise direction and descend via the blue-marked path.

162 Black Bear Mountain Ski Trail

Trail, cross-country skiing
5.8 miles, 2²/₃ hours, 300-foot vertical rise, maps XII and XIV

This trail climbs over the northeast shoulder of Black Bear Mountain, and while it doesn't rise high enough to have any views, it does go through some interesting terrain east and south of the mountain. That section is prone to blowdown and is the roughest part of the trail. It is not recommended for beginning skiers and is almost too rough and wet to serve as a hiking trail. It has yellow DEC ski trail markers, but there are places where they are scarce, so pay close attention to the trail.

The first section of this trail follows the route of the yellow-marked foot trail from NY 28 as described in section 161. From the junction at 2.2 miles with the yellow-marked trail from Uncas Road, section 169, the ski trail turns left and descends along that trail for just over 0.3 mile to another junction where it turns off to the right. It descends to a wetland at the headwaters of No Luck Brook, which lies in a deep, narrow valley. Dead, standing timber gives this area a mysterious quality. The trail turns southwest and follows the edge of the wetland, coming to an extremely dense area of hardwood saplings at 3.5 miles. The trail meets the path from Seventh Lake at 3.7 miles, and the two routes coincide for 100 yards. Leaving the path, the ski trail joins an old road and begins a gradual descent to Cedar Brook, passing beneath the rocky southern face of Black Bear Mountain. The trail crosses Cedar Brook on a deteriorating bridge just below an old beaver meadow at 4.7 miles.

The remaining 1.1 miles follows a series of roads so you must pay careful attention to signs and markers. An arrow directs you to turn left off the road, five minutes past the bridge, and you follow another road to a small clearing. Go straight along the left edge of the clearing, and reenter the woods. You reach private land in less than five minutes and ahead, at a fork in the road, you must bear to the right. The trail passes through an interesting cedar swamp for ten minutes, then emerges out on NY 28, near a telephone utility building. There is no formal trailhead here, so you should ask permission to park near this point. The Black Bear Mountain trailhead turnoff is 0.5 mile to your right and the center of the village of Inlet is 0.3 mile to the left.

163   Black Bear Mountain from Seventh Lake

Path, hiking, views
1.7 miles, 1 hour, 630-foot vertical rise, moderately steep grades, map XIV

An old path leads north from Seventh Lake Road to Black Bear Mountain, joining the old trail from NY 28 just below the summit. It is marked by occasional axe blazes and red paint, and its maintenance is unreliable. Seventh Lake Road forks left off NY 28 just past Drake's Inn, 1.4 miles north of the intersection in the center of Inlet. It crosses the channel between Sixth and Seventh lakes on a narrow bridge at 0.5 mile and passes through a gate at 0.8 mile. Another gate is located on a driveway to the right. The path starts about 100 feet beyond the gate, on the left edge of the road, just before a solitary hemlock. It is easy to miss, but if you look closely, you will see an arrow carved into the surface of the road. Unless you can get permission to park near one of the camps, your only alternative is to park at Payne's Boat Livery, 0.3 mile from NY 28, for which there is a charge. This will add 0.5 mile to the hiking distance.

The path ascends easily for 400 feet to the state land boundary, then steepens considerably as it climbs to the top of a ridge in fifteen minutes at 0.5 mile. After a few easy ups and downs along the ridge, the path descends and at 1 mile crosses the snowmobile trail that connects the Uncas Trail with Seventh Lake Road, section 170. After thirty minutes, at 1.1 miles, the Black Bear Mountain ski trail, section 162, joins in on the right in a wet valley. The two routes swing left and coincide for 300 feet before the path forks right and begins a moderately steep ascent of the mountain. After fifteen minutes of steady climbing, the path ends at a junction with the old blue-blazed trail from NY 28, section 161. Turn right for the final steep ascent of the mountain.

164 Seventh Lake Path

Path, hiking, lean-tos, camping, swimming, picnicking, fishing
1 mile, 30 minutes, relatively level, map XIV

Seventh Lake Road ends at the boundary of state land, 1.4 miles from NY 28. An unmarked path leads to the edge of the lake and passes two lean-tos and several campsites that are usually used by boaters and canoeists. All have good places to swim. Unless you can get permission to park nearby, you will have to park at Payne's Boat Livery, 0.3 mile from NY 28, for which there is a charge. This will also add 1.1 miles to your hiking distance.

From the end of the road, the path swings right, passing through tall hardwoods behind a private camp. White birch and pines punctuate the woods, and in five minutes, you arrive at the first lean-to. It, and its privy, are in good shape and the setting is picturesque. A large rock known as Arnold's Rock, protrudes from the shore providing a good place to picnic, sunbathe, or enjoy the view of Seventh Lake Mountain across the way. The path continues on to a large hemlock grove ten minutes past the lean-to. There are several good camping spots, and the area seems to be stable. The second lean-to is not far beyond the grove, and it is a double-sized one capable of holding a dozen people and their gear. It is also in good shape as is its privy.

The path ends five minutes later at a large campsite past a big boulder. The lake is shallow here, stumps protrude from the sandy bottom, and you can sometimes walk across to the island 100 yards away.

165 Cathedral Pines
Path, maps XIV and XV

Just under a mile southwest of the Eighth Lake Campground or 1 mile northeast of the Seventh Lake fishing access site, there is room on the shoulder for several cars to park on the north side of NY 28. From here you can see a few really tall pines towering above the forest on the knoll to the west of the road. A footpath marked informally with blue paint circles the western slopes of the knoll and leads past the largest of the pines. A fifty-foot spur from the upper part of the path ends beneath one of the giants, which is more than four feet in diameter. A plaque on a dying pine on the lower part of the path memorializes a pilot shot down in World War II. The loop, which is a little over 200 yards long emerges at the highway, 50 feet from its beginning.

166 Eagles Nest Lake
Trail along old road, bushwhack, hiking, cross-country skiing
0.8 mile, 30 minutes, 120-foot vertical rise, maps XIV and XV

The trail to tiny Eagles Nest Lake starts from the Eighth Lake Campground and follows the route of the Uncas Trail. This trail was actually a stage road that was built by William West Durant in 1896. It led from the Uncas Road between Eagle Bay and Raquette Lake, to Great Camps at Mohegan Lake, Sagamore Lake, and Lake Kora. The trail from the campground to Uncas Road is now marked and used as a snowmobile trail as well as a yellow-marked foot trail.

To reach the trail, drive to the entrance of the Eighth Lake Campground, 6.2 miles north from the center intersection in Inlet on NY 28. The entrance is 4.6 miles south of the intersection at Raquette Lake. There is no day-use charge at the campgrounds for those who are hiking this trail, but you must sign in at a register beyond the attendant's booth. Drive straight ahead past the register, through a four-way intersection to a parking area on the right, 0.5 mile from NY 28. This is not open in the winter.

From the parking area, the trail heads west, crossing the channel between Seventh and Eighth lakes in 300 feet. Markers are quite scarce, but the wide trail is easy to follow. The forest is a notable combination of

View from cliffs above Eagles Nest Lake

mature yellow birch, maple, and red spruce. The trail ascends easily for fifteen minutes, coming to a wooden bridge over the outlet of Bug and Eagles Nest lakes at 0.7 mile. Just before the bridge, a trail branches off to the right, also following yellow markers. It leads 0.1 mile through a muddy section, and branches just before reaching the edge of Eagles Nest Lake. The right fork goes to an opening on the brushy shore of the lake. The left fork goes to the outlet, which you can cross on rocks and logs. It then continues, climbing up a moderate pitch to a large campsite on the southeast edge of Bug Lake, 0.1 mile away, section 167. It then turns southwest, crosses the Bug Lake Outlet and rejoins the trail.

A steep cliff across the lake rises over eighty feet. To reach it, you must cross the outlet, then bushwhack along the western edge of the lake, working your way to the cliff top. It will take you about fifteen minutes to get through the dense growth to the top and once there, be very careful since the cliffs are sheer. The view is limited by the nearby hills, although you can see as far as Seventh Lake Mountain to the south. The sight of the lake below is quite nice, however, and the variety of trees found on the cliff top includes fine specimens of red pine, white cedar, and white birch.

167 Bug Lake

Trail along old road, path, hiking, cross-country skiing, canoeing, camping, swimming, fishing, hunting
1.1 miles, 45 minutes, 190-foot vertical rise, maps XIV and XV

Bug Lake is popular with anglers since it is usually stocked with trout. The approach over the wide trail is short enough that carrying a canoe into the lake is not too difficult. Hunters also enjoy the area since the trail allows game to be easily dragged out. Eighth Lake Campground extends its season in the fall with limited facilities for the sportsmen's benefit.

The yellow-marked trail continues past the bridge over the outlet of Bug and Eagles Nest lakes, section 166, 0.7 mile west of the trailhead. It ascends steadily for ten minutes, leveling off at 1 mile where the upper end of the side trail to Eagles Nest Lake rejoins on the right. If you turn right and follow the side trail from this end, you will come to the outlet of Bug Lake in 0.1 mile. The trail crosses the outlet on stones and comes to a large camping area under a tall grove of hemlocks and pines. For the amount of use this area receives from sportsmen and hikers, it is very clean and is a good example of proper camping practices. The side trail then swings away from the lake and drops down to the outlet of Eagles Nest Lake. A herd path continues along the southwestern edge of Bug Lake, ending at a campsite on a broad peninsula, 0.2 mile from the outlet.

The main trail swings north from the junction with the upper end of the side trail and follows the west shore of Bug Lake. At 1.2 miles, the water comes close to the trail and provides a good place to launch a canoe. At 1.8 miles, the trail leaves the shore and heads northwest to Uncas Road, section 170.

Eagles Nest Lake

168 Canoe Carry from Eighth Lake to Browns Tract Inlet

Canoe carry, snowmobile trail, hiking, cross-country skiing,
lean-to, picnicking, swimming
1.2 miles, 30 minutes, relatively level along the carry, map XV

The canoe carry between Eighth Lake and the Browns Tract Inlet crosses the divide between the Moose River and Raquette River basins. It links the West Central region with the river systems to the north and makes an enjoyable walk, whether you have a canoe over your head or not. It is accessible from NY 28 by driving 2.3 miles north from the entrance to the Eighth Lake Campground to a wide turnoff on the west side of the highway. This is 2.3 miles south of the intersection for Raquette Lake village. The carry comes out to the road at this point, and there is a register down to the left. The trail is marked with canoe carry and snowmobile trail markers.

Turning left, it is 0.5 mile to the north shore of Eighth Lake where the Dunning Lean-to is located. It is named after the hermit Alvah Dunning, who had a shanty located in this area. It and its privy are in good condition.

If you turn right from the parking turnoff, you will parallel the highway for ten minutes before the carry swings left following a stream. In two minutes, the snowmobile trail turns off to the left and goes to the bed of the Raquette Lake Railway, section 174, 0.2 mile away. The carry continues straight ahead and passes a privy on the left before following a long wooden walkway out into the inlet where you can put in your canoe. This is 0.7 mile from the highway turnoff and 1.2 miles from Eighth Lake. Those using the carry from Eighth Lake to Browns Tract Inlet make the whole 1.2-mile carry.

A 2.5-mile section of snowmobile trail once ran west from the Dunning Lean-to to the Uncas Trail north of Bug Lake. You could use the southern portion of the Carry Trail above to reach the northern tip of Eighth Lake where this trail begins. It has not been maintained in recent years and parts of it are hard to follow because of blowdown and filling in by saplings, though you can still walk it in two and a quarter hours. It passes through a tall mixed woods and is sparsely marked with DEC snowmobile trail markers and can covers. One stretch high up on the eastern section has a few ski trail markers. Because of the roughness of this route, it should only be attempted by those who are familiar with wilderness ski touring. It does make a good snowshoe trip, however, and except in hunting season, you will probably not see another person.

The trail begins at the left rear corner of the Dunning Lean-to and climbs directly up a shoulder of the ridge west of Eighth Lake. The first 0.2 mile are difficult to follow and in just over five minutes, a path also marked with can covers, turns off to the right, heading toward the Browns Tract Road. The snowmobile trail turns left, heading west and becomes easier to see. After twenty-five minutes, it levels off, and at 1.1 miles, you pass a wet area with tall spruces and hemlocks on the right. Swinging slightly to the right, it avoids higher ground to the south. At 1.7 miles, after fifty minutes, you begin a slow, steady descent that eventually brings you out to the Uncas Trail, section 170. There are no markings at this junction and the abandoned trail is so overgrown you would hardly know a trail ever existed here. Bug Lake is about 0.3 mile to the southeast, beyond the height-of-land.

Along the Uncas-Browns Tract Road

THE UNCAS ROAD was built in the late 1800s so that camp owners and their guests could travel from the boat landing at Eagle Bay on Fourth Lake to Raquette Lake. When the Raquette Lake Railway was built in 1899, it roughly followed the same route. In 1914, a road to the north, paralleling the railway, was built from Raquette Lake to the Browns Tract Ponds, connecting with the Uncas Road. Today that half of the road is known as Browns Tract Road and shouldn't be confused with the earlier Browns Tract Road from Moose River Settlement to the Herreshoff Manor near present-day Thendara. The whole stretch is seasonally drivable today. It turns left off NY 28, just over 0.2 mile east of the intersection of Big Moose Road in Eagle Bay.

It is an adventure to drive the road, and the western end has a canopy of tall maples that makes it quite beautiful in fall. Hunting camps have been built along the narrow strip of private land near the western end of the old railroad right-of-way. North of it, Eagle Creek flows west beneath the cliffs of Cascade Mountain. Uncas Trail, section 169, heads south at 2.9 miles. Camp Buck Horn, behind which begins the path to Ferd's Bog, is 3.5 miles from NY 28 and 5.85 miles west of Raquette Lake. Starting from the boat launch at Raquette Lake, Browns Tract Road forks left at 0.3 mile, a roadside rock has been painted to enhance its resemblance to an Indian at 1.5 miles, Browns Tract Ponds Campground is at 1.8 miles, and the trails to Shallow Lake and the Railroad right-of-way beside Browns Tract Inlet are at 2.85 miles.

169 Black Bear Mountain from Uncas Road
Trail, hiking, views
2.2 miles, 1¼ hours, 590-foot vertical rise, map XIV

This approach to Black Bear Mountain begins at the point where the Uncas Road originally turned south and went to great camps on Mohegan

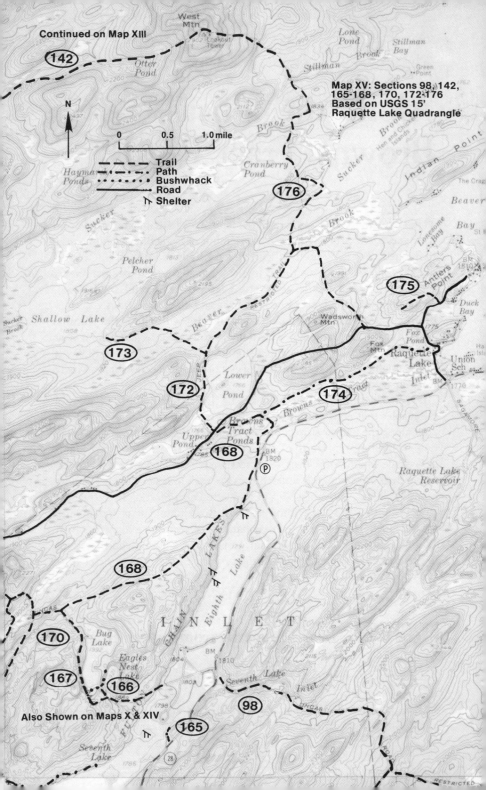

Lake, Sagamore Lake, and Lake Kora. When the Raquette Lake Railway was built, Uncas Station was built here. Known as the Uncas Trail, it is now marked and used as a snowmobile trail as well as a yellow-marked foot trail. There is room to park off to the edge of the road at the trailhead, 2.9 miles east of Inlet.

The trail ascends gradually, passing a yellow barrier in 50 yards, then crosses a stream. You next pass through a section that tends to flood easily from beaver activity. Swinging first to the left, then right, the trail rises over a knoll and begins to descend, coming to a junction in twenty minutes at 0.9 mile. The Uncas Trail continues straight ahead while the trail to Black Bear Mountain, also having yellow markers, turns right and descends to two wet stream crossings. As you begin to ascend, the ski trail, section 162, enters on the left at 1.2 miles. The two trails climb together to another junction at 1.5 miles where the yellow-marked trail from NY 28, section 161, enters on the right. The remaining way to the summit is described in that section.

170 Uncas Trail and Seventh Lake Snowmobile Trail

Hiking, cross-country skiing
3.5 miles, 1³/₄ hours along Uncas Trail; 2.5 miles, 1¹/₄ hours along trail to Seventh Lake; moderate grades; maps XII, XIV, and XV

Beyond the Black Bear Mountain trail junction at 0.8 mile, section 169, the Uncas Trail continues its descent, making a sharp right turn and crossing No Luck Brook on a wooden bridge at 1.1 miles. Climbing up onto a spruce and balsam lined hogback on the opposite side, you reach an unmarked junction, 0.1 mile beyond the brook. A snowmobile trail branches right, going 2.5 miles to Seventh Lake Road. The Uncas Trail drops off the hogback to a low spot, then swings left and begins to climb along the side of a ridge. Tall yellow birch, maples and beech dominate the hillside, but in the lowlands to your left, dense conifers proliferate.

The trail bends to the right, climbing away from the lowland, and at 1.5 miles, it passes an unmarked junction. The abandoned snowmobile trail from the upper end of Eighth Lake, section 168, comes in at this obscure junction, about 150 feet up from the bend, but it is virtually impossible to find. After leveling off at 1.7 miles, the Uncas Trail drops to the northwest edge of Bug Lake, section 167, forty minutes from Uncas Road. The trail continues on another 1.8 miles past Bug Lake and Eagles Nest Lake, section 166, ending at the Eighth Lake Campgrounds. The snowmobile trail to Seventh Lake Road is rough and winding and has a few wet spots, yet as of 1987, it was brushed out and used regularly. Leaving the unmarked junction on the Uncas Trail at 1.2 miles, it heads southwest, following the hogback to a wetland at the head of No Luck Brook. This is the same wetland that the Black Bear Mountain ski trail follows on the opposite side. The trail continues on through a varied woods, passing some mature white cedars in twenty minutes. The Seventh Lake Trail to Black Bear Mountain crosses at 1.2 miles, thirty minutes from the Uncas Trail. Past this intersection, the trail climbs moderately for fifteen minutes in a tall hardwood forest, entering private land along the way. After cresting a hill, it winds down among other private trails to a sharp bend on Seventh Lake Road, 0.7 mile from NY 28.

171   Ferd's Bog
Nature walk, birding, map XIV

An exciting and fragile bog lies along the headwaters of Eagle Creek. A path leads to it from behind Camp Buckhorn, see above, and while crossing the 50 feet of private land to the path on state land is permitted, parking can be a problem. Do not block access to any of the camps. There is a small area 150 feet east of the camp for one or two cars. The state has acquired several lots to the west and according to the Unit Management Plan will build a parking area and access. Trailhead signs should be put up shortly.

The current path, unmarked, leads over a small hardwood ridge, and down into the valley past a hill of tall balsams, then through a stand of smaller balsams with a great array of mosses beneath. It takes but ten minutes to walk the 0.4 mile to the bog. The footpath leads into the bog, but at times the path is flooded and walking farther into the bog is sure to trample something rare. However, from the borders you can spot white fringed orchis and buckbean in summer, pitcher plants and sundew, pale or bog laurel and sheep laurel, bog rosemary, bog wool, and leatherleaf grow in the sphagnum. This was once an open pond with sphagnum borders that have gradually filled in with dead sphagnum or peat, leaving a spongy moss base, a true quaking bog, and a very small residual pond. Pine and red spruce ring the bog, tamarack and black spruce grow sparsely through it.

Most people visit the bog for its birds, for this is a site where both the black-backed and northern three-toed woodpeckers breed. They nest from mid-May through June and into July. In addition to boreal chickadees and grey jays, numerous other boreal species can be found here.

172 Browns Tract Ponds and Sucker Brook Bay Road

Public campgrounds, canoeing, swimming, picnicking, fishing, old road, hiking, cross-country skiing
3.2 miles, 1¹/₃ hours, easy grades along the road, map XV

The Browns Tract Ponds lie to the north of Browns Tract Road, west of Raquette Lake village. The Lower Pond, which is the larger of the two, and its surrounding land, comprise the Browns Tract Ponds Campgrounds, operated by the DEC. The Upper Pond, lying to the southwest, is bordered mostly by Forest Preserve land. An old road leaves the Browns Tract Road at the east end of the Upper Pond, 6 miles from Eagle Bay and 2.8 miles from Raquette Lake Road. It was constructed in the late 1890s to give access to Sucker Brook Bay on Raquette Lake from Eagle Bay on Fourth Lake. Today, the roadway is the boundary between the Pigeon Lake Wilderness Area on the north and the Fulton Chain Wild Forest Area on the south. It serves primarily as a snowmobile trail, but all-terrain and four-wheel-drive vehicles use it occasionally. A yellow barrier stands across the road and there is room for three or four vehicles to park off to the right.

The first 0.1 mile of the road is wide and sandy with an extensive beach along the Upper Pond on the left. You can swim, picnic and put in a canoe here, but camping is not allowed because of the close proximity of the campgrounds. The pond's outlet is crossed in five minutes, after which the road begins an easy ascent. The Lower Pond soon appears to your right and in under twenty minutes, at the 0.9 mile point, you will be in the vicinity of two hard-to-spot forks. Just after the last sight of the Lower Pond, a worn log on the left edge of the road indicates the Shallow Lake Trail, section 173. That log is all the warning you have of the first fork. A few steps farther up the road takes you to a second hidden fork. Here, a path turns right, drops to the edge of the Lower Pond following axe blazes, and continues on to campsite #69 in two minutes. The Shallow Lake Trail fork may not remain hidden much longer since the Pigeon Lake Wilderness Area Unit Management Plan calls for its marking and maintenance.

The Sucker Brook Bay Road continues on through unchanging forest for another 1.5 miles to a bridge over Beaver Brook. The West Mountain trail, section 176, joins in on the right just before the bridge and the two routes coincide for the remaining 0.8 mile north and east to Sucker Brook Bay.

173 Shallow Lake

Trail, hiking, canoeing, camping, swimming, fishing, hunting
2.2 miles, 1 hour, easy grades, map XV

Before the Pigeon Lake area was classified as wilderness, Shallow Lake was a favorite spot for float plane landings. Outfitters would fly in hunters, fishermen, supplies, boats, and canoes, and many locations along the shore became popular campsites. Unfortunately, a few visitors were careless in their actions and today, you will find broken coolers, mangled folding chairs, and many empty bottles and fuel cans. This is a shame since the lake possesses such a wild beauty and peaceful atmosphere. It deserves better. The surrounding woods are quite thick and often tangled so the ideal way to get to campsites and explore the lake is by canoe. If you are planning to spend any fair amount of time in the area, you should consider hauling a canoe the distance. The benefits are well worth it.

An existing foot path to the lake is the logical way to approach it today. It is an old route, marked by axe blazes and is generally easy to follow except for occasional blowdown and a very wet and hazardous crossing of Beaver Brook. The Pigeon Lake Wilderness Area Unit Management Plan has a provision for its improvement and maintenance, and it may become an official trail soon. As of 1987, however, it will take at least an hour to reach the lake from the end of Sucker Brook Bay Road on Browns Tract Road.

From the junction on Sucker Brook Bay Road, section 172, at 0.9 mile, the trail heads northwest through a dense, rocky woods reminiscent of a High Peaks trail. The forest opens up briefly then, after ten minutes, the trail descends to cross Beaver Brook. This is no place for a trail! Entering a dense spruce bog with a deep sphagnum floor, you must try to walk on logs, not just to keep your feet dry, but also to keep from damaging the fragile bog environment. Both are unavoidable, however, and you will soon forget about your feet and start worrying about the rest of you, when you

Shallow Lake with West Mountain in the background.

come to several thin logs heaped across the ten-foot-wide channel. The water below is at least four feet deep in summer and great care is needed to cross safely. The woods on the other side are wetter than at first, and the trail is hard to see. Blazes lead you to the right, then the trail swings left and leaves the 200 yards of wetness behind.

The remaining 0.9 mile to the lake presents no great difficulty and can be covered in less than thirty minutes. The trail stays along the side of a hill where the hardwood forest is easy to navigate through. By paying attention to the foot tread on the ground, you will have no problem staying on course. The trail ends at a little sandy beach where a sign on a tree urges you to keep the area clean. Across the water, along the rocky shoreline, are the nicest campsites; a canoe is the best way to get to them. It is possible to bushwhack along the lake's edge to the right and work your way over to them, but it involves a tricky crossing of the swampy Pelcher Pond Outlet. Off to your right, several rocks lie out in the water and from one of them, you have a picturesque view of West Mountain to the northeast. Other campsites can be found on the northwest and southern shores, and you may wish to try paddling Sucker Brook.

174   Route of the Raquette Lake Railway beside Browns Tract Inlet

Hiking, birding, nature walking
2.7 miles, 1 hour, level, map XV

This raised route along the abandoned railroad tracks is a boardwalk through the swamps and bogs that border Browns Tract Inlet. A wonderfully varied world of water-loving plants lies on both sides of the roadway. At the eastern end of the route, you pass Fox Pond, then walk beside a bog that lies below the handsome cliffs on Fox Mountain. More open swamps lie to the south of the road in the next mile, and a few tall pines dot the hummocks while tamarack fill the lowlands. Beyond, the bog returns, this time with labrador tea, leatherleaf, and pale and sheep laurel in the sphagnum. Only a few mature cedar trees are mixed with the spruce, but the marshy area is carpeted with young cedars.

The western mile of this route passes through a red spruce swamp; in one patch, *usnea*, the lichen known as old man's beard, drapes from the spruce branches in long wispy grey-green strands. This lichen, once much more common in the Adirondacks, is rarely seen in such profuse strands today; lichens are very susceptible to acid deposition and some, like this *usnea*, have been much affected.

From the roadway you can sample the understory of the spruce swamp that contains trailing arbutus, bunchberry, creeping white winterberry, and evergreen woodfern.

Grey jays and boreal chickadees can be seen along the roadway. The road makes it very easy to bird here. And, the walking is level and easy.

The only drawback to the route is that it passes right through the closed Raguette Lake landfill, 1.1 miles from the eastern end. The landfill has been covered, but not seeded and stabilized; and the sand covering has eroded in places.

The eastern end is known as Dillon Road, which begins beside the library in Raquette Lake, just north of the boat launch area. To find the western end, take the dirt track south just opposite the eastern end of Upper Pond on Browns Tract Road. This point is 2.55 miles from Raquette Lake Road. The track heads south for 100 yards and splits; the way west leads to a private house, the way left, to the railroad, is barred by an enormous sand pile designed to prevent vehicles from using it.

You may want to start from the western end to avoid the dump, though a through walk is quite delightful. A trail forks south, 0.5 mile from the

View from West Mountain toward Raquette Lake and Blue Mountain

western end, and leads to Eighth Lake, section 168. Just east of it there is a bridge over Browns Tract Inlet. This bridge will probably last for a few more years, but if it is not replaced, crossing will be difficult at best, and to enjoy the longest stretch of road, you will then have to walk in from the east.

175 Hedgehog Mountain
Bushwhack to cliff tops, map XV

A surprising ten- to fifteen-minute walk brings you to the top of the cliffs that line the southeastern slopes of a small, unnamed hill north of Raquette Lake. There is no path, but there is a great view of the southern end of the lake and of Blue Mountain. This is the easternmost point in the chain of steep-sided hills whose cliff tops yield views of the Fulton Chain Lakes.

There is a sandpit on the road north from Raquette Lake, 0.3 mile north of the turn to Browns Tract Road. Just north of it an old tote road heads northwest, uphill. In 250 yards, a five-minute walk, it seems to disappear, so take a compass bearing toward southwest. This leads you up along the back of the hedgehog, behind the cliffs for 300 yards to an opening with views. In the foreground, you see Duck Bay with Big Island beyond. To the south you can pick out Estelle Mountain with the Blue Ridge to its west. Beyond, Wakely is distinguished by its tower and long profile.

176 West Mountain

Trail, hiking, camping
4.9 miles, 2³/₄ hours, 1140-foot vertical rise, map XV

The trail to West Mountain starts on the north side of Browns Tract Road, 0.7 mile from its eastern end on Raquette Lake Road. You can park on the south side of the road at one of two turnouts just east of the trial. The first 1.4 miles of the trail has not been maintained for the past few years. The middle 1.9 miles follows old roads and is quite easy, if not very interesting. The final 1.6 miles has not been maintained either and though there is little blowdown, a few wet areas will give you some difficulty. The Pigeon Lake Wilderness Area Unit Management Plan states that the trail will once again be maintained, so in time, it may greatly improve. You can avoid the first section by taking the Sucker Brook Bay Road from the Upper Browns Tract Pond, section 172, since the two routes combine at Beaver Brook. It is about 1 mile longer but is much easier.

There are actually two starts to the trail that meet in 0.1 mile, but neither is marked on the road. The westernmost one has red DEC markers and begins by a tree with nails in it, probably the ones that once held the trail sign. This trail drops into the woods heading north and intersects an old road in 0.1 mile. The second trail starts where this old road comes out to the main road, less than 100 feet east of the red-marked trail. Boulders indicate the end of this road and blue DEC markers follow it 0.1 mile to the point where the red trail comes in. The foot trail, now with blue markers nailed over the red ones, heads north away from the road, passing through tall spruces to a stream crossed on old planks. You cross two more old roads in the next ten minutes; then a moderate climb at 0.7 mile takes you over the shoulder of a hill. The trail drops into an area of dense saplings where you must watch the ground for the tread. Blowdown complicates your efforts here also. In forty minutes, the trail nears Beaver Brook and swinging left, it joins the Sucker Brook Bay Road, section 172.

Beaver Brook is crossed on a sturdy wooden bridge and the route beyond is uneventful as it heads northeast. There are fewer markers since they are not needed as often along such an obvious road. At 2.2 miles, the road ends at Sucker Brook Bay where there is a nice view of the Santanoni Range. This is the point where canoeists should land if they wish to climb the mountain. A small campsite is located on a knoll to the left of the road.

The West Mountain Trail turns northwest 100 yards before the bay and follows another road. Swinging north-northeast, the road crosses Sucker Brook after an hour and a quarter and 3.1 miles. Along the road ahead, you may see signs saying Do Not Enter or Road Closed. There are several private parcels in the area and presumably these signs are intended to discourage motorized trespass.

A confusing intersection comes up five minutes after crossing Sucker Brook. The road swings east and leads to private land along the shore of Raquette Lake. The trail turns left at a junction marked by a metal arrow and heads north following red markers. If you were to continue on the road for three more minutes, you would see another trail branching back to the left. This one has blue markers and is in better shape. These two side trails come together in three minutes and turning north-northwest begin the final approach to West Mountain. Markers are more frequent now, but both red and blue ones will be seen.

After going over a small hill, you come to a difficult wet section at 3.7 miles where the trail crosses Stillman Brook. A long ascent now begins, starting with easy grades as you follow a small stream on your left. The forest becomes dominated by mature hardwoods and after fifteen minutes, the ascent steepens. The route becomes tiring and unchanging, but occasional glimpses through the trees let you check the progress of your ascent. Finally, forty minutes after the ascent began at Stillman Brook, you emerge in a grassy clearing just below the summit. This is where the observer's cabin stood, but now only a small shed remains off to your left. The trail crosses the clearing, passing a large boulder and climbs up between rocks to a junction where the trail from Higby Road comes in on the right. To the left, a 200-foot-spur trail goes to the summit, described in section 142.

References and Other Resources

References

Beetle, David H. *Up Old Forge Way and West Canada Creek.* Old Forge, NY: North Country Books, 1972. Reprint of 1946 and 1948 editions, printed by the Utica Observer-Dispatch, Utica, NY.

Colvin, Verplanck. *Seventh Annual Report* of the Topographical Survey of the Adirondack Region of New York. Albany: Weed, Parsons and Company, 1880.

DeSormo, Maitland C. *The Heydays of the Adirondacks.* Saranac Lake, NY: Adirondack Yesteryears Inc., 1974.

Donaldson, Alfred L. *A History of the Adirondacks,* Volumes I and II. Harrison, NY: Harbor Hill Books, 1977. Reprint of 1921 edition.

Dunham, Harvey L. *Adirondack French Louie.* Sylvan Beach, NY: North Country Books, 1978. Reprint of 1955 edition, privately printed.

Gilborn, Craig. *Durant.* Blue Mountain Lake and Sylvan Beach, NY: North Country Books and The Adirondack Museum, 1981.

Grady, Joseph F. *The Adirondacks, Fulton Chain-Big Moose Region, The Story of a Wilderness.* Old Forge, NY: North Country Books, 1966. Reprint of 1933, privately printed edition.

Harter, Henry A. *Fairy Tale Railroad.* Sylvan Beach, NY: North Country Books, 1979.

Kudish, Michael. *Where Did the Tracks Go?* Saranac Lake, NY: The Chauncey Press, 1985.

Marleau, William. *Big Moose Station.* Big Moose, NY: Marleau Family Press, 1968.

Department of Environmental Conservation.
Adirondack Canoe Routes, pamphlet.
Moose River Plains, pamphlet.
Unit Management Plan for the Ha-de-ron-dah Wilderness Area.
Unit Management Plan for the Pigeon Lake Wilderness Area.

Other Resources

Adirondack Mountain Club, 174 Glen Street, Glens Falls, New York, 12801.

Department of Environmental Conservation, 50 Wolf Road, Albany, New York, 12233.

Ranger John Seifts, Piseco, 518-548-5794.

Ranger Tom Eakin, Lake Pleasant, 518-548-4132.

Ranger Gary McChesney, Raquette Lake, 315-354-4611.

Ranger Gary Lee, Inlet, 315-357-4403.

Ranger Douglas Riedman, Old Forge, 315-369-3463.

Ranger Terry Perkins, Stillwater, 315-376-8030.

Bridge at the headwaters of the West Canada Creek

Index

Guidebooks from Backcountry Publications

For information on other regions of the Adirondacks covered in the "Discover" series, please see the back cover.

Walks & Rambles Series
Walks & Rambles in Dutchess and Putnam Counties, by PeggyTurco $11.00
Walks & Rambles in Rhode Island, by Ken Weber, Second Edition $11.00
More Walks & Rambles in Rhode Island, by Ken Weber $11.00
Walks & Rambles in the Upper Connecticut River Valley, by Mary L. Kibling $10.00
Walks & Rambles in Westchester (NY) and Fairfield (CT) Counties,
    by Katherine Anderson, revised by Peggy Turco, Second Edition $11.00
Walks &Rambles on Cape Cod and the Islands, by Ned Friary and Glenda Bendure $11.00
Walks & Rambles on the Delmarva Peninsula, by Jay Abercrombie $11.00

Hiking Series
Fifty Hikes in the Adirondacks, by Barbara McMartin, Second Edition $13.00
Fifty Hikes in Central New York, by William Ehling, $12.00
Fifty Hikes in Central Pennsylvania, by Tom Thwaites, Second Edition $12.00
Fifty Hikes in Connecticut, by Gerry and Sue Hardy, Third Edition $12.00
Fifty Hikes in Eastern Pennsylvania, by Carolyn Hoffman, Second Edition $12.00
Fifty Hikes in the Hudson Valley, by Barbara McMartin and Peter Kick $14.00
Fifty Hikes in Lower Michigan, by Jim DuFresne $13.00
Fifty Hikes in Massachusetts, by John Brady and Brian White, Second Edition $13.00
Fifty Hikes in New Jersey, by Bruce Scofield, Stella Green, and H. Neil
    Zimmerman $13.00
Fifty Hikes in Northern Maine, by Cloe Caputo $12.00
Fifty HIkes in Northern Virginia, by Leonard M. Adkins $13.00
Fifty Hikes in Ohio, by Ralph Ramey $12.95
Fifty Hikes in Southern Maine, by John Gibson $12.00
Fifty Hikes in Vermont, by the Green Mountain Club, Fourth Edition $12.00
Fifty Hikes in Western New York, by William Ehling $13.00
Fifty HIkes in Western Pennsylvania, by Tom Thwaites, Second Edition $12.00
Fifty Hikes in the White Mountains, by Daniel Doan, Fourth Edition $13.00
Fifty More Hikes in New Hampshire, by Daniel Doan, Third Edition $13.00

We offer many more books on hiking, walking, fishing, and canoeing plus books on travel, nature, and many other subjects.

Our titles are available in bookshops and in many sporting goods stores, or they may be ordered directly from the publisher. Shipping and handling costs are $2.50 for 1-2 books, $3 for 3-6 books, and $3.50 for 7 or more books. To order, or for a complete catalog, please write to The Countryman Press, Inc., P.O. Box 175, Dept. APC, Woodstock, VT 05091, or call our toll-free number, (800) 245-4151. Prices are subject to change.

Lee M. Brenning, here shown in his winter "coat," is employed as an engineering technician in Barneveld, New York, and lives in Nobleboro, on the banks of the West Canada Creek. A reverence for the land learned during his youth on his family's farm led him to pursue independent study of local history and the environment. Lee and his wife, Georgianna, are deeply involved with Forest Preserve issues and are continuing their intensive four-season explorations of the Adirondacks.